I0530186

IT'S ME
FROM THE
BIG APPLE
TO
BEAN TOWN

WALTER BENESCH

It's Me from the Big Apple to Bean Town

by Walter Benesch

THE US Review
of Books

book review by Kate Robinson

BOOKWRIGHTS
HOUSE

It's Me from the Big Apple to Bean Town
by Walter Benesch

"Sorry, no UFO contact in this book but there will be a number of interesting incidents which are attributed to reincarnation and a few close calls."

Benesch, a graduate of Franconia College and The New School of Social Research, shares snapshots from his life in the form of letters written to his daughter (some not sent) in this provocative sequel memoir. Beginning with his earliest jobs, such as driving cabs at night in Manhattan and his years-long graduate school studies in anthropology and sociology, Benesch reminisces with an irreverent candor. His early career in social work was accomplished with courageous abandon in some of the most challenging neighborhoods in the Bronx and Harlem. His equally high-spirited pursuit of academic degrees and a long-term quest in the world of advanced Masonry was accomplished with the same unstoppable energy. Benesch also served as one of many caregivers to chimpanzee Nim Chimpsky in the Project Nim study to determine if chimps could master sign language. He eventually retired from a decades-long career in the federal government.

The author's detailed but down-to-earth writing is thoroughly engaging if a bit uneven, with writing conventions occasionally being sacrificed for enthusiastic storytelling. That said, these infrequent issues are nearly unnoticeable because the fascinating narrative is hard to put down. Readers will enjoy the sense of freedom of choice that Benesch had as a white male of his era and the unvarnished rendition of what could have been a more conventional, sanitized memoir. The author's sense of adventure is tempered by a sense of responsibility to society that never wavers despite his freewheeling energy. Benesch's graphic sexual explorations aren't for everyone, but these interludes capture the ambiance of the sexual revolution of the sixties and seventies and his bent for intimate sociological inquiry. The memoir illustrates Benesch's preference to experience life with the volume turned up to eleven and captures well the transformational energy that penetrated the collective American psyche of that era.

THE US Review
of Books

book review by Kate Robinson

BOOKWRIGHTS
HOUSE

IT'S ME

FROM THE

BIG APPLE

TO

BEAN TOWN

WALTER BENESCH

978-1-965552-30-8 (Paperback)
978-1-965552-41-4 (e-book)

BOOKWRIGHTS
HOUSE

admin@bookwrightshouse.com
☎ (213) 286 6700

Contents

Introduction

THIS IS A CONTINUATION of the <u>It's Me: The Early Years, Letters to my daughter</u> book which took readers from my early life through undergraduate work and graduation from Franconia College. Sorry no UFOs contact in this book but there will be a number of interesting incidents which are attributed to reincarnation and a few close calls. Again, these are derived from letters to my daughter while after her graduation from undergraduate college and move to the West Coast.

Though there is an effort to have most sequential, there will be flashbacks and some letters shedding light on events which are remembered after the initial letters covering the same time frames. Additional incidents have been included which were not part of the original correspondence.

It was during this time my daughter "T" started work for Teach for America. She was occupied with teaching elementary school children, participating in co-ed water polo team, while working as a volunteer councilor at an AIDs clinic. It was realized she had less time to read letters. At the same time there were a number of life changes occurring in my life, including divorce from her mother, moving into a one bedroom condo, having a variety of paramours until finding the partner who is truly the love of my life and moving into her townhouse.

As a result there are gaps of as much as months between letters then increased in irregularity once I settled down. Yet when traveling attempts were made to send cluster of letters from as many different Post Offices as possible especially when on trips to different locals.

These letters pick up shortly after my graduation from Franconia College in 1971. Post college dream was to move to the city of my birth, New York and try to create a career. But what job can you have with a B.A. in sociology? That was a challenge. This book will take you through a series of jobs, good and bad, including driving a cab in Manhattan, being a failed street vendor, and work in the South Bronx, first as a volunteer and then as a part of the Youth Services Agency of the City of New York.

There will be references to my work with Nim Chimpsky the chimpanzee that was the subject of Columbia University's effort to teach Nim sign language in a semi human environment. But more extensive details of my work and living with Nim are presented in a what is hoped will be a separate book which includes pancake recipes we created together.

After jobs disappeared in New York it became necessary for me to continue my professional education in Boston. The adventures and misadventures in Boston are described. The book concludes with the necessity to find a job after further graduate work and moving to the next phase of my life. The first letters were actually sent much later, but are placed here in the beginning due to the sequence of events.

Since I have a strong belief that sex and sexuality are a key element in health and relationships, there will be explicit descriptions of various sexual encounters. Some in the form of short essays 'not sent'. This will be applied to the sequence of the letters. Hopefully it will awaken both the sexual desires which should be considered normal and acceptable in a modern society.

This second part of the book, which go beyond the period covered in the letters. The sexual episodes will be included in the narrative. In addition this is taking the point of view as a social worker who at one time was considering a concentration of sexual therapy.

PART I

Letters Continued

Chapter 1

NYC the first years

Hi T:

What do you do after graduation? LOOK FOR WORK!

I was living temporarily on 'The Hill', my mother's place in Connecticut. Having received my Masonic 3rd Degree in February (1971) I was naturally active in the Co-Masonic Lodge, Marie Deraismes #352. All the New York Masons there were giving suggestions. Few helpful. At the same time there was a contingent of the members who were traveling down monthly to Philadelphia to help out the dying lodge there. Since almost all in Marie Deraismes were city dwellers, none had cars. Only a few had driver's licenses. Demetria, Fred N, Edris M, and sometimes one or two others would ask me to drive down to Philadelphia for the meetings if we didn't take the train. If only two of us went down the train was cheaper. Demetria would pay for me.

The Philadelphia lodge met in a regular lodge room not far from the train station. There was an elderly couple who were the foundations of the lodge, having been members since it's founding in the 1920's. There were a two or three others who would occasionally show up. One was a teacher at the Pennsylvania School for the Deaf.

She had met me a number of times when she visited Marie Deraismas Lodge. Her school required her to take additional training every other year to retain her teaching license. The condition the school put on her, was she had to find her own replacement while she was in full time training for those two week. Knowing I had recently graduated, she approached me. It would be a little money for two weeks and might be fun. I would stay in her apartment a short way from the school. It was a deal. Off to Philadelphia.

That Friday she introduced me to her kids. She took off the next day for the training. The class was a high school social studies class most of the kids were 15 through 18 years old. All had their assignments for the next two weeks. Each morning I would put the day's assignment on the blackboard. I was to monitor more than teach. If questions came I attempts would be made to help. With a BA degree in social studies, no problem.

First job, get two things, first the little card which showed the alphabet signs and then the American Sign Language (ALS) book one of signing. I felt learning the signing alphabet for be a good first step. Sunday night before the card was memorized. The book didn't come into my possession until later.

Monday morning I signed "Good morning." to the class. After introductions it appeared that most of the kids were interested in me, partly because I was not much older than them, and at the time, fairly good looking. The girls were especially interested in me. The boys were impressed by my good physical condition. Had NO discipline problems. Some asked in spoke language if I knew sign language. Had to admit not. But told them I learned the alphabet last night.

"Last NIGHT! Man you're good!" one girl replied.

So started two very fascinating weeks. No real incidents. Just fun working with the kids.

There was all levels of deafness. Some completely deft. Most had partial hearing. The latter were evident since they wore hearing aids. Few spoke normally. Most in a slurred or broken pronunciations of words. All read lips. If I spoke slowly they could understand me.

One mid morning one totally deaf girl wanted to get the attention of one of the other classmates to ask question. This was a study time, where all were working out of their books. I was studying ALS from the book, finally obtained. She couldn't get the other girl's attention by waving. Suddenly she **yelled!** I can tell you, you have no idea how loud a yell from a totally deaf person can be. It was so sudden and unexpected I literally fell off my stool. It was like the **BARF** I yelled in Latin class that knocked my old girlfriend Sam off her chair in high school when attempting to get rid of a pesky fly. All the hearing members of the class looked at her. Suddenly she realized how loud she must have been. Looking at me she signed and said: "Sorry." Little did I know these two weeks would be vital to something else years later.

I enquired if there may be an opening at the school. Nothing! They were suffering from budget cuts and couldn't hire anyone who was not already fluent in ALS. So back to NYC. Thank goodness the Eastside Settlement House had apartments on the top floor. Since I had done research there the previous summer, if I volunteered at the Mott Haven Center I could live there. The rent would be fifty dollars a month. Great. I moved at Alexander Avenue, South Bronx.

Love,
Papa

September, 2009

Hi T:

The Temple of Understanding (TOU) was mom's idea for a center for all the world's religions to come together in a center for study and sharing. She felt if they could find their commonalities, the threat from extreme fundamentalism, and radical religious movements would decrease. The source of many world conflicts and tensions would fade.

Norman Artist a former member of Alice Bailey's group had proposed to Mom after her divorce. Mom turned him down. Norman then married a dynamo, Marjorie, who liked to rub shoulders with lots of rich upper class people. Mom invited Marjorie and Norman up to The Hill, in Northwestern Connecticut. For a weekend and shared her concepts with Marjorie. They talked for hours. Marjorie picked up the concept and got in touch with a possible catalyst. One was Juliet Hollister who had many additional contacts and money! Marjorie shared Mom's idea with Mrs. Hollister and by 1960 the Temple for Understanding (TOU) as an organization was started.

I met with Mrs. Hollister and told her my personal religious philosophy and told her kids needed to get involved. Children can easily learn to be tolerant. They can spread what they learn about the commonality of the world's great religions to their parents and communities. Mrs. Hollister appointed me to be the representative to children and teens.

I did keep in touch with TOU, mostly through Mom, and Mrs. Hollister for a short while. One of the first major events the TOU sponsored was a special luncheon (around 1960) at the United Nations for Zulfikar Ali Bhutto. He had been the youngest member of Pakistan's delegation (1957). The TOU wanted to recognize his support since he was to leave NYC to run for prime minister. At this time I was about 11 years old. I always looked older that I was. I was not only invited to the luncheon, but was seated at the head table as the TOU youth representative about 4 seats away from the guest of honor.

I talked with him after the lunch was over. He greatly impressed me. He had done his graduate work at USC – where I obtained a grad certificate years later. I kept track of his political career and was elated when he was elected prime minister. When he as assassinated during a political coup, I really felt the world had lost a great leader. Unfortunately this was to be repeated when his daughter Benazi's life would end in a similar tragic way.

Unfortunately, I never was able to take advantage of my appointment. Locally in Connecticut we did have community forums. When the topics were religion, I would speak up for the TOU. I handed out the TOU pamphlets. That was about the extent of my active involvement. There were no trips or speaking engagements, unfortunately. But I did see Co-Masonry and the TOU as having similar spiritual goals. These would be incorporated into talks given later.

Love,
Papa

Jan. 2010

Me again:

Back in NYC there were no immediate jobs. I tried to several placed. A pawn shop.

"This is a career. Do you really expect with your college education to expect to say in this field?" they asked.

I had to answer "no."

Then came the interview with Sax Fifth Avenue for a sales position. The interviewer was very snobby. It was going decently for a little while. Then he told me: "Of course you would get employee discounts for our merchandise, but at the salary you would be paid, we don't expect you would be able to afford our clothing."

That started a steady decline in my attitude and in the interview. Then he said:

"We have a lot of very important people come in here. How would you treat someone like Senator Buckley?"

At the time William F. Buckley's brother, who was really from Connecticut, had been elected as Senator from NY. The interviewer chose the wrong reference. I met at one time or another all the Buckley's in Sharon, Connecticut. Mostly at the various forums that were held in that section of the state. I detested each and every one of them for their arrogance and the way the patronized everyone. I looked at the interviewer:

"I would treat them like everyone else, politely and with respect."

His response put me over the edge. His next question tipped the scales:

"What you would treat Senator Buckley like everyone else?

"Of course, everyone deserved the same level of respect. Why should a politician be special just because what comes out of us at one end comes out of politicians at both ends!"

The expression on the interviewer's face was worth a 1,000 words. I just got up and walked out.

The next attempt was with an employment agency. They were hiring constantly. The first day was training. They emphasized that discrimination was against the law. So there were a number of key words to be used in taking job references. Bright = White. Energetic = Young. Strong = Male. You get the idea. That immediately set me off a little, but I needed to get some income.

The routine was interview those looking for work and fill out their employment reference cards, using the codes. Next to ask them where they had gone for interviews. Those places were called immediately after the interview to see if the agency could get a formal request. Then use the agency's existing references to see if any of those signed up with us would be suitable for the job listed. I was not doing well. No placements and only a few listing after two weeks.

I remember calling one reference. I had just interviewed a marvelous recent black woman undergraduate. She would have been perfect for the job. On the phone I was praising the girl.

"Well send her over, just be sure she isn't some nigger."

I was mad as hell. It was a perfect match, except for race. The next day I was told I was to be let off. Just as well.

In the mean time I had almost no funds. A little money came from mom and odd jobs. The Pueblo Market at the corner of Alexander and third Avenues, usually had the one meat I could afford. Turkey tails! Back then they were about $0.15 a pound. They became the primary meat source for months, unless I could find something else on sale. Night after night I would prepare turkey tails for myself and Carol. Carol and I had an unusual link. She was my wife in a previous incarnation. When we met she had never thought about reincarnation but after meeting her dream presented a total recall of our life as husband and wife in India centuries ago.

I had been dating Carol since my initial work at the Settlement House. There were curried turkey tails, barbecue turkey tails, turkey tail soup, baked turkey tails, broiled turkey tails, fried turkey tails, usually with onions and other veggies. If something could be made from turkey tails, I came up with it. They kept me fed and happy. Haven't had them in years, at least not as the main course, but when turkey is served at Thanksgiving or other occasion, it is the tail which ends up on your father's plate first chance I can get.

Love,
Papa

April, 2010

Hello Again:

I interviewed at the NYAC (NYC Athletic Club). I got a job as the night desk clerk. Job was to greet members and their guests, check them into the rooms and hand over the keys. I did meet Dennis Day who was famous as the tenor on the Jack Benny program. Of all people Robin Moore came in one evening. I had spent a summer with his family at their summer retreat. I greeted him with:

"Hello Robin."

He just ignored me and pretended we had never met. After all a desk clerk was beneath him. This despite the last time I saw him I was coaching him under a limbo bar with a vodka on the rocks at his parent's summer home on Cuttyhunk Island. After a month it was evident the clientele were all white. I discovered although Dennis Day was welcomed, his boss Jack Benny would not have been. After all the NYAC was an *Exclusive* Club! NO Jews! little less blacks. I put in my resignation. I told them although the job was OK I just couldn't work for a club that discriminates.

The next job interview was for a librarian. Didn't need a MLS (Master's in Library Science) but experience in libraries. Again it was at a private club in NYC for lawyers and professionals. It sounded like a great job. I was still in contact with Tom F from college who was working on his MLS. We had worked together in the Rockford College library until I was thrown out for arrogance just before my senior year. The interviewer told me to come back in two days after they checked my referenced. I came back really hoping to have a job.

"Mr. B, you are really a good fit, but we called the NYAC. I'm afraid we can hire you because we too are an exclusive club."

I shook his hand and walked out disappointed.

I was desperate. Mom was supporting me with the $50/mo rent at the Eastside Settlement House. I was doing volunteer work at Mott Haven Community Center in the evenings with Carol, my major love interest. Finally out of desperation I answered an ad in the NY Times for street vendor. It was to be selling art posters. I got a vendor's license. Then went up the shop that was hiring. They would sell me posters for $1 each. I was to sell them for $2 each. I could pay for half now and pay them the rest later. Deal!

I had brought a large art valise to carry the posters. Soon I had a place staked out, far enough away from the Metropolitan Museum of Art on Fifth Avenue so not to get into their territory. Not far from the Strand Book stalls and the Park Plaza Hotel. Soon I was doing macramé with string to use as bookmarks to add to the posters. Nothing worked. Some of the posters ended up at our yard sales some 25 years later.

I tried to return the posters but the shop had closed. So I pay half price for 100 posters ($50), sold maybe 20 ($40) were sold. More in the yard sale ($25) sales then on the streets of NYC. Hard way to come out with a profit! Only took twenty five years.

Love,
Papa

Chapter 2

Taxi Anyone?

Aug. 2010

Hi T—More adventures:

Let's call this and following letters with a subtitle of: "Hey Lady Need a Cab?"

Carol came up with a suggestion. "Why not drive a cab?"

Well why not. I got to a library and looked the qualifications. First was a chauffeur's licensee. A little extra money but with a perfect driving record, no sweat. Then to take the NY Taxis Commission's test. I knew most of Manhattan but failed the other boroughs. I was shown the answers. I got Grand Central Station wrong! Didn't know the taxi stand was not on 42nd but had it's own little side street that no longer is in use. So I was permitted to retake the test again, 30 minutes later. Having tied to memorize the previous wrong answers. This time I passed. Next take the hack license to a cab company.

The 55th Street Taxis Garage was hiring. Actually they referred me to the Taxi Commission for the test. With everything in hand, I was hired. Day or night shift? Easy, night—bigger tips. Had to work around classes at The New School where I had just been accepted for their graduate program in anthropology. Talked to Howe the manager. It could be worked out. I started the next night. Forty percent of the fares were mine. The other sixty percent went to the garage. Increases depended upon tenure. The rest of your earnings came from tips. For a beginner, tips are critical.

Schedule was Monday, Wednesday, Thursday, Friday and Saturday evenings. Tuesdays were class night. Time 4 p.m.—pick up the cab from the Garage near 11th Avenue. Then work until I felt I needed to quit for the evening. Weekdays I usually knocked off around midnight. Weekends I would sometimes drive until 3 a.m. All depended on the number of people needing a cab.

I told members of Marie Deraismes Lodge I was driving a cab. They thought 'well it's a job.' At least something until another job was found. So for the next seven months I was hacking in one of the busiest cities in the world. Many a cabbie would get into the cab lines at various places around town. I preferred to roam the streets. Brought my old Zenith portable radio from The Hill, and placed it on the dashboard of the cab. Turned to WQXR, of course (the classical station). Many a fare was surprised by a young man's choice of stations. If they were a classical lover it usually resulted in a bigger tip.

Since I wanted to watch out for Demetria and I knew the East Side better than uptown or elsewhere, I cruised mostly between Fifth and Lexington Avenues between 34th and 86th Streets. My first week was fantastic. I was the highest earner in the garage for the week. "Beginner's Luck" they all said. It was.

Love,
Papa

Nov. 2010

Buddy want a cab?:

I actually enjoyed driving the cab. Here is one of the strategies I used. It was fun when stopped at a red light. Sometimes there were three cabs in the front lined up side by side. I would rev up my engine as if I was to peal out once the light changed. The other cabs noticed and would prepare to beat me. In reality I was watching the sidewalks. The light changed. The other cabs shot off. I slowly pulled over towards a couple or individual who had just emerged from an apartment building, bar or restaurant. 'Need a cab?' I would shout. More times than not, they got in.

I remember one night a black hooker flagged me around Lexington and 48th. Some cabbies refused to pick them up. Not I. I pulled over, knowing when a hooker needed a cab it was to get out of the territory FAST as the undercover cops were in the area, about to make a bust. As I pulled over, two jumped in real quick.

"Get us out of here, fast!"

I started to pull away, not realizing the door was still open and a third was trying to get in. Stopping quickly I deeply apologized saying I didn't realize there was a third passenger. I took them down to 34th Street, pulled to the side, got out and opened the door for them. They were really impressed. When not pressed by traffic I opened the door for most of my women fares. They really liked my manners. When I dropped of the gals gave a 100% tip. Best tip ever. Always looking to see if any hookers need a cab from then on. Few did, but I kept my eyes open realizing the inner being, no matter what the outward profession, is a part of the way life ebbs and flows hoping these women will find their inner light and goodness within. After all life is imperfect. The art of life is to make the best of the imperfect and one can never tell what goodness is hidden within.

One afternoon approaching 2nd Avenue there as Demetria and Annette, her partner, walking down the street. I pulled up to say: 'Hi.' Demetria was shocked until she noticed who it was. She admitted knowing I was driving but since she had never seen me in a cab it never really sunk in until that moment. We laughed a little about it. Yet if I had not been so close to them I felt I would have been dismissed like Robin Moore did when I was at the NYAC.

During the brief times in the garage you would have 5 to 10 minutes to talk to some of the other drivers. There was one old cabbie in his late 70's. He had driving all his life. As a matter of fact he started out before there were any motorized cabs. He first drove a horse drawn cab. This was before World War I. He was the highest paid driver taking in 70% of the fares. Only talked to him a few times, but he had stories. Wish I had written some down. He started at a time when the papers were warning that Manhattan would be covered with 5 feet of horse manure by 1929. Like so many futuristic predictions, it didn't take into account the advancement of technology. In this case the automobile.

I remember one cab coming in. It had been hit on the passenger side rear section. Howie took pictures of the damager. Then one of the maintenance mechanics climbed into the trunk, kicked out the dent and the cab hit the road.

"We can collect $100 for that damage from the insurance." Howie told me with a grin.

There was one fare who wanted to go down to the financial district at night. Most unusual. But hey a good fare. So got there with no problems. Now the drive back. There on the corner was a young black woman flagging me down. She wanted to go to 2nd and 86th. Perfect. That was in the middle of 'Little German Town' an ideal place to pick up new fares. I got her up there. She suddenly jumped out of the cab saying she was going to get the fare. Forget it. I waited then realized she was a fare beat. Told Howe. He dismissed the fare but warned me that was the only time. It was the only fare jump experienced.

I remember picking up a couple on Madison Avenue during rush hour. It was in the middle of the block and I was on the left side of the street. The man wanted me to make a right turn at the light, only 50 feet away. That required crossing 3 lanes of heavy traffic. I refused saying it was not safe. I volunteered to turn off the meter until we got to 2nd Avenue where they wanted to go. He got real mad. Ordering me to make the turn. His wife took my side noting the heavy traffic. I went up an extra two blocks and a half, made a safe right turn and dropped them off where they wanted. He as complaining all the way. His wife thanked me for considering safety first. He just slammed the door and gave me a $0.15 tip. I threw it back at him.

Feb. 2011

Hi T–Cab Anyone?:

One Saturday in the late afternoon I was behind the main entrance to MOMA (Metropolitan Museum of Modern Art). They had been having a fund raising afternoon celebration / fair. But by 5:30 the party was over and the various vendors and entertainers were piling out the back entrance.

One woman raised her hand and shouted "Taxi."

I picked her up. She had some Tarot cards, a crystal ball and a few other items in a bag including a fortune tellers costume she had been wearing. She immediately told me she had been the "fortune teller" for the event. She wasn't a real one but felt she was psychic.

"I bet I can read your mind. Let me think what sign you are."

I played along but thanks to Mom and advanced meditation techniques, knew how to deflect psychic attempts to read a mind, or anything else. After putting up psychic protection I started concentrating: 'Pieces, Pieces, Pieces!'

Suddenly she said: "I bet you are a Pieces."

"Nope, sorry, Virgo." was my response.

"Gee I can't understand it, Pieces was coming in so clearly." I just smiled.

"I bet I can guess your name."

That was easy as the hack license was on view in the front. But she had been sitting back and didn't look. I focused on the name 'Ralph, Ralph, Ralph.'

Again I heard her say: "I bet your name if Ralph."

Not even turning I simply said: "Sorry wrong again." As I did I pointed to the license.

She raised her self and started shaking her head: "I just don't understand it. I've been on target all day. Let me guess where you were born."

This time I concentrated on Boston. After about 30 seconds: "I've got this clearly. You were born in Boston weren't you?"

"Nope, right here in Lenox Hill Hospital on Park Avenue."

By that time we had arrived at her apartment. She just couldn't understand how she had gotten everything wrong. I just smiled, helped out of the cab and handed over her bags. Never told her she was a true mind reader. It was just the phony messages she was picking up.

One Saturday night had been busy and profitable. I had dropped off what I thought was my last fare on the upper West Side. Now I just wanted to get back to the garage and call it quits. After dropping of the cab I had a good walk to the subway, then two trains to get to Alexander Avenue. Late at night it could be an hour trip.

On 11th Avenue and was pushing on the gas going well above the speed limit. The "Off Duty" sign was illuminated on the top of the cab. Then I saw a black man waving at me. Being off duty I drove right by. Then it hit me. He had what looked like a Brooks Brothers suit on. What the hell was he doing in this section of town? I slammed on my breaks. Backing up the block plus to where he was standing and rolled down my window.

"I'm off duty but do you know where you are?" I asked.

"Have no idea. I was told to take the crosstown bus to 11 Avenue and then a bus to Greenwich Village, but I haven't seen a bus or anything for over an hour." he said.

I responded: "First realize your are in Hell's Kitchen. Second those busses stop running at 1 a.m. Third you are lucky to be alive! Where do you want to go I'll get you the out of here."

He gave me an address in the West Village, not far from Washington Square. I told him to get in.

"If you can get me there in 10 minutes or less, I'll give you a good tip."

That was usually a 20 to 30 minute drive even more if there was heavy traffic. I knew I couldn't use the then elevated West Side Highway as it was always patrolled by the police. The best way to get downtown, go **under** the West Side Highway! He got in.

"Hold on."

I got the cab up to close to 90 MPH. The only thing I had to watch out for were homeless men who hung out under the highway. As we were close to the piers trucks may be pulling out. I was lucky. No homeless, no trucks, and no cops. Got him to his address in 11 minutes and got a good tip. That was one of two times when I violated the speed limits for fares.

Love,
Papa

June, 2011

T–More Cab Stories:

While cruising on the East Side a woman flagged me down. She jumped into my cab:

"Follow that cab. The one that just pulled out."

OK, like right out of the movies. Even the old timer never got such a call. So off I started. The cab in front must have been told to loose me. This was late rush hour, there was heavy traffic. The driver in front stepped on it. I followed inches from her tail. If she turned, I turned. If we where on a one way street, I would be right off her passenger side tire. If she turned left, I was right behind. She couldn't turn right without colliding with me. Suddenly she turned into a parking lot. This was one on an open block with entranced on both streets. Again I followed. The parking attendance was having a fit as two cabs zoomed through the lot at over 40 MPH and out the opposite street. Then the cab pulled in front of an uptown bus. A man got out and jumped on the bus. I turned to the woman:

"Do you want me to follow the bus or the cab?"

"Follow the cab. I think it will pick him up in a few blocks."

I followed the cab! At the next light, now in the upper 90's, we both rolled down are windows. The black woman driver asked:

"What the hell are you following me for? He took the bus."

"I know" was my response: "but my fare thinks you are going to pick him up later."

She grinned at me: "Shit I'm going back to my garage in Harlem. That honky doesn't have the balls to follow me up there. By the way, you're good."

"So are you" I responded and waved.

I pulled over. "You heard her, she's right. Where do you want me to take you?"

"Back to where you picked me up."

On the way back she told me how her good looking husband was cheating on her. She wanted to find out where his love's apartment was. Felt sorry for her, but realized he must have married her for her money as she was not at all attractive. This from what I observed.

One evening on the East Side an elderly black woman was coming out of one of the more fashionable townhouses. She hailed me. I pulled over.

"I'm going up the Harlem. You'll take me there?"

"Sure, just tell me where and I'll take you."

She looked as if she was in her 80s, still working as a maid. She had two bags of groceries as her section of Harlem had few markets. I drove her home. There on her stoop were three black gang members, based upon the colors they wore. I pulled up, got out of the cab, helped the woman out. Then carried her groceries up the stoop steps. All the while the 3 blacks were watching me. She then offered me a big tip. Let's face it back then 95% of white drivers wouldn't go to Harlem. I looked at the tip and handed it back to her:

"Here you keep it. I think you need it more than I do."

She looked at me with complete surprise then with an expression of thankfulness. As I started back toward the cab, one of the three gang members watching shouted:

"Hey honky."

"Yea what the hell do you want" I responded.

He got up and looked me in the eyes.

"Your OK. I'll get the word out that you can drive in Harlem any time you want."

I smiled and nodded, got back in the cab and drove back to central Manhattan.

Love,
Papa

Oct. 2011

Would you believe–Last Cab Stories (I think):

I picked up a trio of college girls obviously from out of town. Likely on Spring Break. We were driving cross town on 57th Street between 6th and 7th Streets. I was in the center right lane on this two way street. About three cars in front of me I saw a bum trying to cross in between the cars in mid block. Not a good idea in heavy traffic. His coat caught the bumper of the car that just passed him. He was thrown to the ground. The car behind, driven by a woman, was too close and going too fast to stop. Not speeding just too fast to stop in the 5 feet between her and the man who had fallen. Crunch! Her front tire ran over the man's head. She let out a horrible scream. I passed her as she became hysterical. My fare(s) asked what happened. I didn't respond until we were close to 7th Avenue. After we had left the scene I turned:

"The woman who screamed just ran over a man who tried to cross mid block. I think he's dead."

"How do you know?"

"Did you hear a crunch just before the scream?"

They nodded. "That was his skull being crushed."

They looked sick. I dropped them off on Broadway.

A nicely dressed man flagged me outside the Waldorf Astoria on Park Avenue. He wanted to go to LaGuardia. He was late for a flight. I drove as fast as I could through the Midtown Tunnel and out to Flushing. We arrived in record time. He paid me but told me to wait in case he missed his flight. I put on the off duty light and waited. Sure enough about 10 minutes later he showed up.

"Get me to Idlewild ASAP, I might be able to catch their next flight to Germany. It's leaving in a few minutes."

Now I had no idea how to get from LaGuardia to Idlewild, now called JFK. I got on the highway but the wrong way.

He looked at his watch.

"How much longer?"

"Maybe 30 minutes"

"Forget it. Take me back to the Waldorf."

I did. What was interesting the fare was exactly the same as the trip to LaGuardia. He said he would go to a club, get drunk and catch a flight the next day. I think he knew I didn't know how to get to Idlewild from LaGuardia. Still a nice tip and a pleasant conversation.

One night after my shift driving the cab, I was taking the Subway back to the Bronx after getting off around 1 a.m. I arrived at the 138th Street station around quarter to two. The exit was on the same corner as the police station. As I started up the stairs there was a loud racket going on. Loud shouting was accompanied by any number of thuds. I slowly peered out of the stairs before emerging completely.

A riot going on. A yellow cab company had their garage near by. A gypsy cab company had their garage about two blocks away. As was discovered later, two cabs, one from each garage got into an accident right at the police station on Alexander Avenue. The drivers got into a fight. Like a baseball game where the benched clear out to join in the fun, both garages emptied out joining the fight. The police being undermanned were trying in vane to break it up.

I was tired. No way was I going back down into the subway station to get out on the 3rd Avenue exist and walk the extra 3–4 blocks around the riot. So up I went. What was bad. I was carrying a little bag like most cabbies where my radio and container that had my dinner in it on one hand. I looked like a cabbie getting off duty. But then again I could be a night watchman or any number of other laborers.

When I got to the top I started down Alexander Avenue. One man was coming at me with a tire iron. Raising my hand I said:

"Wait! I'm just going home." pointing down the street. "I'm not part of this, go hit him!" He turned and hit the guy I pointed to.

Another man came at me with a knife.

"Hold on, I'm not a cabbie. Go stab him." He turned saw the closest driver from the other garage and tried to stab him. Not sure if he was successful.

By this time I was almost at 139th Street. I side stepped on man who charged, tripping him as he passed. He ended up on the sidewalk. Crossing the street I looked back. Laughing to myself I said: 'Thanks Bugs Bunny, your method does work.' It was like I had been in the middle of a Looney Tunes cartoon where Bugs shouts "STOP" and all action stops allowing him to pass through. Well it worked that night.

Love,
Papa

Jan. 2012

Hi T–Cab Stories Over but…

One night after getting off late. I was on the Number 6 IRT line headed back to the South Bronx. A group of blacks came in the car. They sat across from me. All five were staring at me. They were giving off very bad vibes. I suspected they were gang members. Their leader was staring intently at me. I think he was sizing me up as a potential target for a robbery. I took his staring at me as a staring contest and just stared back. Neither of us blinked for the first few minutes. But being tired I blinked first. Then began to laugh. The others lightened up. The one who had been staring at me started to laugh too.

"Listen guys," I said "lets do this again when I'm not so tired. I've had a long day. If you want come to Mott Haven Center tomorrow and we can continue."

When they heard "Mott Haven" they realized I was not some honky from a safe area. It may have been the conversion, stares turning into humor, or that I was from the South Bronx, all tensions subsided. They got off in Harlem. I continue to Alexander Avenue.

One afternoon I was walking past Sax Fifth Avenue by the side entrance. Rather unexpectedly the side door opened. Three men came out, but all were talking to the one in the middle, David Niven the great actor. Not looking where they were going, David Niven bumped right into me. Surprised he said excuse me. I just said:

"Excuse me Mr. Niven, didn't expect anyone to come out that door."

His troupe went one way and I just continued where I was going. That was my literal run in with a famous actor. I did pick up a number of the stage actors while driving the cab, but none famous.

While driving a cab I always avoid movie crews. All were arrogant and VERY poor tippers. After all it was a privilege for any cabby to have them in their cab. I remember picking up one crew. Each extra bag or case was to cost an additional $0.50. This crew of 3 had three large heavy metal cases. I assumed they contained camera and sound equipment. Driving them to where they wanted I told them to fee and the extra $1.50 for the cases in the trunk. They refused to pay the fee for the cases. I pointed out the sign in the front of the cab which clearly stated all trunks are subject a $0.50 sir charge. They still refused to pay, handing over the basic fare and a small tip. I got out of the cab, opened the trunk and removed each of the cases one by one, dropping them the full height from the top of the trunk to pavement below. Bang! They screamed and yelled. I just got in the cab and drove off. Always avoided movie crews after that.

A few years later and shortly after one of the famous blackouts, I ran into the *Superman* movie set on 57th Street. The power in the city had been restored where the filming was taking place before other areas. 2nd Avenue where I was going, and Harlem, which was having riots, remained without power. The special treatment for the movie set pissed me off and a lot of New Yorkers. As you approached the location, there were signs and tape instructing pedestrians to not cross the lines.

I was not going to go back to 6th Avenue, cross at the cross walk and come back on the other side. They even blocked off half the lanes, so traffic was heavy and solid on the other side. Not safe to cross midway! Realize the blocks between the avenues can be exceptionally long. Especially between 5th and 6th where the filming was taking place.

I was walking down towards 5th. It looked as if the crew and caste were taking a break. I didn't; see Christopher Reeve, nor Margo Kidder but once the movie came out recognized the scene that was filmed shortly after I passed through. The sidewalk was blocked off half way down the avenue. There were police stationed around. These seemed like the desk jockeys cops given an easy assignment. As I walked towards the barrier a cop started to approach. I just went into my South Bronx walk and starred him in the eyes. My pace quickened and became very deliberate. Either I must have given the impression I was insane or part of the set I do not know. He just backed away. I just walked through the set untouched.

Love,
Papa

Chapter 3

YSA Harlem

April, 2012

Hi T:

I had been driving the cab around 7 months when Carol heard the Youth Services Agency (YSA) was hiring. I filled out the job application and actually got an interview. Carol said my volunteer work at Mott Haven and at the Settlement House should help open the door. I think she called someone she knew in the personnel office.

Sure enough after a few weeks I received a call to come in for an interview. On the day of the interview, I dressed in a suit, traveled down to the YSA HQ across from City Hall on 60 Park Row. Ms. Margaret Bebek was the interviewer. Ms. Bebek was not what I expected. She was an older white woman. Later I found out she was an ACSW (member of the Academy of Certified Social Workers) and had worked all over YSA since it was founded. She was impressed with my volunteer work at Mott Haven, also as a recorder for the Area Agency and the White House Conferences on Aging, in New Hampshire and the follow up conference in Boston, which I had done shortly after graduating from Franconia College. Within a week I was hired.

I was told to report to the West Harlem office as a 'street worker' (real title 'Youth Service Specialist'). The office was on Broadway and 94th street, not far from Columbia University. I was the only white in the office.

The week I started work at YSA, all the managers and the director were talking about the annual YSA party that had been held at Bear Mountain State Park. There was a wonderful restaurant which had a large hall for special occasions such as banquets and weddings. It is important to know this was during Major Lindsay's administration which was famous for its unaccounted for spending and wild times at City Hall.

The YSA Commissioner Gross decided to take advantage of the loose accounting and held this party at city's expense up at Bear Mountain. What I heard the first two days in the office was nothing but the goings on at the YSA party for the managers and above. Our director described how one of the women tried to take on most of the men on the stage. Another woman challenged her for attention and did a strip tease which resulted in her being 'raped' my a host of men who wanted to do more than just watch.

According to the talk, the whole party turned into an orgy. According to the accounts few left at closing time but most stayed. Soon almost everyone was naked and having sex with anyone. The Bear Park management tried to stop the party, but were thrown out of their own restaurant. The doors were then barricaded. Both the liquor and food supplies broken into. This went on for the whole weekend. The police were not called in until Monday.

These men were saying things like:

"Did you see what Sally did?"

"Yea man that was great! DP and then some."

"Did you get a chance to f**k Linda?"

"Oh yes, she loved every minute of it."

"How many bottles of the good stuff did you get from the cellar?"

"I got about a dozen, how about you?

"Oh, about half a dozen."

This went on for hours and every possible sex act described in detail. The women who enjoyed themselves at the party dressed in a most provocative way the following week, showing as much cleavage as possible and some not wearing any undergarments as a means to invite continued attention. Later two of the women were found to be pregnant but couldn't identify the fathers. The only thing that you can compare it with would be the scenes from *The Wolf of Wall Street* movie office orgy. Several were arrested, but likely released. As one of them said:

"Hell, I f**ked over a 30 men that weekend.! How could I know who the father is?"

What finally broke it up was the state police were called in on to take back control of the building.

Within days the Daily News and other papers got a hold of the story. The next week the shit hit the fan. Commissioner Gross was arrested. Bear Mountain State Park estimated that the damages would amount too close to $100,000, this is in 1972 dollars. As more and more was being reported the whole agency management panicked. A week later the **very same individuals** who saying how great a time they had were now carrying this conversation.

"Did you go the the party at the Mountain?"

"No couldn't make it, was sick that weekend."

"Do you know anyone who went to the party?"

"No one who I work with went."

This was my introduction to YSA. Months later Commissioner Gross trial he was convicted, sentenced to do time in Sing Sing (yes it does exist). According to an inside YSA story when Gross received his prison uniform and was asked:

"What's your name?"

His response was: "I'm Commissioner Gross."

The guard responded: "Like hell you are n***er. In here you are 986254." Or something similar according to one source who told me.

Thus ended the career of Commissioner Gross and Mayor Lindsey! More on YSA next letter.

Love,
Papa

Oct. 2012

Hi T:

The YSA 'street workers' were assigned a specific area to patrol at night (usually 8 p.m. to midnight). The objective was to observe if there was any gang or youth activities which indicated possible trouble. If spotted, we were to intervene redirecting the teens and gang members to either go home, or at least not break the law. At the time the YSA street workers had a higher mortality than the police and fire departments combined!. Because I was new AND white, they assigned me the southern most area of the unit, from 76th to 90th Streets, from the Hudson River to Central Park West. Actually this was perhaps the most quiet area of all the areas the unit covered (thank goodness). You had to file a daily report of where you covered and any activities you may have seen, if any.

Mostly I reported on the hookers in the area and a few younger kids running around late at night. Over by Central Park West I ran into a small group of hippies who were enamored of a self proclaimed guru. Using this as a point of possible trouble, my report stated there was this one group/'gang' with a leader that had an overbearing influence on his group of followers. I didn't mention they were all white, nor that they were hippies, just that they needed to be watched in case the behavior turned negative. My superiors bought it. So for the next few months, I would patrol the area but focus my attention on this one group that met in the park almost every night. I even joined in some of the meditation exercises.

On Broadway I did get to know one young (early 20's) hooker and would occasionally talk with her in a diner in the neighborhood. It was turning cold. Winter was coming. We would get a cup of hot chocolate in this one diners in the upper 80's. Only natural since we walked the same beat.

What I didn't know at the time was that an older more sophisticated black man who had a private office in the back was reading my reports. After a couple of months he came up to me and introduced himself:

"Hello, I'm Delmar Woods. I am attempting to recreate a social work unit to work with the schools and youth groups around the area. I've been reading your reports, you deserve something better than the unit you are assigned to. Would you be interested in becoming a social worker?"

You can guess what my answer was. Mr. Woods told me to keep it quiet but he would see what he could do. Easy to see why. My supervisor hated Woods. I called the individual who originally interviewed me, Mrs. Bebek. She knew Mr. Woods, informing me he was one of the best social workers in the agency.

After two weeks, I got a note from downtown. I was to be assigned to Mr. Woods and the newly formed social work unit in the same YSA office. I was delighted. No more midnight walks or putting up with the less than intellectual group of street workers–brave and creative, but rarely more than a high school education. This was the opportunity that I had been wanting.

Mr. Woods was an ACSW (member of the Academy of Certified Social Workers). He fell from political grace and given a do nothing desk job in the West Harlem unit. Now the political winds were changing, mostly due to the above incident at Bear Mountain. Mr. Woods got the go ahead to reform his old unit. Our referrals usually came from schools, Boys Clubs and Police Athletic League (PAL) centers when they had a kid acting out and out of control. Our job was to investigate the child, get as much information as possible about them and their family, then refer them over to the appropriate long term care facility for counseling or therapy. It was the job of my dreams.

Of course Carol was told went the reassignment came through. After the first day on the new job, we went out and celebrated. I told her how impressed I was with Mr. Woods and expected to learn a lot from him. We both thought it was the ideal opportunity for an aspiring social worker.

Love,
Papa

March, 2013

Hi T:

The second day in the Social Work Unit, Mr. Woods asked me to come into his office so he could show me how the case folders were organized. He asked me to stand next to him behind his desk where he was sitting so I could see how the case records were organized and lay out in the binders.

Each folder was in six parts, all bound together and with clips on top where you could attached all the papers by the top after punching two holes. He carefully showed how the written referrals were put in the first section when you opened the folder. Next came the initial write up from the referring agency or school. Then in the next section was additional information from the police, schools, of social service agencies regarding the child and his family, at least a must as could be released to YSA. Then came the narrative where we would write up our visits to the family, discussions with the child being referred, etc. Since YSA was not set up to do long-term case work the last section was where our outgoing referrals to long term assistance agencies. The most common were Catholic Charities, Jewish Family Services, Children's Home Society, Foster Care, or adoption agencies, and Child Protective Services: Long term care unit.

As we were going through the layout of the folder suddenly I notice that Mr. Wood's hand was between my thighs. At first it was hardly noticeable. Then the touch became more pronounced that I couldn't help but realize it was deliberate. The hand approached my testicles. That was more than I could take. Politely asking if the example folder could be taken and review in my own office. Mr. Wood's said that was fine. I picked up the folder Then calmly and very nicely walked slowly out of his office, scared of offending him, but also realizing he wanted me for more than a case work unit.

I was in a quandary. I WANTED THIS JOB. Taking the subway south to a cross town transfer and then the IRT #6 back to 138th Street, Alexandria Avenue was a longer than usual. The conflicts within my mind were unbelievable. I just didn't know what to do. I had talked to others including Ms. Bebek. A lot could be learned from him. I didn't tell anyone what had happened until I got home that night. There was no way I would give in to Mr. Woods. I just have no desire to go in that direction. But to keep the job, would I have to give in??? All this and a whole lot more were racing in my mind as I walked the blocks from the subway station to East Side Settlement House. I slowly climbed the stairs to my apartment and waited until Carol was able to get off from work and come over.

Carol came over to see how the first full day went. I told her everything that had happened and how much the job meant. We talked about it for a long time. I was both excited about the job, but didn't want to have to suck Woods' cock off to keep it, or worse. Carol came up with a fantastic idea.

The next day I reported to work as usual. Still reviewing the case work folder if I had a question, I would politely ask Mr. Woods for clarification. Everything was going smoothly. What Mr. Woods didn't know was that since Mott Haven Center didn't open up to the staff until 2 p.m. Carol was going to meet me for lunch, She knew exactly how to dress for the occasion.

Back then the CBS TV series about cattle drives called *Raw Hide* was still popular (Clint Eastwood was the young Rowdy Yates–the start of his career) though in reruns. The the trail boss' saying was "Head them up, move them out." So Carol came over around 11:15 for lunch. She wore the most revealing V neck sweater she had. A very effective Raw Hide bra–one that heads them up and moved out her almost 40" as much as possible. The sweater must have proceeded the rest of her body by at least 4 inches. When I saw her at first I wanted to jump on her to take advantage of her appearance. However, knowing this was for Mr. Woods' benefit I restrained myself. I knocked on Mr. Woods' door. In his usually cheerful voice came:

"Come in."

Upon entering I said: "Mr Woods, I would like you to meet someone."

He looked up with all the anticipated of a five year old opening a Christmas package: "Yes.!.!.".

Carol entered. "This is my fiancee Carol B."

He up beat expression turned into one of utter despair. Carol leaned over his desk to where she was at a 90 degree angle from her hips and her tits touching the top of the desk making them almost bust out of the bra in front of his face.

"Oh Mr. Woods, I'm so happy to meet you. I can't tell you how happy Walter is working with you in this unit." She held out her hand.

Out came a very dejected baritone voice: "Oh h o w d o y o u do" came out of his mouth in mournful manner as he took her hand.

The expression on his face was priceless. He couldn't help but notice her breasts just inches away and her extended hand. He politely shook her hand with a total absence of any sincerity, just barely grasping the finger tips. Then he collapsed into his chair.

"Mr. Woods, Carol and I are going out to lunch together. I'll see you when I get back."

We turned and left. Carol and I had a delightful little lunch in a nearby deli. We laughed about Delmar's reaction. I gave her a kiss goodbye and went back to the office. I walked into his office. After lunch I walked into Mr. Woods' office.

"Mr. Woods, did you get my point?"

"YES they were **BOTH** very evident."

From that point on we had a perfect working relationship. I will always consider him one of my best supervisors in a long and varied career.

Love,
Papa

Aug. 2014

Social work adventures:

You have to understand, our Social Work Unit was not a permanent case work unit. We received referrals from various sources, researched the case and made referrals to permanent units. We rarely worked on a case for more than a few weeks.

There was one referral for our office to attempt to find a missing girl. She was a Puerto Rican, about 13 years old and had not been seen by her family for a couple of weeks. After visiting the school and talking with her teachers, it was learned she was still attending school. She must be in the area. Queries were made about extended family. It was learned that she had cousins on the East Side around 118th Street and 3rd Avenue. After talking with some kids in the area who knew her, an address was given where she might be. The next day I would visit the place to see if she was there.

That day, I worn a nice suit and after briefing Mr. Woods, took off to East Harlem. After several transfers on the busses, the last few blocks had to be walked. As I was walking down the street toward the East River, a very strange sight was surrounding me. There were limos, Caddies, Lincolns, even two Rolls Royces on the block. Every possible parking spot was filled with luxury cars. Looking down the block, a small old church became visible. Outside the church were these two LARGE characters with an extra bulge in their left side watching everything on the block. Both looked like ex Green Bay Packers interior line-men. As I approached the church, with still a block to go, they slowly moved their right hands into their left side suit 'pockets.' Realizing they were mafia, my eyes kept straight ahead. Yes, I was watching them, but not by direct eye contact. As I reached the church steps, the pace quickened. They saw I was not going into the church. Slowly they lowered their hands and when back to just watching' the block.

Later I made queries about what had happened and why the church had so many luxury cars there that day. I was told that one of the old black drivers of the Gambino Family had died. It was his funeral. All the 'family' wanted to show the deceased family how much he would be missed. There may have even been members of some of the other "families" attending as the drive was well respected by all the families. The two outside were the 'guards' for the 'family' and not the deceased's family.

Meanwhile, back to the child search. I got the the address where the girl might be staying. As I entered the building. Interesting all the steps of the stairs were missing. The address given was the 4th floor. Asking one of the tenants how does one get upstairs the response was:

"Use the railings."

So climbing up the stairs using the railing and banister, the 4th floor was gained. Long before the door was reached word got out that some idiot in a suit was climbing the stairwell. By the time the forth floor was arrived at, the whole family was in the hall to observe how the last half flight was successfully gained. I asked if 'Juanita' was living there.

"Yea, she lives here now, so her father can't rape her anymore. What of it?"

I explained who I was and why there. After a few minutes of dialogue I found out food was elevated to the upper floors via pulleys and ropes out the windows. That the landlord refused to keep up the place. All that worked was the electricity and water.

A write up was shared with the school and a full time social worker assigned to the girl. Didn't find out the results but I believe she was either placed in foster care or under the care of the family I visited.

Love,
Papa

Chapter 4

Personal life continues

Hi T:

As you can tell from the letters, Carol and I were getting to be a well known couple. We were together as much as possible and often seen around the neighborhood.

Do you recall how we met? More importantly our connection in India? I had been a Brahman priest. Unfortunately a very poor one and always in need of money. She had been my wife. Remember, keeping with the Indian traditions, our marriage was arranged. There was no love. It is likely we were married while very young and not brought together until she was old enough to bear children. When we did come together, I made a serious attempt to teach her the basics of spirituality—the basic teachings of our Hindu faith. But she wanted no part of it. She was a Hindu atheist if there ever was such a thing.

Children came fairly quickly. When I was in my mid too late 20s some disease swept through the city. I became one of the victims. But when I died, she had refused to throw herself on my pyre as was the tradition. It was a logical choice. There were five young children to care for. What was worse, she never really accepted the spiritual teachings of Vedas which I would be attempting to teach each day by the Ganges. She was meant to learn from me. But owing to my early death this never occurred. It was a karmic debt that had to be paid.

Though not aware of it during our early dating, it became more and more apparent that she was interested in both my beliefs and activities. She now accepted reincarnation, having recovered many of the memories of our previous life together. I took her to the Arcane School meetings a couple of times, but that did not appeal to her. She had never had any exposure to meditation nor was she familiar with the Alice Bailey books nor Theosophical concepts. She did become interested in Co Masonry. She would meet me after the Co-Masonic meetings for dinner, often with some of the members. Soon she wanted to join.

She must have been one of the first petitioners outside of the close circle of CoM family members to petition for years. She and I were certainly the youngest members, at least once she was admitted. Her joining was connected to the old karmic debt. Co-Masonry was to be her introduction to the spiritual teachings she refused to accept all those centuries before in India.

Her petition was accepted. It was one of my greatest joys during our time together. To be the Senior Deacon and conductor during her initiation was a joy. Besides it was fun! Actually it was also amusing. If you ever go on the internet and look up Masonic initiation you can quickly learn the candidate is told to put on a special robe, while exposing their left knee, and left breast. The robes in Co-M were not like the ones used in the masculine lodges. The robes usually had a fairly large cutouts in the breast areas. With Carol her breasts were so large and sagged down so far, you couldn't actually see a little more but the rounded flesh that was only slightly exposed through the hole in the robe. So only part of her left breast was made bare for the ceremony. Still it went very well and the lodge had a great celebration after the ceremony. It was a great day for Marie Deraismes Lodge #352.

As for Carol, after reflecting upon the ceremony and the overall experience, it was as if this was an introduction to something that had been missing from her life. Or in our case–lives! She fell in love with Masonry and the idea of a school of philosophical and spiritual teaching without the dogma of any particular religion. It was a perfect match for her at this time in her life.

Love,
Papa

Sept. 2014, #2

Hello again:

Before you get more about Masonry here is a little bit of fun Carol and I shared.

Neither Carol nor I were earning enough to afford the great white way of the main Broadway theaters. So we would try to find less expensive entertainment. During the summer months this was easy with all the concerts and activities in Central Park and elsewhere. But during the other months we had to keep it cheap! We found the perfect solution (OK a film list is coming).

There was a little movie theater near Times Square that was showing Japanese films. The price was right, only a couple of dollars and usually a double feature. The favorite films were the popular ones from a few decades earlier, especially those directed by Akira Kurosawa. But they would also show films by other great directors of the 1950s and 1960s. The Bijoux (not sure of the spelling) movie theater on 46th Street, where the Lunt-Fontanne Theatre is now, became a favorite destination on either Friday or Saturday nights, at least once a month, if not more.

It was there that we first saw the *Seven Samurai*, still my favorite, as well you should know. It is interesting to watch *The Magnificent Seven* the dramatic Western with the great caste. Note in the credits the acknowledgement to the Toho Company of Japan because it was a copy of the *Seven Samurai*. This was the movie that made me love Takashi Shimura (wonderful in *Ikiru*) as the samurai who shaves his head like a monk to rescue a kidnapped boy. But this and many of the other films had Toshiro Mifume turned him into my favorite actor of all times. I remember his staring in a number of American films: *Hell in the Pacific* with Lee Marvin is excellent. But I loved Inagaki's *Samurai Trilogy*. Mizoguchi's *Ugetsu*, and *Sansho the Bailiff* were memorial. Teshigahara's *Woman in the Dunes* certainly left an impression as did *Bushido* and the *Samurai Saga* by Tadashi Imai. *Sword of Doom* was a favorite, staring Tatsuya Nakadai who also appeared in some of Kurosawa films.

Kurosawa became my favorite director. We tried hard never to miss one if his films that were being shown. *Rashomon* has to be one of the greats of all times, made into an American version. It tells the same story from the perspective of the mugger, the rape victim, the husband's ghost, and a witness. NONE of which match any of the others. Wonderful psychological tale. I loved *Yojimbo* and it's follow up *Sanjuro* both of which stared Toshiro Mufune. *Red Beard* is great! Later, after leaving NYC I loved *Dodesukaden*, *Ran*, and *Kagemusha* which were released in the late 1970's and 1980's. If you ever can't think of a present for me, see if you can find *Red Beard* or *Sanjuro* which I would love to add to my collection of movies.

There were fun films too. Zatoichi the blind masseur/gambler was always amusing. These were a series of films which started to come out in the 1960's but continued for some time. They were always a mix of sword fighting and satire. Zatoichi, being blind, used his cane as a sword. But when challenged, became an unbeatable dualist who always defeated the enemy. One of my favorite of these films was *Zatoichi Meets Yojimbo* where Shintaro Katsu, the actor who made Zatoichi famous is challenged by Toshiro Mifune to a fight. Mifune makes a thrust into Zatoichi's body and Zatoichi pretends to curl over in agony, only to reveal that Yojimbo's sword was captured in his cane's sheath.

When the Zatoichi films were shown, it was usually a double feature as the films tended to be shorter than the Kurosawa films that would last up to 3 hours.

Love,
Papa

Oct. 2014

Hi T:

Got to finish the previous thought on Japanese food and movies:

What just as fun, the Sushi Genza restaurant had just opened up, just across 7th Avenue and Broadway on the opposite side of Time's Square as the Bijoux. Thus dinner and movie evenings consisted of going to the Sushi Genza and then to the Bijoux or to the Bijoux and then to the Sushi Genza. What was unique about the Sushi Genza, it was the first sushi restaurant for the working class. There were other sushi restaurants in New York, but they tended to be VERY expensive and quite exquisite. The Sushi Genza was a small place with only around a dozen tables and a sushi bar with no more than 8 seats. This is where the lower income American-Japanese would go for dinner.

Carol and I discovered the Sushi Genza after walking back from the Bijoux movie one night. It was perfect. A Japanese dinner would be the perfect cap to a Japanese movie. So we went in. Now you must realize sushi was not the common fair it is today. Back then you would have a hard time finding any but the expensive Japanese dining rooms offering any sushi. When we entered we just stared at the chef preparing the raw fish. Neither of us had ever seen this before. Of course on our first visit we ordered tempura. Not enough courage to try raw fish, yet.

If we saw the movie first I would always strut over to the Genza in a samurai stride. If the film was the *Seven Samurai* the music theme called the parade of the samurai would be running through my head as I walked. Carol thought this was fun and the walk just added to the theme of the evening.

After a couple of visits, I finally got up the courage to order sushi. IT WAS GREAT. I was a convert. Carol tried it, very gingerly at first. But she began to love it too. Soon that was all we would order. Of course the miso soup came with the meal along with the hot green tea. This became our monthly night out. Dinner and a movie, both being Japanese. Of course the staff at the Sushi Genza got to know us and would warmly welcome us every time we entered. It felt we were part of their family.

One of the funnest things that happened was when a Puerto Rican family came in. It was a couple with a young son and daughter. They four of them were seated at a table near Carol and I. They looked at the menu and couldn't imagine eating anything that was listed. The father insisted upon a family dish of fried rice. The poor waiter tried to explain that fried rice was a Chinese/American dish. This was a Japanese restaurant. They didn't have fried rice. The father got more and more insistent:

"You Asian, all Asian restaurants have fried rice." He was raising his voice and was getting more and more belligerent.

I beaconed the manager over to my table.

"This guy has a hungry family but doesn't know one dish from another. Just fix your mixed vegetable tempura, then toss it and a large bowl of rice into a frying pay with soya sauce and serve it to them. They won't know the difference."

The manager told the waiter to take the order. Then they did exactly as was suggested. It was a mix of shrimp tempura, mixed vegetables and regular white rice all thrown all thrown into a wok pan with soy sauce, tossed up and down a few times and served in a large bowl they almost never used. The family was perfectly happy.

The manager thanked me for helping out. It reminded me of the Rockford Collage disaster were they served uncooked fried rice the the Japanese consulate for a 'Japanese Night' at the college.! The college chef refused to take my advice to serve tempura or other Japanese dishes, insisting that fried rice was perfect. Problem was, he didn't even know how to prepare it. That meal was a disaster!

Love,
Papa

Not sent

On my birthday two couples including Randy and Doris came over with Carol to the apartment on the top of East Side House Settlement. The other couple were married. I had seen them on several occasions. They were close to Randy and Doris. Carol knew them. The two young teenage girls accompanied them were friends. They also came as an adventure to spend an evening in the heart of the South Bronx. The occasion was to be a surprise birthday party. All that knew me had a gift. One was a record. I love records. It was from the married couple who's names I have forgotten. Of course being a lover of music, especially classical I quickly unwrapped it. Much to my surprise it was a album of the Kinks. I had never heard of the group.

"Walter we think your are kind of a kinky guy. So we thought this was a perfect album for you."

I thanked them, trying hard not to show my disappointment. I don't think the album ever got played. The other gifts were small items, a tie, candy and other items, all appreciated more than the record.

After a pizza dinner and a few drinks, we were trying to determine what to do for entertainment. The only game in the apartment was backgammon. Not appropriate for eight people. Randy said let's play spin the bottle. After a few spins and almost everyone having been kissed. Someone suggested making it more interesting.

Whoever was chosen had to remove an article of clothing. Though there were a little hesitant all agreed to the new rules. This began a game of strip spin the bottle. From the beginning the bottle seemed to point to myself and Doris more than the others. In no time I was nude followed by Doris on the next spin. Doris admitted being embarrassed at first, but after a few minutes was walking around with no hesitation. She was an attractive woman of average proportions. Nicely formed breasts and hips. Of course I had no problem being in the natural state. Remember the art class where I posed once in the nude back in college when the class asked for volunteers to pose. I was the only one who did pose.

Soon the other two men were down to their undershorts. When the wife of the man who gave me the Kink's album had to take off her bra, she quickly shook her long blond tresses in front of her breast. It was then we were told they had a baby at home and she was breast feeding. Her husband said it was fun squeezing her breast, watching the milk shoot out. Much to his wife's surprise, he grabbed her breast and projected some of her milk towards my mouth. It was funny to both of us, but she was very embarrassed.

The next person down to her bra and panties was Carol. When the bottle pointed to her, she was very hesitant to expose her massive mammaries. I suggested she take off her panties if she was too shy to expose her tits. This put the reluctance over the edge. She got up and took off her bra. The gentleman who's wife had just squirted some milk, gave a loud cheer. They were the largest breasts he had ever seen. Carol shook them to the amazement of the rest of the group. The two teenage girls who I did not know, also became topless, but like the mother, had long flowing hair to cover themselves. While this was going on I was walking around. There had been no decision as to what would follow being deprived of all clothing.

I did see Doris laying on her stomach on the carpet. A though entered into my mind to jump on top of her. But being unsure how Randy and Carol might take it, decided not too, even if only as a joke. The suggestion that the girls be blindfolded and have to guess who's penis they were touching was rejected. The younger girls were just too reluctant. The same suggestion was made for the men to feel the exposed breasts. Carol said it would be too easy for all the men to tell it was her. The lactating mother would have also been easy to tell. Much to the dismay of the men, that addition to the game was rejected.

As for the mother, her husband said she was shy because even while lactating, her breasts were still relatively small. She really felt inadequate after seeing Carol. I sat next to them and told her that small breast were very attractive and usually much more sensitive. I convinced her that she was a very attractive woman and with beautiful small breasts. What could have turned into a very sexual adventurous evening, fizzled out.

Chapter 5

YSA again, Co-M, and Kali

Jan. 2015

Hi T:

The adventures in the Social Work Unit were many.

In the mean time, the work in Harlem started to pick up. There were several cases referred to the social work unit. Mr. Woods would give me the information about the kids in trouble and ask me to check it out.

One of the first cases involved a kid who was constantly acting up in junior high (now called middle school). What was unusual was he was white of German background. Since we had a written referral, I went to visit the school. The vice principal was the only administrator in the school at the time. This VP was a small white man, no more than 145 lbs and around 5'6". He was shown the referral letter. I asked him if he could tell me anything about 'John.'

He told me how John disrupted the class. Something had to be done about his anger and acting up. Asking about John's siblings he told me there was a history of problems with the whole family. I asked if he would make the John's files available to me.

"No they are confidential."

He was willing to talk the boy but not share the files. Just then there was an announcement over the speaker:

"Intruder has been seen in the building."

He said very quietly "Oh dear" under his breath He was visibly scarred.

I chimed up: "Would you like me to accompany you in your search for the intruder?"

"Oh would you be so kind."

We walked all the corridors and halls. No intruder was found. Who ever it many have been likely realized he was in the wrong building and left. This was a relatively small school in a crowded neighborhood so possible mistake. Either that or it was a parent who picked up his child and left without checking in at the office.

When we returned to the VP's office he thanked me profusely. I leaned over and gently patted the back of his hand. Then said in a very gay manner:

"Well I am JUST so happy you helped me. If there is ANYTHING else you may want, just let me know" as my loving squeeze was applied to his hand.

I gave him a loving look saying:

"May I see any of the files on the family?"

He led me to the office and pulled out not only John's files but the files of the whole family. It was a really troubled family. I read the files, made notes and when finished went back to his office to thank him.

"Oh I'm so happy I was able to be of help, I do hope we can get help for John."

He got up and came over very close to me, stroking my shoulder: "When can I see you again?"

I turned to him and said: "Sorry but my feathers just don't go in that direction. Bye honey!" I turned and walked out. His look of frustration was unbelievable.

When I got back to the office I told Mr. Woods EVERYTHING that happened and how I was able to get to read the files. He laughed long and hard. When he was able to regain composure he turned to me: "Walter, you are going to make one of the best social workers in New York City."

He did his best over the next few months to help me anyway he could. I got back to the office and did the write up. After a home visit I found a 7 year old girl in the home under the kitchen table. Still in diapers and unable to speak. It appeared the father didn't feel a girl was worth any attention. It was a classic of psychological cruelty. Eventually all 4/5 (?) children were removed from the home and the family kicked off welfare. Just one of the early cases referred all the children to Child Protective Services. There were many more cases and incidents but these stand out.

There was the Hispanic woman who wanted help. She had 7 children and an abusive husband. There wasn't anything we could do so Mr. Woods suggested she go to Catholic Services. When her husband found out she went to ask for help, he started hitting her. All the children started to cry. Since she was in a project building, she took the elevator to the 20th floor, walked up the stairs to the roof. and jumped out in a way that her family could see her go splat on the sidewalk below their window. One solution to her problem.

Love,
Papa

March, 2015

Hello There:

One night after a date with Carol I dropped her off at her apartment. She lived in one of the Mott Haven Project buildings on 143rd Street and Willis Ave., across from Alexander Avenue where East Side House was. It was a tall building, crime ridden, and across from Mott Haven Community Center where she worked. I would walk through the project drive ways back to East Side House,. It may have been more dangerous, but most in the area knew me. Besides when I walked Carol home, I carried my old rock hammer I had when in high school and with a 9" knife on my belt on the other side. Can't carry a gun in NYC! If you are not a crook! There is nothing about carrying other weapons! Seldom did I had any problems. If there was a "feeling" of danger, the knife would be drawn out and in my left hand, in full sight, while the pointed end of the rock hammer was even more threatening. Nope—rarely had any problem.

As I was approaching Alexandria Avenue, I heard a little tiny thin "meow." It sounded like a small kitten. I looked in the bushes. But didn't see anything. Making the little noises I do when calling a pet, suddenly this very little kitten meowed again and came towards me. She could not have been more than 4 pounds. There was little doubt that someone's cat had kittens that were likely put in a bag and thrown out. This little one somehow escaped and made it to the bushes. She must have heard me coming and started to meow in hopes there would be some kind person to rescue her. She was cold, underfed and wet. I picked her up and put her in my jacket. Had no idea how I would be able to keep her but had to give her shelter for the night.

When we got inside I poured a bowl of milk for her. The whole bowl disappeared FAST. So I gave her more. After petting and talking to her for a while, she began to purr like she was really happy. Most likely she was! She started to stretch and flex her claws while in my arms. She gave little love bites since her teeth were small–those little bites hurt. Still they were love bites and she meant no harm. It was late while not having a litter box, I just took it for granted that she would piss somewhere in the apartment and I would just have to clean it up in the morning. A couple of pillows and a mini blanket were made for her bed. I also blocked the hall so that she would only have access to my bathroom, common room and my bedroom. When she saw me climb into bed she curled up and went to sleep.

When I got up in the morning I fully expected to find a mess somewhere. Looking all over the area where she had access to, there was no sign she relieved herself. She was fed some cooked eggs and more milk. Then she stated to mew as if she wanted something. Realizing she had not gone to the bathroom since picking her up, and not having a litter box, I found a box lid and tore up a newspaper into the box top. She watch closely. I stood up and said: "There." She jumped into the box and everything she had been holding inside came out. Here was a little tiny kitten who was so house broken that she refused to soil the rooms of her rescuer. It was at that moment I realized she was to be **my** cat.

Carol came over in the morning and I introduced her to the kitten. She immediately curled up in her arms and started to purr. She was at home with both of us. I told Ruby, who lived in the other apartment on the same floor. She had no problems about a cat living on my side of the apartment. Bill S, the head of the Settlement House was notified. No problem either. Now for a name. Thinking about how she showed affection through those sharp claws and little bites, the logical name was Kali, the Hindu goddess and wife of Shiva. That afternoon after a trip to the store a proper litter box was prepared and put in the bathroom. Kali would usually sleep at the foot of my bed, which was not possible if Carol spent the night. On those nights she was happy on her little bed of the mini blanket. She was home. I had a pet.

In no time Kali was very comfortable at the apartment. She made friends with Rose who actually liked her once she became use to having Kali around. Kali became my second favorite pet after Lilly, my Irish Setter in Connecticut who had been taken away from me when I was young.

Love,
Papa

April, 2015

Hello T:

Carol took to Co-Masonry as if it was a long lost salvation. She loved the elderly members. Of course they loved her. She loved the rituals. She took to studying the catechisms and progressed as fast as the time limits permitted. In Co-M, or at least in Marie Deraismes Lodge, you had to wait at least 5 months before you could put in the "Bag of Propositions" a request for examination for advancement to the Fellow Craft (FC) Degree. I loved going over the rituals with her. We would spend time working on the catechisms when she was ready to put in a request for promotion.

As an aside I felt it was necessary to provide a greater understanding of what was happening. This letter hast to provide a little more information about Masonry in general and Co-Masonry in particular. To understand the Bag of Propositions you must understand a little of the ritual. At the closing of the lodge, there were two bags (literally little cloth bags) pass by the Senior and Junior Deacons. The Senior Deacon had the Bag of Propositions. The Junior Deacon had the Bag of Benevolence. Each Deacon would walk around the lodge to each of the members and collect a dollar (or whatever they wish to contribute) in each bag. In the former (B of P), members would put in cash to help support the lodge along with any proposition they would want the lodge and the Worshipful Master to consider. This would include the requests for advancement. The Bag of Benevolence was to collect funds for any charitable cause that would come up for consideration. The latter was deposited in a separate account. Should a member of the lodge need some special assistance, the Benevolence fund would be the source. If the fund exceeded a certain amount a charity would be considered and voted on in the Lodge for a donation. After the bags were circulated the Worshipful Master would examine the B of P to see if there was any written propositions in it. He or she would take out the proposition and read it to the lodge. If action was required, it would usually take place at the next meeting.

Another point needing clarification is Co-M meets and does business in the 1st–Entered Apprentice (EA) Degree. This has to be mentioned because many of the masculine lodges in the United States meet and do business only in the 3rd Degree (Master Mason's Degree). Virginia is a good example of working only in the 3rd Degree. In the lodges that are maintaining the tradition of only meeting in the MM Degree (except for degrees), the EAs and FCs are not permitted in the lodge meetings. The more progressive lodges in the USA are moving towards doing business in the EA Degree. Many of the lodges in Washington, D.C. are good examples. This allows even the newly initiated EAs to participate and observe the workings of the lodge immediately. It is interesting in visiting different lodges those that appear to be growing tend to meet and work in the EA Degree. Those that are stuck in the old traditions of only meeting the the MM Degree are just barely maintaining status quo, or slowing dying though there are a few exceptions.

In Co-M the EAs are permitted to observe the meetings, but may not speak on any business items. In theory they are not to speak at all unless addressed by the Worshipful Master of the Lodge. The FCs may contribute to discussions within the lodge but are not allowed to vote. It is only the MMs are permitted to vote. This combines some of the old traditions whereby only a MM is considered a full Masons, while still allowing those who do not have the 3rd Degree to participate. It works well.

Love,
Papa

Chapter 6

Flashbacks and other adventures

May, 2015

How about a series of flash backs:

Pawtucket was experienced in my Junior year as an undergrad but where not included in the earlier letters. As a result the adventures in Rhodes Island are narrated here in a series of letters:

In the letters about my college forgot my summer jobs. One because they are fun and second, after seeing the movie Selma, I have to report my encounter with Georgia Governor George Wallace. So this is where we will start.

Once upon a time I told you about being in Rockford at the end of October and saw Presidential Candidate Herbert H. Humphrey. He was behind in the polls but was beginning to turn it around. What killed him was the violence and riots that occurred after the killing of RFK and Martin Luther King, Jr. allowing old "Tricky Dick" (Richard Nixon) to win. This was just days before the election and when I asked what would he most want. "One more week." was the response. In the book It's Me The Early Years there is a photo of HHH in the back along with a photo of Mohammad Ali, both of which I took at the rally.

What is interesting was my summer job that year. Mom was working for a character who owned a string of small newspapers. Mom asked if one might be willing to hire me for the summer. Thus I got a summer job with the Pawtucket Times in Rhodes Island. Mostly as a 'cub reporter' taking the obits and small news items on the candlestick phones. Since I had a camera and was interested in photography I did tag along with Flash, the lead photographer on some jobs. This way many of the other phototogs got to know me, those from the Boston Globe, Providence Journal, etc. We covered mostly disasters but other stories as well.

One job I was on my own. The old racist George Wallace was running for President as an independent. He actually carried 5 states, all in the South. He was having a convention in either New Port or Providence. I was assigned to cover the event. I had the Press credentials and badge. The convention was filled with Rhode Island red necks but in the back of the hall there was a large group of mostly Black and a other demonstrators. The photographers roped area was right in front of the speaker's podium.

I took some photos of Wallace, one of which was used on the front page. It showed him with one of his typically ugly sneer and his finger pointing down at an angle. Great photo showing him at his worse! Then I slipped out of the photographer's area towards the demonstrators. They were getting more vocal and as I approached, the Wallace goons locked arm in arm, and along with the rent-a-cops they started marching in on the demonstrators, who had NO WHERE to go. As a result, they were being packed in like cows in a cattle car off to the packing plant.

Suddenly one black women fainted. One of the goons behind the front line shouted:

"Get her, she is trying to break the lines."

The 'security officers' started hitting her with billy clubs and kicking her while she was down. I tried to take a photo of the incident (unfortunately it didn't come out due to the movement of the camera and being pushed). But a rent-a-cop shouted:

"Get that kid and his camera!"

The next thing I saw a half dozen goons after me. I jumped on the tables and leaped from one table to another with the thugs right behind me pushing seated people to one side or another. As I approached the photographers roped off area, they were within a few feet of me. I shouted: "**Help!**" and made a huge leap towards the other phototogs.

Two of the photographers resembled interior linemen of a major league football team caught me in mid air. They quick stood me on my feet and faced the goon squad.

"If you want this kid, you'll have to come through us!"

They were much larger than the goons and now the whole photo corps was looking at us. Wallace's men turned swearing. I thanked the guys and told what happened. They continue to escort me safely to my car.

The next week the rumor was The Pawtucket Times photographer was to receive an award for the best photo coverage of the Wallace Convention. Then when they found out it was a summer part-timer, the award quietly disappeared into the atmosphere.

Love,
Papa

July, 2015

More Summer Job flashback:

The summer in Pawtucket was interesting in more ways than one. Although I really wanted to work as a photographer. They labeled me as a 'cub reporter.' Primary duty was to take ads and obits over the phone. What was interesting was they used the old fashioned candlestick phones. You quickly learned how to hold the phone's mouth piece between your ring and little finger, while pointing the speaker towards the ear with the rest of your hand. All in the left hand. This freed the right to take notes.

Whenever there was a chance I would tag along with the principal photographer. Flash the photographer who tucked me under his wing was really a great guy. The first week there, Flash came running out and said:

"Come on Walter."

We ran to his car. There was a Corning Glass factory fire. When we arrived the factory managers were organizing a press tour. We got in the back of the crowd. Suddenly Flash bent down to tie his shoelace. He was taking his time.

"Flash, we'll be separated from the group."

He just smiled and nodded. Soon the press tour group had disappeared. Flash said:

"OK, let's go."

He got up and went in an opposite direction. We saw firemen and rescue crew coming up from a staircase. Flash motioned downward with his fingers. Soon we were in the middle of where the molten glass had spewed out of the furnace. There was hot glass everywhere. Since we both had press badges no one paid any attention. He took photos of the glass now all over the factory floor. He turned one corner and got a picture of a man being carried out on a stretcher, a large part of his leg encased in glass. Flash turned to me:

"Never follow the crowd, you'll will never get the great shots."

Flash and I often went around the corner to a little diner for lunch. Their speciality was hot dogs. You could get a hot dog for $0.35 or two for $0.50. I asked why are they so cheap. He pointed out that next door was a meat packing plant.

"Don't look too closely at the dogs you are eating."

Sure enough, after a number of lunches at the diner, I had pulled out dog and cat hair from one dog. A rat tooth from another.

"Well it's all meat."

When pointing it out something strange in the bun on another day Flash he said:

"Ever notice there are so few stray animals in town. Well since these hot dogs don't cross state line, they don't have to be inspected. What you are eating is meat. Just don't ask what it is from."

I didn't. We kept having lunch there for the rest of the summer.

The evening photographer was much younger than Flash. He used to tell me tales of different jobs. His favorite was when he had to take a photo of a car twisted around a telephone pole. The car was actually completely wrapped around the pole with the front and read bumpers over lapping. While positioning himself for a better shot his foot kicked a cloth bag. A fireman ran up to him:

"Don't kick that bag, that's the kid's head!"

I had a similar job. A group of kids stole a car and decided to race along an abandoned railroad track. They thought they could jump over the old RR bridge. The only problem the tracks and bridge no longer existed. They thought if they went fast enough they could make the jump in the car. Almost succeeded! The roof made it. One of the kids was still alive with the rescue crew arrived, but not for long. The driver's body was mostly in the gas tank, or at least what was left of it. The other passages were found in the engine, in the trunk, and with body parts scattered all over. The speedometer, when found, showed that when they hit the abutment, the car was going over 95 mph. Fortunately by the time I got there, most of the body parts had already been collected. I took photos of what was left of the car and where the impact was on the stone. It was unbelievable to me that they didn't even try to build a ramp to make the jump. More on the paper next letter.

Love,
Papa

Aug. 2015

More about Pawtucket:

One of Flash's favorite stunts was to wash out the chemical cans which contained the developer and hypo used in developing film. These usually have the poison warning posted on each can. In fact the chemicals are highly poisonous if ingested. We would then use the cans for drinks. He had a favorite joke. Couldn't play it on the old timers as they had seen it a thousand times. So he waited until one of the newer reporters or managers would come into the photo lab and ask for something. Flash would then grabbed the can filled with soda and shout:

"I can't take the pressure of all your demands anymore."

Whereupon he would down the fluid and fall to the floor. Most had already seen this before. He did scare the hell out of some of the newer staff. It was always a good laugh. We really did use the cans to pour the large bottles of soda which had been in the fridge for us to drink out of.

One of the things Flash taught me was to get greater contrast in my shots. If the negative was not as crisp with its black and white contrast, he showed me how to burn in various areas. This could be done with cardboard with various holes which you would hold between the enlarger and the paper. The light from the enlarger could then expose just the areas of the paper that needed to be darker. Flash never used the cardboard. Instead he would cup his two hands together burn in the areas to be darkened. It was soon after learning these tricks. I did away with the cardboard using my hands as he had demonstrated.

That summer saw a great improvement in developed pictures. Partly due to better equipment. Partly due to practice. A lot due to his coaching. The technique and striving for good contrast was re-emphasized when a photography class was taken with a 'professor' who had studied with Minor White when at Franconia College a two years later. Minor White was one of the great photographers on the earlier part of 1900's and helped create the 'zone system.' If you ever see your grandmother's light meter, on it you will see the zone system contrast guide glued to the meter. Match the shade of what you are photographing with the shade on the meter to get a better contrast on the finished print. All of this doesn't matter anymore with Photoshop and the other digital photo tools. It was important in the 1960's when black and white photos were king.

While in Pawtucket I was staying in the YMCA only a block or two from the newspaper. It was an interesting experience. The room was small. Bathrooms were shared. They would supply new towels and sheets once a week. Most of those staying there were long time elderly residents. Some transient workers. There were a few others who had been there for some time, mostly because it was cheap. The man in the room next to me, must have been a little older than I am now. He would sit by the window watching. When asked what he was looking for the answer was always:

"I'm waiting for my wife. She said she would pick me up any day."

Apparently he had married a much younger woman who stuck him in the Y. He had been there for at least 3 years possibly more, looking for the return of his wife. She never came. But day after day he would sit by that window looking for her.

There were a number of body builders who would work out in the gym. These guys looked a lot like Charles Atlas (famous body builder of the 1950's), this was before Schwarzenegger became well known. They hung out together and seldom talked to anyone outside of their group.

One of the more interesting characters was a middle aged man who had a regular job. He was a little slender and fairly good looking, with a full head of hair and dark eyes. Never learned what kind of job he had, but it was regular employment. After stopping for dinner somewhere, he would retire to his room. He would come to the Y and change into tux shirt, tie and jacker—no pants. He would then walk the halls until he was tired and went back into his room for sleep. It was amusing seeing him with full formal wear from his patented leather shoes, over the calf socks, held up with garter belts on both legs, then nothing from the top of the garter belt to the bottom of his shirt. Overall you could say many of the residents in the Y were perfect candidates for mental facilities. But there were few psychiatrists or mental health professionals who would have taken on these cases.

There were a number of high school aged boys would come to the Y because of the gym and body building equipment. Three I got to work out with. A few admired several of the well built men working out regularly. We were talking one afternoon. All were amazed at this one individual who was preparing for body building competition. This was a period when gays were not seen nor accepted as they are now. They were considered abnormal and deviant. The boys said how much they wanted to be like this one individual. I asked if they liked boys more than girls? They didn't understand the question. I told them that I had never seen any of these body builders with women. They often hang out by themselves. Isn's that a little strange.

"Take a look at their legs. You don't see any hair do you. What real man shaves his legs?"

They looked. "You mean that are gay?"

Looking at them myself: "What do you think?

Hated to bust their bubble. The boys no longer idolized that body builder. How things have changed, dramatically over the years.

Love,
Papa

Sept. 2015

Still in Rhodes Island:

That summer was remarkable for many reasons. Once with Flash we were out on a shot. He saw some hippy girls with very dirty feet. He asked when they had taken a shower. One said the night before, they had just been walking all day in the streets to get to a festival. Actually it was the New Port Folk Festival. Flash turned to me:

"You can't tell me she showered last night with her feet that dirty."

It was a wake up sentence. From that point on whenever someone started with 'You can't tell me….' I never did. That is a clear sign of a closed mind. By the way, my feet would be just a dirty after a day walking bare foot, especially if walking on the roadside as she had done.

Towards the end of the summer I hooked up with some Baha'is. Likely through the job. But one weekend they were going to the Folk Festival and invited me along. This was actually a multi-day trip making it a long weekend. On the way to New Port we stopped by an elder black woman's home for lunch and to pick her up.

Dorothy was in her 60's and had joined the Baha'i Faith a few years before. She was never happy with the traditional Christian nonsense and had been looking for something else. Baha'i offered her a more positive faith. She and I started talking, separate from the group. It quickly became evident she had past life memories. I held her hand and starred into her eyes. Images of other life times came to me. I would describe what the 'impressions' were. She sat up and confirmed each image I was picking up on. Each was in her mind since she was a young child. But growing up in the South and part of a Baptist family, like my experience with my dad, she quickly learned that such memories were not welcomed. She soon shut them out of all her conversations. Sitting with me, they came flooding back.

We they got in the car to pick up some more to go to the Festival. Dorothy and I continued our conversation in the back seat. The more we talked the more light shown in her eyes. It was as if a shroud had been lifted and a bright new soul was allowed to shine through. When we arrived at the Festival, knowing that she was not going to walk all around like the rest of us, she turned to me:

"Are you HE?"

"Who?" I asked.

Dorthy: "Are you the returning Christ?"

"Dorothy, I am no where near that high. I'm only one who also remembers and is here to help others."

By this time tears of joy were in her eyes. As she hugged me good-bye, she thanked me for explaining what had been with her all her life, but never understood. It was a moving moment. I kissed her on the cheek and tried to generate a chi energy blessing as we parted.

Later in the Festival as we were moving from one stage to another I ran into an old acquaintance, William F. Buckley. Remember he was from Sharon, Connecticut. I had met him and the rest of the family in some of the local discussion groups held by various forums in NW Connecticut. He didn't remember me. He as too busy putting down someone who didn't have the ability to challenge him at his level. Few could. I chimed in with a few terse comments that shot down some of his arguments turned and left before he could counter attack.

As we were moving to another impromptu performance, suddenly I felt a huge push from behind me. Nothing physical. It was pure psychic energy. Someone with the most powerful aura was behind me. I asked:

"Who is coming."

Some of the others felt the same energy. They turned me around. There was Pete Seeger. It seemed as if a halo was surrounding him. He was the most spiritual being I had ever seen. AND HE WAS AN ATHEISTS! He was moving through the crowd. If a group was not drawing an audience, he would ask if he could join them. None would refuse such an offer. He would give them a mini workshop. Make suggestions. Then as they jammed together, a larger crowd would gather. Once they had audience, he would bid them good-bye and move on to the next group.

Some would follow Pete, but there was always a larger group that stayed behind before he joined in. I watched him do this with 5 different groups. His soul's light was the brightest one could imagine. And he wasn't even aware of it. He was just being Pete! What a great soul.

Love,
Papa

From Detroit #1 Oct. 22, 2015

Interesting Job:

There were photo assignments that were fun. I remember be given as assignment to photograph Miss Pawtucket who was to compete in the Miss Rhode Island Beauty Pageant. She was a cute dirty blond with a nice figure. I was to take a few glamor shots for the newspaper. She was posed on her front porch, then in a hammock. This latter photograph was the best and printed for the paper. They actually wanted more with different outfits on. It didn't occur to me to ask her to change so the evening photographer went back out to take more shots. When they reviewed my favorite shot, it was rejected because 'it showed too much leg.' Her short skirt was well up her thigh, a little too high apparently. Interesting in that if she was in a swim suit, it would have shown a lot more leg. That shot was not selected, but two of mine and one large one of the other photographer were selected in the spread on this local beauty queen.

Another interesting assignment was the news a local teenager had purchased a hurst and turned it into a hippy mobile. According to neighbors and others it was really well decorated and a major spectacle. I can imagine what the back was used for, since it had been roomy enough for a coffin, it was a perfect "F*#*–mobile." When I arrived at the home of this kid, he and the car were absent. Both his parents were home. His father said the kid was expected soon. So we sat on the front porch and talked, and talked, and talked.

The father was born in Maine, grew up in a logging family and became a logger himself. He met his wife in high school. They were married after their senior year. The oldest child was the boy with the hurst. Suddenly a girl of about 9 came out and asked him for something. Don't remember what. He turned to me and said:

"She has been a very interesting child."

When asked why, he started telling me a story from when she was about 5 or 6 years old. Apparently she would occasionally ask her mother of father for a play toy which she didn't have. When they said: "You don't have X."

She would turn away sadly but then come back saying something like:

"Oh that was before I came here."

As the dad spoke, he seemed to open up to me more and more. He said most interesting of these episodes. One Sunday morning the girl came running into the kitchen and said:

"Mommy, Daddy, it's Sunday, can we go for a ride in the surrey?"

Her parents didn't know what a surrey was. Her mother turned to her asking:

"What's a surrey honey?"

She turned to her mother and said:

"I'm sorry mommy that was when I was a little boy a long time ago. Before I came to live with you and daddy."

After realizing her parents didn't know what a surrey was, she gave them a complete description. Later she tried to draw one. For a 6 year old the drawing was fairly accurate. Interesting in that she had never seen a surrey in this lifetime.

There had been other memories of what must have been a previous life. Speaking with the dad, he had begun to do a little research and learned a tinny bit about reincarnation. We spoke for some time. Some of my experiences and those of others I had come into contract with were shared. Over an hour went by. It was time to leave. He thanked me. For the first time he finally understood the memories of his daughter. The conclusion together with the impressions from the girl herself, who by now had joined her dad to listen to me, was that she was a boy likely living in the 1890's. 'He' must have died of a disease or accident while under the age of 10. Based on some of the conversation, a disease was the likely cause of death. Every Sunday her previous family would go out for a ride into the country side in their surrey. This was the most happy memory of that life and she really missed it in this life. I may not have gotten the photo of the hippy hurst but the conversation with the dad and his girl likely was worth more than any photo of a car. He really appreciated my sharing thoughts on reincarnation.

Love,
Papa

Detroit #2 Oct. 23, 2015

Last on Pawtucket. End of Summer beginning of new school year:

I was trying to call your grandmother. Some how I had a feeling things were not going well. Yet I couldn't get anything from her when we talked. But there was something she was hiding from me.

By the time my summer job was over she picked me up and we drove back to Connecticut. It was then I learned that she had been fired. We were broke, again. I was a little worried about her facing real poverty again. Just as I was about to return to Rockford College. We talked about it. She knew opening up the Letter Shop again would not provide her enough to support herself and the expenses college would take.

The first move was to attempt to get an increase from the Tabor Fund scholarship. She talked to Dr. Joe and was able to get a bit of increase that would cover books and housing. That was the first step. Dr. Joe talked to Missy Hart about mom working for her full time. In the past mom had done little jobs for Mrs. Hart, as part of the secretarial service. Dr. Joe knowing that Missy wanted to do a biography on her father, Adm. Bronson, suggested mom may be the person to help. By the end of September she was hired full time by the Adm. and Mrs. Hart.

This actually took a great deal of worry off my shoulders. Knowing she was working at a decent salary was a great relief. This enabled me to concentrate on school. It also enabled me to use some of my summer money for the first purchases of serious art. Tom, Kirk, and I decided to start the Dorm B Art Gallery. Tom already had a good collection of art including a marvelous copy of Titian's *Flora* which was the crowning piece of the gallery. We supplemented it with posters and the typical 60's psychedelic art. It was about that time the head of the art department, Phillip Dedrick introduced us to Mr. Lasurre, from Australia. He was the individual who first started trading art with the natives of Papua. We all bought a few pieces.

Then went a regular art dealer came to campus, Dr. Dedrick made sure that Tom and I were the first to see his collection. As we were looking at the collection including *Durer's Four Horsemen*, which I couldn't afford but still wished I had purchased. It was while looking at these pieces, his buyer came in with a folio of new pieces. He had just flown back from Europe and had a huge collection of art. I started going through the pieces that had not even been priced. I pulled out the small late impression of *Durer's Jesus' Entry into Jerusalem*. They only wanted $40 for it since it was a late impression done after Durer's death. Then I spotted several pieces of Callot's passions. There were sheets which had 5 and 10 of these small etchings from circular plates, too expensive. This was what was described as part of the 20 passions of Christ. Twenty individual tiny circular plates what would be printed on paper in different formats. I found a small one with only 3 of the prints. Talked them down to $50 and set it aside.

Then *St. Jerome* by Ribera caught my eye. It was Saint Jerome Reading with a lion and a skull on either side of him, ca. 1624.

"How much?"

"Well we haven't priced it yet." was the response.

"What if I offer you $75 would you accept it?"

"Well since they have just come in and your are friends of Phillip you can have it for that."

Three down, one to go. That is when I spotted Giovanni Battista Piranesi's *Capitoline Lapides*. I didn't know it at the time, but this was the largest engraving ever done by Piranesi who was famous for his dungeons and architectural etchings. Again I asked what he wanted. They told me $200.

"Too much, since I've already purchase several pieces, would you accept $90."

SOLD!

That is the piece was given to the Detroit Art Institute <u>this weekend</u>. So this was the beginning of your father's serious art collection. By the way the Dorm B Art Gallery became famous.

Love,
Papa

On way back from Detroit #3 Oct. 22, 2015

T:

You got the letters related to the summer of 1968, now for summer of 1969. It started with a letter to the Pawtucket Times asking if I could come back for the summer. Never got a response. So had to find another job.

Mom wanted me to learn more practical skills, such as woodworking. She got me a job at Salisbury Artisans. This was a small shop, owner and principal carpenter, where a variety of small hardwood products would be made. There was one problem. I had NO experience that would help. Two weeks in I accidentally damaged one of their seal imprints. They said I had to go. At least they found another job for me.

It was on the opposite side of Salisbury in a little factory called the House of Herbs. The House of Herbs was a spice company. They packed high quality spices, all kinds, into their square base bottles. They also sold custom spice racks to hold their jars. Your mother, Marisol, had that rack in the kitchen at one time. It may still be there.

The House of Herbs always hired a group of high school students and occasionally a college student or two to learn the routines. Then in August, the students to take over while the whole regular staff took vacation. This particular summer I was the only college student. They assigned me to the shipping department. I quickly learned how they packed the spice jars into their boxes to be shipped all over the country. I was assigned there because it was the one job with the greatest of importance. It was certainly an easy job, but critical for the company. Not only did we ship out the spices, but would confirm the payments and work with the accountant to be sure the books balanced concerning the purchases. We where also the quality inspectors.

The storage area for all spices was the floor above the assembly line. There was a double door that would open with an earthen ramp leading up to the second floor storage room. When a large shipment came in, the truck would back up to this door. I would get the fork lift and move the pallets of spices to the appropriate place. This room took up the whole length of the factory. It was a good planning to be above the assembly line. All we had to do was to open up a door in the floor, dump the spices into the chute leading to the conveyor belts where the bottles would pass under. Each container received the appropriate amount of the spice to fill it before passing to the next stage where the tops were placed on the bottles.

The worse part, was it was summer and there was no AC in the factory. This was particularly bad one day when the store room told us we were almost out of black pepper. We had received about ten 40 lb bags of fresh fine ground black pepper. Two of us were told to go upstairs, bring the bags to the shoot and dump them as needed. The idea was to pack all but one or two bags into the bottles by the end of the day. There was one problem. It was a **hot** day. The attic must have been close to 95°F. As we brought the canvas bags to the chute, they would be cut open. The black pepper was then dumped down the chute. The fine powder of pepper would be flying all over the air. We were sweating like crazy. Every grain of pepper in the air would land on our sweating arms, legs, head, in our eyes, hair and nostrils. No matter how hard you tried to avoid it getting on you. It stung like hell. The pepper was getting through long sleeves. This made you sweat more. In your pants burning your legs. Every inch of our bodies was on fire.

Downstairs, there were few problems. The chute was well insulated. Very little spice would fly into the air on the main floor. Not so for the attic. By the end of the day, I was covered with black pepper. The stinging was terrible. Once we were finished for the day, I jumped into the car. Driving as quickly as I could towards Lakeville Lake, with eyes stinging with pepper blurring my vision. I parked close to the lake as possible. Ran to the water. Jumped in with out changing into a bathing suit. Swimming, including under water with eyes open to wash them out. After 30 minutes in the water I felt better. I got out of the water and drove home.

Love,
Papa

Nov. 2015

T–more House of Herbs:

Before the regular staff went on vacation, they wanted me to experience all aspects of the process. Including a week on the assembly line in different positions. BORING! The beginning of the line, you grabbed bottles from boxes and placed then on the conveyor belt. The next stage was to be sure they moved under the chute and were filled at the proper levels. The next worker supervised the labels. They would move down a little ramp, pass by a brush that wet them, and then slapped onto the bottles. The next phase was the tops. First they had to be loaded. Next as the bottles came under the caps, the machine would screw them on each bottle. Then all packed into boxes.

As I stood there loading the bottles one morning, my whole thoughts was how dull this job was. The fact some of these workers had been in the plant for 30 years was almost beyond comprehension. As I watch the summer kids manning each position with the adults standing behind, the repetitiveness was putting me to sleep. Then it came to me. Don't think of them as humans. Visualize each as a chimpanzee. Each with their own peculiar mannerism, own expression, all knuckle walking from one position to another. Looking at each of the line workers as if they were a chimpanzee, started making me laugh. No one understood what I was laughing at. I certainly did want to tell them. Little did I know that in a few years I would become part of a real chimpanzee's life–Nim.

August came. The regulars all went on vacation. Things went smoothly. The first interesting thing was a shipment coming in which was exceptionally valuable. I was told it would arrive Monday or Tuesday. Expecting a large truck with containers or bags of some special spice the shock when a UPS driver knocked at the front door. He handed me a box about 12″ x 8″ and about 3″ thick. I was then asked to sign the receipt of the box. I looked at the packing slip, IT WAS INSURED FOR $30,000! This in 1969! It was the finest quality of Saffron from Spain. Not only from Spain, but from a certain locale where the best was grown. Looking up the directions for packing the saffron, the book said: '22 twigs of saffron in each bottle.' It seems a bit silly but there we were, pulling 22 twigs of saffron by tweezers and placing them into bottles. Even taking the twigs off the tape holding the lid were bottled. This job could not be done on the assembly line but by hand. Each bottle with 22 twigs sold for over $10.

The funnest adventure was when one of the kids read that nutmeg could give you a high. We were closing down for the weekend. I turned off everything and said good night to all the kids, thanking them for all their help. I forgot to count to be sure all were accounted for. On Sunday I got a call. Where was 'Tommy?' (not real name) a parent asked. He had never arrived home. Driving to the plant, I couldn't imagine him being there. The whole plant was searched. Nothing. I then went upstairs. There laying on some of the sacks of spices was Tommy. He was totally out of it. All I could get out of him was a long:

'OOOOOOOOH.'

He had put about 1/2 a cup of ground nutmeg into a glass of milk and downed it. Lucky it didn't kill him. Lifting him up, half carrying him, half making him walk, we got downstairs by the truck ramp as the stairs were impossible for him to negotiate. I called his parents. They picked him up. By then he was able to speak a little. They carted him off the Sharon Hospital. He took one day off but was back on Tuesday. He had little memory of what had happened. All he remembered was there were lots of colors floating around the attic. Interesting because all the walls were plane brown unpainted wood. All the storage containers were either wooden barrels or light brown burlap sacks. No colors! But he sure saw a lot of pretty rainbows full of colors after taking the nutmeg.

Might add upon the return of the staff and seeing my reports on both the packing and shipping of the spices, including the saffron, I was lauded as being the best summer manager they had ever hired. By the next summer the House of Herbs was in a loosing take over battle with McCormick spice company. McCormick took over promising to keep it open as a high end product. Within a year the plant was closed. So much for that promise.

Love,
Papa

Chapter 7

Back to work

whenever, 2015

Hi T:

T back to the South Bronx and more on the gangs:

Patterson Projects were a block behind the Settlement House. The Black Spades claimed that area for themselves. I could see the tall project buildings from my window. I knew that was where the gangs with 'contracts' to kill me hung out. Why? you'll to find out latter. Near by were the Ghetto Brothers (I think), who occasionally would team up with the Spades if they had a joint objective, major break in/robbery or if confronting another gang.

Now realize the names of the gangs have changed and morphed over the years. The names given here may not refer to the gangs with the same names today. In the Mott Haven projects the Spanish Mafia, and a Puerto Rican gang were two smaller gangs that often teamed up for self defense against the Spades. On the other side of Alexander Avenue another small gang which I think was called the Hispanic Aces hung out. These three latter gangs would come to Mott Haven Community Center in the evenings. I knew, at least by sight most of them. The Center was often the focal point of disputed territory between all of these gangs.

One day the Black Spades caught one of the opposing gang members. Which gang I didn't know. One side of the project building was almost pure brick, with only a window or two on the upper floor. Most likely where the elevator shaft was inside. They tied up the kid they captured. Hammering spikes into the wall they tied his hands to the spikes. One of the Spades had obtained a rapid fire machine gun (now it would be an AK47 or better). They were going to kill this kid as a lesson to his gang. Once tied up, the Spade who had the machine gun carefully put it tight to his shoulder, aimed and pulled the trigger. Bullets went flying all over the wall. The key to a machine gun is the kick. Unlike most rifles and shotguns, you do not want to hold a machine gun tight to the shoulder! The recoil will make you loose control.

Well, the kid kept his finger on the trigger until all the rounds were spent. Since the Precinct building was only 4 blocks away that many shots drew attention fast! Within seconds of expending all the rounds you could hear the police car sirens. The gang members split in all directions. When the police arrived they saw the kid tied to the wall. Surely he must be dead. But when they got to him, all he had a few cuts from flying brick, but not a single bullet had hit him. So much for the execution.

Thanksgiving was coming up. Carol wanted me to fix the dinner in my apartment and then carry it over to Doris' for the actual dinner with Randy and her. Doris and Randy were her closest friends. It was to be a first class dinner. There was duck and pheasant for main entree choices. For both the start and the finish pumpkin soup and pumpkin pie were prepared. There were 4 kinds of bread / rolls, all made from scratch. Two yeasted and two quick breads out of biscuit flour. Then came a variety of vegetables such as green beans with mushrooms, squash, sweet potatoes and as the main starch wild & brown rice combination. I also made condiments for flavor.

The pumpkin and apple (for those who did not want pumpkin) pies were baking in Doris oven while we at the main dinner. All toll there were 22 different items for that feast, all coming out at just the right time, at just the right temperature for the perfect meal. Even Carol said I outdid myself. The meal started around 3 and we didn't move from the table until after 6 or 7 p.m. We ate until we could hardly move. It was the best Thanksgiving meal ever prepared outside of a 5 star restaurant.

Meanwhile back on the job there was a host of case referrals. One of a young boy acting out in school. The first job was to interview the parents if available. In this case they were. Off I went to interview the parents. While sitting at the kitchen table I noticed something moving under the table cloth. Picking up the table cloth there was a girl, about 7 years old and wearing dippers. She was shy and didn't speak. The parents seemed very defensive once she was discovered. When asked why she wasn't in school there were an exchange of blank stares between the two. Basically the only excuse was they didn't want to bother cleaning her up. Besides that would require her to be toilet trained. Then they would have to teach her to speak. But after all she was just a girl, it wasn't worth the effort. This was one of those cases where I really had to check myself to prevent beating both parents within an inch of their worthless lives. After the field visit to the home the whole family was referred to Child Protective Services. Within a day or two all 4 children removed from the home. The parents welfare checks were stopped and they may have been under investigation by the police. After receiving confirmation that Child Protective Services had custody of the children, my interest ceased. A lot of my friends and others would ask if this was a black family. I told them:

"No they were German Americans!"

Love,
Papa

Late Aug. 2015

Back to the work place:

After Mr. Woods acknowledged the fact that I was not to become his lover. He accepted it and really helped me whenever asked. But he must have felt an inner need to find another way to have fun in the office or at least surround himself with other gay friends. I continued to learn the more and more from him about doing social work. I tried my best to do what I could for the kids that were referred to us.

In the mean time, Mr. Woods wanted someone of his old unit to come work with him. Mr. X (can't remember his name) soon showed up. He was over 6' tall, dressed in only the best suits, had a beautiful baritone voice, even deeper than Mr. Woods', and was very distinguished looking. He was also a flamer! despite his very masculine outward appearance.

As Christmas was approaching, Mr. X would show up in the late mornings and bellow "NOEL NOEL!" as he walked down the hall to his office. He and I rarely spoke but were always on friendly terms when we did get together. I actually liked him and his outrageous actions. It was never boring with him around. He was also a good social worker when he concentrated on the cases given him. Most were the more difficult cases. Though I was quickly proving myself in an ability to assess and write up a case some needed more experienced attention. Later Mr. Woods told me he would chime out the 'noel noel' if he had scored with someone that afternoon. He liked white men, like Mr. Woods.

The funnest thing that happened with Mr. X was the time Mr. Woods was standing by his window and we were having an informal staff meeting. Mr. Woods looked across the street, and noted there was a man standing nude in his window. Mr. X ran over to the window and with an enthusiastic voice said:

"Where?" as he almost pushed Woods off balance.

Mr. Woods pointed, and X just stared. I decided discretion was needed and quietly left the office. The door was closed and I have no idea if anything happened, but they were there together for some time.

After being assigned to a case X would go out 'on case work.' Noting our co-worker would be absent for most days as December progressed and not being aware of any new referrals coming into the office I asked Mr. Woods what cases? Woods was honest with me. During this time of year *Mr. X* would go down to the Wall Street area and look around for catering services delivering food. His modus operandi was to follow the caters into the office where there was a Christmas party going on and join the party. Since he was dressed in his usual impeccable style, there was never anyone who challenged him as he went into an office. This was an excellent way to pick up young men of similar persuasion. Mr. Woods said he would either give and or receive several fucks / sucks at every party he attended.

One December week I only saw him in the office once. When I did, he had a huge grin on his face.

"Walter, know now how easy it is to get fucked in the Wall Street parties? This is the greatest part of the year! I had three young white guys yesterday and loved every minute of it!"

I just smiled and told him it was great he had so much fun. Unfortunately that was the beginning of the end of the unit. Not immediately but eventually.

The last referral we received was one where a grandmother was asking for help with her teenage granddaughter. It appeared the girl was acting up in school and at her home. Unlike most of the referrals, this was a solid middle class black family. I went to visit the family and explained the role YSA Case Work Unit would play. We would see what the problems were to determine how to best help the family. Most long term care referrals were made to either Catholic Charities or Big Brothers/Sisters organizations. They were staffed with full time long term social workers who could do more intensive one-on-one with families than our unit.

At first the girl was very reluctant to cooperate. Her grandmother's biggest concern was the girl not washing our the bathtub after taking a shower. For some reason that stood out in her mind. But the girl rarely did her homework and was anti-social in school, disruptive in classes and getting into fights with other kids. After two visit, I was getting no where. Then I got a call from the grandmother. She was suspended from school again. Could I come over?

I raced over to their nice apartment on the upper West Side, not far from Central Park. I was there before the girl arrived. This must have impressed her as for the first time she actually sat down and talked to me. She hated being an only child with a father who disappeared and who's mother died. I tried to tell her how much nicer her home was home was than most others that were referred to our unit. By relating my own history seemed to open her up.

She had a father who deserted her. So did I, kind of. My dad never did anything to help mom and I out. She had a mother who died, but she had grandparents who cared for her and were trying to give her a nice home. All I had was a drunken mother throughout my high school years.

She was beginning to see I had a worse childhood than her. I must have spent about 2 hours with the family at home. When sitting with the grandmother and the girl together we opened up the one tipping point in the problems, the bathtub. By the time I left she agreed that she would clean it out after taking a bath in the future. The grandmother called me a few days latter saying how much I had helped.

I was planning my next visit when we got notice the social work unit was going to close. I sent her a letter notifying them of my transfer, I would no longer be able to see the family. Right after receiving the notice a the letter was sent, Mr. Woods asked if they were notified of my transfer. He said if they had not, he wanted to take on the case himself. Too late, but I dearly hope things improved.

Love,
Papa

Chapter 8

Ft. Apache

Sept. 2, 2015

Hello T:

Picking up where we left off in the previous letter and our VERY gay co-worker it is important to realize this was the early 1970's will little tolerance for gays. Complaints were likely made it down to HQ. I suspected my old street workers unit's manager complained as every time "X" came into the office. One could see the scowl on his face whenever X passed his office. Never found out directly, but some how word got out the unit was just a bunch of queers.

Sure enough early the next year the Social Work Unity was to be disbanded. I was to be reassigned to another unit. At the time YSA wanted to get rid of a white male in an agency that was over 80% black and Hispanic. They figured if I was sent to the worse area in the city, good-bye Walter. If I didn't quit, someone would shoot me and they would be rid of me that way. After a week of indecision Mr. Woods told me where I was to be re-assigned. The Agency was going to send me to just outside the Ft. Apache area of the South Bronx to an emergency relocation hotel on the Grand Concourse. As a matter of fact it was the Grand Concourse Hotel just a few blocks from Yankee Stadium. Not quite Ft. Apache, but back then the whole area was considered pretty dangerous. What they hadn't looked at was the address where I lived.

I liked living on Alexander Avenue. Sometimes it was a little noisy. Many of the Hispanics (about 60% NewRicans) would have impromptu street parties with mostly percussion sections, using trash cans and lids, a few guitars, and other odd instruments that were around. This sessions would last well into the early morning hours, especially on weekends. But you got used to it. It too was on the boarders of the true Ft. Apache.

What was funny to me was that an Hispanic reporter for one of the channels was assigned to actually live on Alexander Avenue for one week. He came back reporting in the news one evening, it was one of the starriest places in the city. There were gun shots almost every night of the week he stayed there. There were illegal gambling (the only kind back then) in the form of crap games all over the area. He found a cock fight in one of the basements (news to me, but then I didn't hang out with the older Hispanics). All told he reported that he felt lucky to be alive. They was hilarious to me as I had been there more than 2 years.

The transfer was walking distance from East Side Settlement House where I lived to the Grand Concourse Hotel. All I had to do was to go towards the subway station turn right, go a few blocks, turn right again and that would be the start of the Grand Concourse! Or one could take the subway to 143rd and the Grand Concourse saving a few blocks. However, that was not the safest way as the gang in Patterson Projects was one of the gangs that had a contract on me.

Mr. Woods seemed to be concerned.

"Mr. Woods, do you realize where I live? They are throwing Br'er Rabbit into the brier patch."

To understand that you need to be aware of the Disney 1946 cartoon 'Song of the South' where Br'er Rabbit escaped the Br'er Bear and Br'er Fox by pleading with them to do anything but throw him into the brier patch. Of course that is exactly what they did. Upon landing in the brier patch Br'er Rabbit started to sing: "Born and raised in the brier patch…" and got away. So Mr. Woods just smiled and settled down at ease.

As for that Christmas—nothing special can be remembered. I think Carol got a very fancy Singer Sewing Machine for a present, but it may have been the next Christmas.

Love,
Papa

Chapter 9

Demetria, the gangs, and more Co-M

Hi T: Ready for some Bread?

It was about this time that Demetria from the Lodge asked if I would be interested in inventing bread recipes for possible bread cookbook. Demetria knew I loved to bake bread. On weekends, Carol and I would come up with various breads and muffins for our friends. If there was a meeting, I would sometime bring in some rolls or other snacks for after the meeting.

Demetria was the cooking editor for Parade Magazine, the Sunday supplement for many different papers around the country. Her name de plum was Beth Merriman. She had the column for over 30 years by this time and was well known in the world of cooks and editors. Demetria suggested that if I could invent somewhere between 75 to 100 new recipes, she could pull together an equal amount from her old files. Together that would be enough for a bread cookbook.

Naturally I jumped at the chance. It would be a way to work with Demetria and have a joint project that might even proved profitable. Every weekend Carol would come over and help with the recipes. I would break out the various flours and other ingredients. Then would make up a new recipe. Each were tried by Carol and most by Demetria. Those which came out great were to be included. These were a combination of quick breads (baking soda & baking powder) in just about every combination you can imagine. Many of these became the muffins or pancakes your classmates loved when you had sleep overs. Mind you, none were from the official recipes, but the combination of ingredients.

The one problem with creating a recipe was measurement. Carol would be sitting at the kitchen table. There in the small kitchen on the top floor of the East Side House Settlement, she would be trying to write down all that I was adding to the recipe of the day. Suddenly an idea would flash before me. I would grab a spice of additional ingredient and put some into the mix.

"Wait! How much did you put in just now?" she would ask.

I would hold open my hand in a cupped position: "Oh about this much!" If it was a spice "A pinch or two." We finally narrowed it down. A handful was a third of a cup. A pinch was an 1/8 of teaspoon. As for larger amounts of spices it was easy to estimate the amount in the palm of my hand as it was added to the dough.

Eventually Carol and I had close to 100 recipes. Many were tested with our friends and co-workers. I would turn over the recipe cards to Demetria for filing. As I was working on the breads, many a weekend afternoon was spent at Demetria when not out with Carol. One day while looking around the apartment, there was a picture on the mantle of a young man in uniform. I asked Demetria who it was.

She told me it was the love of her life. He had been killed in the Battle of the Bulge in 1994. I stared at the photo for a long time. It looking like a familiar face. That night it came to me. We were both in the same Division when the Germans broke through. Our lines were dissected by the blitzkrieg of panzer tanks. A vision of Demeteria's old lover came to me. We promised if one of us didn't make it the other would take care of those closest to us.

He promised to visit my family down in the Southwest and try to comfort them as best as possible. My promise was to take care if his girl back in New York. She was a cooking editor. Her name was Demetria. Suddenly all became clear. I was meant to be with Demetria. It was a karmic promise from my previous life. Now that she was advancing in years, it was my duty to watch over her as best I could. Our attachment towards each other had started in 1944, before I was born, before mom even joined Co-Masonry. But there it was. I was fulfilling a long held promise which spanned across death.

Demetria felt there was a stronger than usual connection between us. When I told her of the vision I had, she sat quietly for a few minutes. She looked up:

"I think you are right. It just feels that we have this connection which spans across time beyond your years."

I kept a close eye on Demetria until I left NYC for graduate school in Boston. I always hoped I would be with her in the end, but during my second year, while talking with my internship advisor my ankle gave way. I fell on one knee. He looked at me:

"You OK?"

Getting up I said: "Yes but something just happened, I just don't know what."

That evening I got a call from mom. Demetria had died that afternoon. Due to her weight problems and diabetes, it was always he ankles that would give out if she was having an attack. My ankle gave way in Boston, at the same moment she died in New York.

Love,
Papa

Chapter 10

More on Work

Hi T:

Even when I found work at YSA I continued to volunteer with the East Side Settlement House activities. Nights that were free, often found me still working with the kids at Mott Haven Community Center. Still tutoring and teaching art.

About this time there was a major effort to work with the gangs in the area. Remember two of the gangs had a 'hit' on me while 3 others were trying to protect me. This needs a brief explanation. One evening while volunteering at Mott Haven Community Center, several of the hispanic gang members came running into the center. The leader said the Spades were after them. He and this friends needed protection.

Mott Haven Center had two sets of double doors which were about 4 feet apart. The outer door did have the capability to be barred by a metal plank which fitted into the slots like those seen in the movies with a castle door being barred against an enemy. The problem was the first of the Spades was already at that door with about 6 or 7 others close behind. Seeing the situation and knowing they had to be pushed out before the plank could be inserted, thereby locking the door something had to be done quickly. I had a crazy idea. I told the hispanic members to open the inner door when I yelled. Carol stood by a door which lead to the auditorium. I got about half way down the aisle and then yelled:

"Open the doors!"

Carol opened the auditorium door just as I was running full speed towards the main entrance. Then the hispanic gang members opened the inner door to the entrance. At this time most of the Spades were at or partly inside the outer door. Suddenly here came a 200 lbs ex-lineman for a high school football team running full tilt towards them. Letting out a huge yell, I threw a cross body block against all the Spades at once. None were expecting it. It was like a bowling ball hitting the head pin and following through for a strike! All were pushed outside. As I scrambled to my feet, Carol and director of the Center quickly closed the outer door and secured the plank to prevent the gang from entering.

The local Hispanic gangs spread the word what I had done. There were 3 in the neighborhood. All were committed to help me. As for the Spades they joined with the other gang to put out orders to have me killed. Thus began a cat and mouse game which lasted until I left the South Bronx.

There was a major effort to bring in local successful blacks as mentors for the kids to try to convince them to abandon gang activities. This included a major planning effort including a brain storming activity to be held in one of the local community centers' basketball courts. An outside agency was put in charge of the initial effort. Chairs were arranged in a semi-circular position around a group of four chairs in the front for the discussion leaders, most of whom were from the other centers in the South Bronx. The individual who initiated was the manager of the center. He asked us to welcome the former football player to the session who would lead the discussion session.

Willie, a former National Football player was either guard or tackle position on one of the teams. It may have been the Giants. I just don't remember. His fame was he was from the South Bronx and proved to be successful. He had been retired from football for a decade. The problem was his intake of food continued at the same pace as in his playing days. I remember when he came in his 6′3″ height was overshadowed by his 450+ pound body. He was almost as wide as he was tall, or at least it seemed that way. Now I understood why there were 4 chairs in the front. One was for the center's manager, the other three were for Willie. As he waddled over to them, he carefully arranged all three and took up every inch of each.

The next two hours was as basic brain storming session on how to deal with the gang activities. There were few new or creative ideas. As I was a guest from Eastside House Settlement and not a regular worker in Mott Haven. I mostly listened. Carol had asked me to take notes and report back. What struck me was that none of the gangs would pay attention to Willie due to his weight. He would have been the object of ridicule if they were permitted to speak. As a result, if he tried to take any suggestion but the gangs were not there, at least not consciously.

Here was a government grant funded session which gave a good salary to the leaders to come up with ideas to reduce gang activities. Yet after a day's efforts, there were little new or innovative ideas and nothing I could take back which were not already in practice in at Mott Haven and the other centers under the East Settlement House management chain. My conclusion, a day's waste of time and money. This would not be the first of such sessions which I considered not worth the money or effort.

Love,
Papa

October 30, 2015

From Philadelphia #1 mailed while Charlene is running

Hi T Back to the Bronx:

The Grand Concourse Hotel had once been THE hotel for the Bronx. In the 1920's through the 1940's it was considered the most luxurious hotel to be found in the Bronx. It was the place that many of the baseball teams coming to the Bronx to play the Yankees would stay. On the top floor Babe Ruth had his permanent apartment. This was perfect as it was only a block and half from **The Stadium** (Yankee Stadium, or *The House that Ruth Built* to novices). Famous individuals would use it if visiting the Bronx if they didn't want to stay in Manhattan.

By the 1950's the Bronx had started to decline. It was becoming more black and Hispanic. The middle and upper middle class Jews who had dominated the Grand Concourse's apartment houses and luxury homes were moving out in droves. As they did, blacks and Puerto Ricans moved to the Concourse. Soon the neighborhood was no longer considered safe by most whites. All that was left was the hotel and the Bronx Borough President's building, diagonally across from the hotel and up the hill from the Stadium.

There were a few bars across from the Stadium which still catered to the old clientele, especially on game days. You could tell which they were as they were filled with autographed photos of great Yankee players going back to the Babe and before. Since the Giant football team played in the stadium there were photos of many of their famous players as well. The bars were almost always dominated by caucasian clientele. Minorities were discouraged from entering. Not from anything that might be said, but slow service and a basic ignoring their attempted to get the attention of a waiter or the bar tender.

Sometime in the 1960's the hotel gave up on trying to continue as a viable public hotel. On the top floor a few of the long time permanent residents were permitted to remain. But all the floors below, were turned over for the city to house displaced families with children. Most were homeless due to fires or declarations of condemnation by the health department of their former residences. Most were owned by the typical absentee landlords who would rather collect the rent than provide any services or repairs.

My job was simple. Keep control of the kids and prevent the gangs from entering. Our unit was The Youth Services Agency unit. Charlene Casey was the supervisor. There was one young slender woman named Cynthia, who from her light skin had been a product of a mixed race relationship. No one could have imagined that years later I would marry another Charlene who's sister's name was Cynthia! Another woman named Lucy who was older black woman with huge breasts. She was always concerned about the children, but seldom obeyed basic rules.

My first day on the job I appeared in the unit with a suit and tie. They looked at me as if I came out of a circus. All were dressed very casually. It was apparent this was NOT a suit and tie environment. After a long conversation with Charlene she told me I needed to focus on the pre-teens and teens. Get them occupied with various activities and when the weather permitted take them across the street to play softball. If the weather was bad, create activities for a few of them to get involved within the office.

I would focus on the boys. Lucy and Cynthia would focus on the girls. The hours were from 10 or 11 in the morning until 6 or 7 p.m. at night. Whenever possible we would obtain subway passes to take the kids on trips when school was not in session. I was told to keep in contact with the Bronx Borough President's office to see what they could offer. I actually got to know the office quite well.

The head of the Bronx at the time Mario Cuomo, the father of the New York State Governor in the 2015. It was there where we were able to get tickets to Yankee games, which was done as often as possible. This would allow me to take a hand full kids, usually boys to The Stadium for daylight games. Sometimes Saturday game tickets were obtained, when I would work a little extra to let the kids too enjoy time out of the hotel. What was interesting was the ticket takers for the bleachers got to know me and the kids. After the start of the third inning, if I had 4 or 5 kids that wanted to see the game, we were let in ticket or not. If night game, sometimes I would go by myself for free. That year saw 22 games.

Love,
Papa

Halloween, 2015

From Philadelphia #2 mailed while (the current) Charlene is running

Hello there:

Work at The Concourse Plaza had many of its own adventures. One of the early things I started was tutorial sessions for grade schoolers. Most of the kids in the Hotel were considered below average learners. Like you when you were teaching, I found it to be a more a result of prejudice by the teachers and low expectations. This says nothing about the shit schools in the South Bronx. There were three days a week that I would offer tutoring for grade schoolers in the office. Once some the parents heard about it, we had about a dozen or more kids join in. Most focus was on reading and math. If a mother requested special help for their child, efforts were made to accommodate them.

One under performer named Jesus came to the tutoring sessions. One afternoon I asked what he wanted to be when he grew up. His answer was that he wanted to study architecture. Considering his grades were Ds and Fs I asked how would he be able to do that if he didn't improve his grades and study habits. He thought about it.

It was during these years I had a MOMA (Metropolitan Museum of Modern Art) membership. One afternoon after visiting the museum including the gift shop, a series of construction toys were purchased. The next tutoring session with Jesus he was introduced to the toys, AFTER working on both his reading and math. There were other games from MOMA that were included when working with Jesus. About a month of working with him, I asked if he knew of any architects.

"I think Frank Lloyd Wright is the greatest."

This shocked me a little. Apparently he knew the Guggenheim was designed by Wright and in some magazine he had seen a number of this other buildings. In my collection of books there was a copy of Frank Lloyd Wright Autobiography. Would he be able to handle this? I had to give it a try. I told him he could read my copy, but only if he would report to me what he had read at each tutorial session. If he needed help in the book, he would receive it during our sessions. This way his reading progress would be checked while allowing more time to focus on math. Slowly his grades began to improve. It took the whole academic year, but he finished the autobiography. His mother was so happy at the end of the school year she gave me a hug and a kiss on the cheek. Jesus' grades were now all As and Bs. He had become a star student.

Later, when they moved out of the hotel, they happened to move into an apartment in Mott Haven public housing, in the building next to Carol's. I continued to see them, now informally. Jesus had an older sister who has just turned 13. She was well aware of the gangs and the dangers surrounding her. She knew the possibility of being raped, especially due to the fact she was rapidly developing into a fully developed woman. She approached me and suggested I take her up to my apartment and de-flower her. It was an awkward moment. She was attractive. But we sat down on a park bench and I told her why I could not do that. At the same time she was told a lot more about the facts of life than her mother ever had. I just felt it was necessary. I gave her a hug and said good bye. We never were together again, but I would wave when seeing any of the family on the streets.

One of the major activities was to take a group of kids across the street from the hotel to play softball in the park. It was not really big enough for a true softball park, but for the younger kids, it was perfect. We were able to get balls and bats with an odd selection of mostly used, but decent gloves through the Agency. The games were regular on almost every decent day in the afternoons all year around. At least when there was no snow on the ground. Games took place for an hour before the tutoring sessions.

I do remember when one of the janitors from the hotel asked to take a hit. He clobbered the ball. The ball sailed high over the park and came down on a car parked across from the Plaza breaking the car's window. Another time a bumper was hit by a hotel worker wanting to join in. After those two episodes we stopped letting adults join in the games.

The most interesting rookie was Little Juan. His family who arrived only a few months before from Puerto Rico. They had been burned out of their apartment. Juan had never played softball. He was just a little over 3 feet tall. Someone told me he was in the first grade, so likely around 7 years old. Juan had little but stocky body. We showed him how to hold the bat. He was told how to hit the ball by swinging the bat. He took a few practice swings while the game was proceeding. Then we let Juan come to bat. I asked the boy who was pitching to toss him an easy ball. WHAM!! Juan killed it. The ball traveled over the heads of everyone in the field. Surely this was beginners luck. Next pitch. WHAM. Another home run. Every pitch that was over the plate was hit. He was an instinctual softball hitter. His family moved out only after a few weeks. Sure hope he joined a real team when old enough. His older sister would accompanied him to the park. I told her to tell their mother Juan was a natural for baseball.

Love,
Papa

November 1, 2015

Hello there:

I loved working at the Concourse Plaza. It was great getting paid to play with kids!!!! When not playing, tutoring, which was mostly fun too. What was nice is that on fair weather days I could walk to work. Just had to watch which way. Had to go in the opposite direction to 138th Street to catch the beginning of the Grand Concourse Blvd. This would take me past a few gas stations.

It was 1973. OAPEC started an oil embargo in their attempts to raise the price of oil from $3 per barrel to four times that price. This produced major shocks around the country. In the Bronx, the few gas stations suddenly had long lines of cars trying to get gas. I would walk past blocks of cars waiting to get gas. When a station pump was dry–a black flag was put on the pump. When the flag was on the station's sign next to the road, this meant the station was out of all gas.

This was at a time when the USA had increased its imports of oil to record levels. To resolve the crisis Nixon sent in Henry Kissinger to negotiate Israeli troop withdrawal from the Sinai Peninsula which was one of many reasons for the oil crisis. The result was the taking of control of oil out of the Western oil companies hands, placing it into the hands of the Arab countries and other members of OAPEC for the first time. Something that has largely continued to this day. It changed the world.

As for the hotel, the gas had no effect, we all took the Subway! This was a time when I was going to The New School of Social Research in the Village for my MA in anthropology. There was one family with three older boys. The two oldest were in their late teens and I had little contact with them. The youngest was a 13 year old, 6'3" and over 250 lbs. His name was James, but due to being slightly retarded, everyone, including his family called him Duffy James. James was constantly getting into trouble. I would take him out to play ball. Despite his size, he couldn't hit very well and lacked the coordination to catch and throw as well as the younger children. Soon he stopped playing ball. He had one friend in the hotel.

One day as I was walking into the hotel, James was yelling at his friend. It didn't take much to get James off. A little comment he could take the wrong way. Any negative talk about his family would set him into a tantrum. Calling him retarded to his face (which was common) had the same effect. Having no idea what started this and knowing James rarely stopped at yelling, I started walking over. Sure enough James starting hitting is friend. I pulled James off. He threatened me. I grabbed him by his coat. Placing my elbows under his rib cage, I used all the strength I had to slam him up against the wall of the hotel, with his feet about 4 inches off the ground. Then placing the left hand on his sternum holding him firmly against the wall, my right was in the form of a fist.

"Cool it right now! Or I'll put your head through this damn wall!"

James realizing his feet were off the ground and he was at my mercy, looked down and then into my eyes: "I'm sorry Walter. I OK now."

I let him down, made sure both were alright and went to my office.

A few weeks later I got a call from the hotel manager. James was causing a riot up on the 5th floor. Sure enough when I got off the elevator, there was James confronting a girl about his age. The one advantage for the girl, she had a broom handle in her hand. James would charge her swinging his fists like a windmill. As he approached her, she would hit him in the head with the broom. He would stagger back. Refocus and charge again. Only to be hit again. I could see this happening from the elevator down the hall. James was bleeding from several gashes in his head. I quickly grabbed James yelling at him to stop. I then turned to the girl, telling her I would control him. I took him down to the office and we bandaged him up. His mother didn't want to take him to the hospital–which was more dangerous than the streets.

Mott Haven Community Center still saw me most nights. Carol and I were becoming engaged. I bought her a diamond ring from Bergdorf Goodman. It was a raw diamond, 6 carats, with 2 emerald chips and 3 diamond chips surrounding the central stone. I have never seen any ring as beautiful since. The diamond was in its natural crystal structure. The cut emerald and diamond chips accentuated the main stone in a most unique way. The whole ring was set in white gold. Carol was also into sewing. I got her the latest Singer deluxe for Christmas. So you can see my savings were not accumulating as much as they should have with all these purchases. She was progressing through Co-M becoming a Fellow Craft (2°). Everything was going well. The job, Masonry, volunteer work and my relationship with Carol. It really was too good to last.

Carol's mother was blind and very paranoid. One night we took her out to a small Chinese restaurant. Carol and I were sitting side by side with her mother on the other side of the booth. Suddenly her mother gets up and starts swinging her purse at the man in the booth behind her. Thank goodness she missed but I had to grab the purse from her while Carol tried to calm her down. She thought the man was plotting to kill her.

Another time I was walking Carol back to her apartment. When Carol opened the door her mother was right there. She started yelling at me claiming I was insulting her by having sex with her daughter in front of her because she was blind. She kept telling me to stop screwing her daughter. Carol tried to tell her we were not having sex in the doorway. We hadn't had sex at all! Her mother refused to believe it until Carol grabbed her hand putting it on her pants which were fully zipped and buttoned up. That was what Carol had to put up with all the time while living with her mother. Never did find out what happened to her mother after Carol left.

Love,
Papa

Series of letters sent from Williamsburg

November 13, 2015

More of Duffy James:

Attempts to help James with school work were largely unsuccessful. I did take him on a few of the trips, but had to watch him closely. Eventually he considered me a friend. Then one day just as I was studying for finals, I noticed my briefcase with all my books and notes was missing. Lucy said that James had been looking for me. I rushed out and hoping that he just hid the case I checked the stairwells and all the corners where a briefcase could be hidden. No luck. I knocked on his apartment door.

"James, you came looking for me earlier, did you see my briefcase? It is missing I have to study for my tests tonight."

His response: "I didn't see anything Walter." But from the look in his eyes I knew he was lying.

"James, the books and notes are very important. I need to do well at school."

At that the time one of this older brothers came to the door. He overheard some of the conversations. James turned to him and said something inaudible to me. He then volunteered to help look for the briefcase. After looking down the same halls where I had already looked, he suggested looking in the stairwell.

"James I've looked there."

"Well Walter maybe you missed it."

He opened the door to the stairs. There on the first step was the briefcase. I turned to James and thanked him for his help. I showed him the books and notes showing how complex the courses were. He actually seemed interested in some of the pictures (I believe it was my archeology course book). I was VERY relieved to have the books and notes back. Did well on one test, the other not so well on the second.

James was not the only problem in the hotel. Zachary T was another character. He was a little smaller than most of the boys his age (12). He was trouble! While playing ball, he would push smaller kids around. He would cut lines for activities. His school grades were poor, but he seldom showed for tutoring sessions. He was one of the kids I would take to The Stadium for the games. One sunny afternoon he had grabbed a number of mustard packets and started stamping on them with his foot, making them squirt all over the seats and anyone who happened to be in the path of the flying mustard. Three times I told him to stop. Three times he ignored me. Finally I grabbed him.

"If you won't listen to me you are going to watch the rest of the game next to me."

Whereupon I grabbed him and put him into a head lock. For the next 4 innings Zach watched game from my head hold. If he couldn't see a play, I would reposition my lock, raising his head so he could see the action. Whoever said you can't lay hands of kids as a social worker, never dealt with these kids.

One day while playing softball Zach starting coming towards me with a very aggressive German Shepard. It was his cousin's dog who was walking next to him. Zach told me to be nice to him or he would sic the dog on me. The dog was acting very aggressively, pulling at its chain and growling.

"If you do, I guarantee you that the dog will be dead within one minute. Now get that dog away from the game."

Looking him straight into the eyes and realizing I was dead serious he and his cousin turned and walked away.

One of the kids came up to me and asked: "How could you kill a dog like that?"

"Easy, I would let him bite my arm, then grab the jaw and yank it downward. This would break the jaw and possibly push the bone into the skull, killing the dog. If not, the dog would be seriously hurt and harmless."

One of Zach's friends told him what my strategy was for disabling the dog. Zach later came up to me an apologized for bringing the dog and threatening me.

Back in the office my co-worker Lucy one day came up to me.

"Walter you have a lot more education than I do. Can you explain why I have so little feeling in my breasts? Men love playing with them but I get little enjoyment from it."

Not being an expert in the field, I thought for a moment. "Lucy, it may be due to their size. Your nerve endings are limited. It may be that they are too stretched, decreasing sensitivity."

Never found out if I was correct. But Lucy thought about it and thanked me. Was the only logical explanation I could come up with.

Love,
Papa

November 14, 2015

The worse case:

The most tragic incident involved 3 abandoned children. It was a hot summer day. Most of the rooms had no AC. Someone outside the hotel, came in and told the management that 3 children were hanging out of a 5th floor window. The management asked us to investigate with them.

Charlene and Lucy went upstairs. A few minutes later 3 children were brought into our offices. The boy was the oldest, around 7 or 8. The girls were about 6 and 4. All had lice in their hair. Each was dressed only in a nightgown. They smelled like the cat house in a zoo in the middle of summer. They had not had a bath for weeks if not longer. All were malnourished. I went out to the local deli and got some food and milk for them. Everything was perfunctorily devoured like a wild beast. It was as if they had not eaten anything in a week. We asked the boy, who was the only one who could talk clearly, when was the last time they had a regular meal. He couldn't remember. They had been eating the plaster off the walls to keep their bellies feeling full. The problem is the paint on the walls was lead based. All were suffering from lead poisoning. The youngest most severely. She couldn't talk intelligible. Lucy and Cynthia gave the girls showers and found some second hand clothes. Child Protective Services was notified immediately. That was easy. They had the back office.

Jim was head of Child Protective Services. He was an older gray bearded white man who lived in Harlem. He was a very mild mannered individual. His main job was to check out if any children appeared to be mistreated or were not getting the right amount of food and clothing. Whenever a family in the hotel was referred to him by us (YSA) or the management he would check it out. His major concern was children. He had an old dog that would occasionally accompany him to the office.

He inspected the children. Then the apartment. Upon returning to his office he started working on some paperwork. He checked the welfare records. All the children were on welfare. BOTH parents were listed as in the home. He called some friends in the courts and foster care services.

He told hotel management the second the parents came into the hotel to send them to his office. Several hours later the parents entered our offices. They were impeccably dresses with the latest fashion. The father in a very nice suit. The mother is a beautiful dress with lots of jewelry dangling from her wrists and fingers. One could immediately tell where all the welfare money was going. Certainly not for the children's food. I directed them to Jim's office. They took seats across the desk from Jim. I stood in the door. Jim asked me to be a witness and to prevent them from leaving.

He looked at them. He looked as clam as usual. But there was something I noticed in his eyes which told me furious:

"We found your children dangling dangerously from the apartment windows, which were not locked. The children are seriously malnourished. Your son couldn't tell us the last time he was fed a decent meal. I consider you as unfit parents. Mr. and Mrs. *ABC*, I have prepared papers here for you to sign your children over to Child Protective Services immediately. Welfare has already been notified. You have been suspended from receiving any more checks. Once you sign these papers you are to never see your children again. You are never try to regain custody. All this is included in the papers you are to sign RIGHT NOW!"

He placed the paperwork in front of them with a pen on top.

The father jumped up: "You can't make us sign those papers."

The mother: "We refuse to do it and you can't make us."

Jim very quietly leaned over to the side of his desk and pulled out a pistol.

"You are going to sign those papers RIGHT NOW OR SO HELP ME I WILL PUT A BULLET IN EACH OF YOUR HEADS."

He then pointed the gun at the father.

The mother screamed: "You wouldn't dare! We have a witness" pointing to me.

Looking them in their eyes I responded in a soft voice: "You're absolutely right. Some how Mr. ABC got a hold of a gun and threatened Jim. In the struggle he was killed instantly but not before another shot hit you." Then looking directly at the wife: "in the heart which unfortunately killed you as well. I'm sure you want to sign those papers."

Jim smiled. I stood my ground as if to tell them there was no way out of that room without either signing or being placed in a body bag.

They signed. Later they tried to protest but never got anywhere. Jim told us the results of medical tests. The boy had about 30% of his brain destroyed, the older girl roughly 40%, the youngest over 50%, all due to the lead poisoning. They would all be functionally disabled for the rest of their lives. The youngest not much more than a vegetative state, estimated IQ of less than 50.

Love,
Papa

November 15, 2015

Even more about the Concourse Plaza:

One interesting character in the hotel was Mrs. Killebrew. She had five children, most likely from their appearances from different fathers. She was an over weight black woman in her late 40's or early 50's. Her two youngest boys were often with me on outings or playing in the park. What always fascinated me was the Masonic ring she wore on her little finger. Never asked if she or possibly one of her husbands was a Mason, but by her behavior, seriously doubted it. She use to drive the management crazy. At least once a week she would call the front desk and asked for breakfast in bed. There was no food service. This was a welfare hotel. She knew that. It didn't matter. She wanted breakfast delivered to her in her apartment. It never happened. Usually within a few minutes of her calling the front desk, we would get a visit from the manager.

"Would you please tell her not to ask for breakfast or any other special services from the front desk."

When she emerged from her apartment she was reprimanded. She would promise that she wouldn't do it again. Then in a few days, the front desk would be requested to bring a breakfast up to Room 634 (her room). The management was VERY happy when she was moved out to a new apartment.

It was about this time Charlene made me the Assistant Director of the unit. Partly due to my education, partly due to my experiences also because I was cool under stressful conditions. About a month later Charlene went on vacation. It was clear that I was in charge. Everyone was told to notify me if they were going to be absent. Likewise if they were to take any leave, or had any problems. Everyone was to complete the time sheets every Friday by 2 p.m. Cynthia cooperated fully. The first week went smoothly. The second week not so much.

Lucy went missing for a full week. I didn't have her home phone number. Cynthia tried to call her but didn't reach her. As Friday came, there was still no sign of Lucy. She had not called. No one had heard from her. Time sheets were due. I put on Lucy's AWOL (absent without leave). This would forfeit any pay for the week. Monday Charlene came back. She was told about Lucy's absence. When Lucy showed up she was almost out of control. She wanted to physically attack me. I sat down and told her that we did not hear from her for the whole week. She had not called in as instructed. I had no choice but to put her down as AWOL. Charlene backed me up. Lucy appealed declaring that she was working for another unit during that week. We knew is was pure BS. But somehow she got away with it. Eventually the pay was restored.

There was one day when we were playing ball in the park. Over by some bushes was a couple making out. They were on the ground and likely thought the bushes concealed their activity. It didn't. Upon closer look, it was evident that both were women. Some of the boys spotted them and looked at me. I shrugged.

"Some girls like other girls." and left it at that.

Since we had been getting subway passes and tickets from the Bronx Borough President we thought it would be good if a picture perfect family from the hotel could be found to take them over to the offices to thank the Borough President in person. There was a perfect black family. The father had some college. The mother was smart, exceptionally well spoken and polite. The oldest girl, Victoria was a straight A student in middle school. Her younger sister was likewise a very good student. Both were exceptionally nice and always tastefully dressed. They loved to read and would come in for tutoring mostly to get hands on new books I would bring in. The youngest was a boy, Jimmy about 3 years of age. He was cute as anything. His smile would bring most women to tears with loving kindness. But Jimmy had a bad habit. If not watched, he loved to walk behind people and give them a bite in the ass. Not a play bite, but a real chomp! He bit me once. Charlene more than once, and Cynthia several times. Lucy avoided him all together. Even Jim got a bruise on his ass from a bite.

We scheduled the meeting with Bronx Borough President–Mario Cuomo. Yes, he later became the Governor as did his son. I took the kids over.

"Please keep an eye on Jimmy for me will you Victoria."

She promised she would. Cuomo met with us. He was impressed by the girls. Jimmy just smiled his adorable smile. We thanked him for all the help and the tickets. As Victoria was talking to him, I couldn't see Jimmy. Suddenly there was a scream from Cuomo. Jimmy had bit him hard in the ass. There Jimmy was with a big smile on his face as Cuomo was rubbing his sore ass. Victoria grabbed him. She chastised him in front of everyone. It was not the impression we wanted. But Victoria was so apologetic that Cuomo seemed to get over the incident. We still got tickets, but made sure Jimmy was never introduced to the public again.

Love,
Papa

Thanksgiving, 2015

Concourse Plaza Esoterica:

Would you believe there were individuals who were attractive to me much the same way as Doris was in Pawtucket years before. Sometime during the years at the Concourse Plaza there was a worker in one of the other agencies who started talking with me. When the skies were clear and the weather warm, we would take bag lunches to a park on the other side of the Bronx Bureau building and sit in the park which had a little hill. There there was as much privacy as one could expect. Unfortunately her name escapes me. We would discuss meditation at first. What made her interested was a simple demonstration of cloud zapping. Soon she was able to accomplish it too.

Word got out to some of the kids. Soon there were a bunch of girls who despite their personal anti-white attitudes, started hanging around me. There must have been between 8 to 15 that joined our luncheon forays. Each was eager to learn how to zap clouds. Of course many don't believe it is possible that by staring at a cloud and concentrating on it while mentally saying:

"My will is stronger than yours. You will disperse and disappear."

Time and time again, our little group would make clouds vanish. Meteorologists will say this is a result of the wind dispersing the clouds. In some cases yes. But there was a much too consistent result when the focus was on a single cloud. Often other clouds around the targeted piece of water vapor would remain in tack. But the cloud being concentrated on, though usually a small one, would dissolve far more rapidly than any others around it. This of course was taught to me by Marcia Moore way back in Concord when living with her family. Remember her children, Loulie, Chris and Johnny were all taught this. So it was common practice among the Moores.

Soon the sessions expanded. Now the focus was on temper control. By learning some basic breathing and simple meditation techniques, the girls found they could control their anger and emotional outbursts. There was never any advanced techniques taught, just basic breath control, rhythmic breathing and mental focus on something with a positive meaning.

As more and more girls came to these sessions, my co-worker became fascinated with why some of the children were being attracted to me. Using a technique of holding hands and focusing on the third eye, impressions sometimes inter into my thoughts. If the focus is on a previous reincarnation, then bits and pieces of the other persons former lives start to pop into my head. This way I was able to get my co-worker to open up to her previous life. Soon she started having memories, much like Carol did when I first met her. She called me her personal mystic. When she returned from Mexico on a vacation, she presented me with a little totem figure, holding what looks like an offering bowl in its hands. This small figure, no more than 5″ tall has remained in secretariat for many years. It is the only physical memories that has been retained from the Concourse Plaza.

What happened after I opened her up, suddenly other children started coming to me. Almost none were able to express why. Many even refused to admit they wanted something from me. Yet they came. Again mostly young girls. When they were alone with me in the park of some place quiet the conversation always started with my asking:

"Do want to talk about memories you can't explain?"

Never once did any ask what I meant. For each of these children, ages from around 8 to 15, they would start asking questions: "How can I remember XYZ?"

"Mr. Walter, is it possible to remember something I couldn't have experienced? Why do I remember being another person?"

Almost always, these questions were followed by asking them questions: "Do you think you may have had another life sometime? Were you seeing a place you have never been? What do these images tell you?"

Almost all soon started believing they had lived before. The word reincarnation was seldom used, but here were as many as 20 or more children who were attracted to me. All for one reason. Here was a source to help explain what their every day world, everyday religion, everyday faith, everyday family could not. By talking they all learned they were not crazy. Their memories just might be real. Of another life. One note, NONE were exceptional lives. All were most common. A few as the opposite sex to what they were now. More often another race or different cultural background. Never were any record kept. Just happy with being able to help. Looking back, wish notes had been made. Just never expected to have so many come to our sessions in the park (sometimes in the office where tutoring took place).

Love,
Papa

November, 2015

End of the Concourse Plaza, end of a life:

After the baseball season of 1974, Yankee Stadium was scheduled for a renovation. When taking the subway I would watch them tearing down the old Stadium. It was sad, seeing the old seats being taken left the cement exposed. Then the field was dug up. Lastly the old traditional facade was taken down. When that happened I was almost in tears. There was my beloved Yankee Stadium, the house that Ruth Built, being torn down. Soon all that could be seen was the outer walls and the inner hole in the ground. It was the saddest two seasons I experienced. It was just too far to travel to Shea Stadium to see the games where the Yankees shared with the Mets' stadium. Plus there was no place to take the kids after the 3rd innings!

One good thing during this time was the hiring of another man to work in our unit. John was from Harlem. He had been working as one of the 'street walkers.' Remember the job I first had in YSA? Since he was a little older than me, and over six feet tall, we put him in charge of the older teen boys. Together we would take groups for bus trips, when available (which was rare) to other places around NYC. We would take them to Central Park using the Subway passes. We worked well together. One trip was to the Natural History Museum. Great success. He was a great addition to our unit.

It was while the Stadium was undergoing renovations that everyone was notified that the Grand Concourse Hotel would be closing for renovations too. It appeared there were complaints about this famous hotel being used as an emergency welfare residence for burned out families. There was a group of buildings being developed at 725 Fox Street where the families would be housed. The other advantage it was around the corner to the Lynch Police Athletic League (PAL) center.

Headquarters was trying to make an agreement with the Lynch PAL to allow the kids from the new shelter to use the center after school and in the evenings. The biggest handicap was Fox and Simpson Street intersection was the location of the Ft. Apache Precinct office. 725 Fox was only a few blocks away. The shelter would be in the very heart of Ft. Apache. At the time it was the most dangerous section of NYC. We were given a month to clean up and prepare for the move. This included notifying the families that it was necessary they find new apartments ASAP.

The permanent residents of the hotel were notified that would have to move. Remember the top two floors stilled had the long time residents. There were a number of women who lived alone. But the most remarkable individual up there was a dwarf. At first the kids would tease him and make fun of how short he was. I made an extra effort to get to know him. He was really delightful. He had retired from Ringling Brothers Circus, 'The Greatest Show on Earth.' For some 30 years he had been one of the clowns.

After a few meetings with him, I got him to agree to meet with some of the kids, especially those who made fun of him. We would get the kids to sit in the lobby or occasionally in our offices with him. He would tell about his adventures in the circus. All the great performers he had known. The wild animal acts he participated in. Tales about accidents and when animals didn't behave as planned. A runaway elephant. A tiger that got out of a his cage. They were wonderful stories. The kids got to know him and he them. Soon when someone new would make fun of him, the kids who had met with him would come to his defense. After about a month, no one, not even the older teens or parents would say anything negative.

The dwarf had trouble figuring out where he was to move. He had no family nor relatives. He had been there since his retirement. He knew of no where else to go. Written requests for exceptions for him and one other woman were submitted downtown to allow them to stay during the renovations. No luck. An appeal ended with another rejection. I even wrote how much he had contributed to helping with the kids. Still no deal. The management made multiple appeals themselves. They said the rest of the hotel could be renovated while these two seniors remained in their apartments, until new apartments would be available for them to move into. Again the appeal were ignored.

It was the day before the closing of the hotel. These two people were the only ones who had no where to go. Phone calls were made pleading their case. Later that day the assistant manager said he had not seen the dwarf all day. He went up to check on him. He returned, white as a sheet.

"He's dead!"

The little guy just couldn't bear to leave. He hung himself in his closet. About two hours later, the result of the final appeal came in. He and the woman would be permitted to stay! Two hours too late. As the kids were moving out, some asked where the dwarf was. I had to tell them the truth. Soon about a dozen of the kids were in the lobby, all crying. Some left little drawings, other flowers in his memory. It was one of the saddest days of my life. I hated bureaucracy! Still do when it makes no sense.

Love,
Papa

November, 2015

Still me:

It was about this time that the Youth Services Agency wanted to have all their units trained on the importance of good planning and leadership. It was a two day retreat. There were about 6 units per session. Our unit, Charlene, Cynthia, and myself were all together for one session. One of us was left behind to hold down the office.

The whole session of the first day was a team building effort. The day was basic lectures on the importance in having a plan and leaders to help execute the plan. It was very basic information on planning and management. The idea of putting it together for everyone in a day retreat was relative new at this time. The trainers felt a major new concept in team building and planning training would prove beneficial. It was an informative session for that time. In today's culture, it was nothing exceptional. Still for the time it was considered something revolutionary, especially for social service agencies.

The second half of the second day was an exercise to prove the point that planning and careful directions are better than just random, chaos. The group was divided into two teams. Charlene and I were in the control group, the group with no instructions. The 'select' group were given packs of 3x5" file cards and a multi page set of instructions. Our group received the same number of file cards but no instructions. The object was to build a stable, attractive, and high construction out of the file cards. The tallest and most distinctive would be the winner. The other group even had diagrams to guide them. We were given 2 hours. GO!

Charlene immediately yelled to our group: "Put Walter in charge!"

None challenged her suggestion. I quickly divided the team into those who would build little box structures using 6 cards. These would be the basics of the structure. Another group was to put the cards together from the first group for form the base for the larger structure. These were stacked on top of each other, each level slightly smaller but taller than the previous. As I was telling them what to do, I made a rough diagram of the building (resembling, a little, the Chrysler Building). One person was told to build the top tower. This included some triangular structures to break up the right angles. These were put around the basic square tower structure. As we were progressing Charlene was grinning ear to ear. She kept sneaking a peek at the other group. If we were equal or doing better than them, I would get a thumbs up.

By the end of the first hour we had a very solid three level basic structure. The last hour was putting together the tower and the elaborations. The sculpted cards would interrupt the basic rectangular lines and shapes to give the structure a more aesthetic appearance. As the time was down to the last 10 minutes the facilitators were looking desperate. They were looking at what the group designated to be the failure group was doing. The problem **we were't failing!**

TIMES UP! The two structures, which were constructed on plywood sheets, were brought together. Our structure was taller! Only by two inches, but it was taller. One point. Equally stable if not more, though the facilitators refused to admit it. Two points. As for the appearance, the group that followed the instructions, it was a typical box structure. It looking like a multi level housing project structure. Boring! Ours had the basic box underneath, but we had the added features of triangles on the tower, which was topped by a semi cross style decoration. That should have been the final point for us. The facilitators refused to admit our structure was better looking. When they remeasured our structure, they didn't measure from the plywood base but cheated on their group by a good 3 inches to give their team the point.

Our team erupted! We had clearly won all three elements of the exercise. Charlene shouted:

"You just don't want to admit the control group out performed your instructed group. WE WON, all three points!"

Our team shouted them down. Charlene turned to the lead facilitator:

"It is not planning and instructions, it is choosing the right leader."

Have always loved proving the 'experts' wrong! Wouldn't be the last time.

Love,
Papa

Chapter 11

Back to Fort. Apache

December 17, 2015

It's me again:

Remember my co-worker John who had joined the unit? He actually had a car. One day a week before the move, he drove to the new digs at 725 Fox Street. Taking a look at the new location he drove back to the hotel. When he returned he looked like he had lost most of his blood in his head. Despite being a very dark black man, he looked pale. Upon returning to the office he immediately turned to me with a special request:

"Please find me another place to work. Transfer me to Harlem or Bedford Sti in Brooklyn, BUT PLEASE DON'T MAKE ME GO TO FOX STREET!"

Charlene and I made some calls. There was one unit, much like the one I was at on Broadway in south Harlem. They were short of staff. Especially staff willing to work in the heart of the bad sections of Harlem. We got him transferred to a Harlem unit. We saw him once after the transfer. It worked out well for him, as he was closer to his home. He knew the neighborhood and some of the other workers. He even knew some of the leaders of the gangs in the area. Didn't ask how. Knew better. An ideal location for him.

The actual move was easy. The new digs were converted row houses. A better description is rebuilt brick buildings. There was no evident of the old buildings remaining. The exceptions may have been the infrastructure. Child Protective Services had two rooms. Jim was not going to the new location. New staff were assigned. There was a new department added. Two truant officers assigned to the relocation shelter. They had their own little office. Their duty, see all the children in the shelter were reassigned to the local school as long as they were residing there. They were a help especially with the educational efforts I continued to offer. They would often assist in the tutoring, providing school materials and course materials when needed.

The YSA offices had little or no files, except for time sheets and a few personnel files. However we did have the largest staff. So we were given a number of offices for our desks, files and more important places for counseling and tutoring. Charlene and I had one office as the Director and Assistant Director of the unit. Cynthia and Lucy were given another room to use as an office and council any girls that needed redirecting.

We soon got Neighborhood Work Corps workers. They included a couple of Viet Nam vets. One had been a combat Army. The other was also Army but in logistics, mostly just unloading and distributing supplies as they came into Saigon. I tell everyone when comparing notes, I was shot at more than a Viet Nam vet. In truth it was this latter vet. He had never been shot at during his tour of duty. As for you father being a target, though shot at from a distance a couple of times, the closest call will be coming soon.

The focus of our job remained the same. Keep a lid on the kids and get them involved in positive activities. This proved to be easier than at the Concourse Plaza. The Lynch PAL Center was just around the corner. I was over there more than in our offices. Soon they almost considered me a part of their staff.

The apartment buildings were only a four stories above the ground floor where the offices were located. The other attached (721 & 723) buildings were for the managers and maintenance staff. All the rest were apartments, both on the first and upper floors. Within a week we were close to full. The only problem with the Fox Street location, I could no longer walk to work. I would have to take the Pellam Bay #6 IRT line to Longwood Avenue and Southern Blvd. Then walk the few blocks to Fox Street shelter. The buildings on Southern were full of tenants. As for the block on Fox Street, our buildings were the only ones that were decent. To the right was a concrete open area, fenced in. Then slightly elevated from Fox was the side/back of the PAL. Only part of the front wall was still standing. The rest had been reduced to rubble. The building next to ours was in bad shape but standing and occupied. Nest to it was a building with part of the front wall still standing, the back totally demolished. The end of the block was a pile of rubble that must have been a building once upon a time. Across the street were mostly shells of buildings, if even that much. Most were reduced to piles of bricks and junk. This was Fox Street in 1970s. You couldn't recognized it today. There is even a tennis court across the street!

It was about this time Helen Wycherly the American head of La Droit Humain wanted to set up a Royal Arch Chapter in New York. A special convocation was held in which several of the Master Masons of Marie Deraismes where exulted to the Royal Arch Degree. Among them were Demetria, my mother and myself. Fred N had already received it, though I am sure if it was in Larkspur at the old headquarters. Fred was studying the Kabbalah in the Jewish traditions and had taken some advanced courses. He felt the Royal Arch Degree and the Kabbalah were closely linked, being related in both the ritual and symbols. It is important to realize the symbols contained in Masonry are a way to express the nature of man and the universe. The have preserved the hidden truths and are a guide towards higher spiritual realization.

One of the members of Marie Deraismes, Aggie was about to go into the hospital for a hip replacement. The doctors told her the recovery in the hospital would be at least three to six weeks, at which time she may be able to leave with the help of a walker. Fred came up with an idea. It was to meet at Demetria's and perform the section of the Royal Arch Degree where 'we three or such as we...' form a triangle. But rather than just practicing this part of the rituals Fred felt it could be used to generate healing power which might help Aggie heal.

We three would gather at Demetria's and perform that particular of the ritual. But the focus of the ritual would be to generate energy and then send it out to Aggie. When we did this, within minutes Demetria's phone would ring. It was Aggie! It is important to know she was not one of the members who had receive the Royal Arch Degree when offered. In the phone call she would cry out:"

"What are you doing to me? I can feel heat in my hip."

We only did this three times, but within a little over two weeks time Aggie walked out of the hospital trilling her cane on her fingers. Yes! there is more to Masonry than what most are aware of!

December 18, 2015

Dear T:

I must admit my years at Fox Street were certainly some of the most memorable. There were lots of adventures and interesting incidents. I will try to recall as many as possible. Others may occur to me later, some may appear as back flashes.

The place to start is really with the Lynch PAL. The director of the PAL was Bill Rainey. Bill was a tall black man, likely in his 40's, though not sure. He was friendly. Well educated and a good conversationalist, he was also good with the kids. The assistant director was Pablo (don't know his last name). Pablo was originally from Puerto Rico and spoke with a strong Spanish accent. There was a boxing coach, Frank Rodriguez. He was in his 70's, short and likely not much more than 120 lbs, but had more New York Golden Gloves winning boxers than any other boxing coach in the history of NYC. Frank was so well known, Howard Cossell, the famous sports broadcaster, hosted his retirement dinner. More on Frank later.

When the YSA staff started to bring over the kids to the PAL, they were more than happy to receive us. One of the conditions was YSA was to provide at least two of our staff with the kids. Most of the boys who had any talent for boxing wanted into Frank's classes. A schedule was developed which included all of our staff as support. Most of the night shift was assigned to myself and our two Viet Nam vets to allow the women to get out before dark and back to their families. Let's face it, the neighborhood was NOT safe after dark. Come to think of it daylight too.

The PAL's main floor was where their offices were, Bill's on the right as you entered the door, Pablo's on the left. There was a front desk where someone was to check kids as they came in, which was rarely done. Then beyond Bill's office was a library / study room which had a piano. There were a number of desks and a small conference table with chairs around it in case there was a group tutoring session. I don't remember but either the bathrooms were on the left of down the hall to the right after the study room. To the left was the pool room. It had two pool tables. The rules for the pool room was NO SWEARING, no gambling, and good behavior at all times. Overall these were the rules for the PAL in general, but in the pool room it was more important as sometimes some of the egos of those being beaten in a match came to the surface. Not always in a friendly way!

Upstairs was a stage and the basketball court. It looked like it may have been a school at one time. When basketball was not being played, we would put up two ping pong tables. If only a few were playing b'ball, then it was be set up as a half court with at least one ping pong table off to the other side. In the winter time, this would also be the kickball court for the younger children in the afternoons.

In the basement was a whole other world. To the immediate right as you entered, was a ceramic studio. No one had used it for years. But there was a kiln, a wheel, and a closet filled with supplies. Next to it was a darkroom, with enlarger and likewise supplies not used for years. No one had used either because no one had those skills. You can see where I fit in real quickly. At the end of the basement hall was the boxing ring, showers, and workout room which took up most of the basement. Frank had a few assistants (I think they were volunteers). Likely most were former students and former Golden Glove champs.

The PAL usually opened around 1 p.m. The boxing area would occasionally be opened earlier if tournaments were to take place. It was never empty.

Love,
Papa

December 19, 2015

Hi T:

In the PAL one of mine main duties was watch the kids. Many soon got to know me. Both those from the relocation shelter around the corner and neighborhood kids would listen to me. I would tell them I was once homeless (Concord). That I grew up poor, making the cheapest meals possible to survive (tuna & apple curry on rice). I told them how my school tried to keep me down, because I didn't fit the WASP ideal. [In case you are not familiar with the term WASP it stood for "white, Anglo-Saxon Protestant—of the upper middle and upper classes mostly.] I would tell them about the discrimination and classism I faced in Connecticut. Some who knew about the March on Washington, would love to hear about my being there to hear Martin Luther King's famous speech. All these life experiences were related to the kids in Ft. Apache. That plus the fact I was still living on Alexander Avenue earned their respect.

Soon there were a group of kids that were constantly surrounding me. Bill thought I was one of the best influences and role models for the kids. Not because I was white, but because I had gone through many of the same challenges they faced daily. When things were quiet at Lynch PAL, he and I could be found either playing ping pong or chess. In ping pong Bill always loved to use the OLD sandpaper paddles. With his long reach, he was able to serve the ball way below the table (something not exactly within regulation rules), disguising the spin he would put on the ball. When the ball hit his side, it would have either side, back or top spin which would occur so fast, my successful returns were less than 50%. At the same time, being a pen grip player, my spin serves proved difficult for him to return. Overall he likely won about 60% of the time, but we always had fun.

It was during these games we would discuss either our own lives, or possible problems with some of the kids in the center. This proved to be a far more congenial way to discuss the kids' problems than a formal sit down meeting in an office. Of course sit down meetings were held, but over a chess board. Again Bill likely won more than half. Neither of us were great players, but we both loved the game. One kid who was called Fat Willie loved chess too. Bill suggested I play him as he was at a level comparable to our skill level. So Fat Willie and I became regular chess players. Sometimes in the corner of the b'ball court upstairs, sometime in the tutoring room, even on the front steps of the PAL. We were very evenly matched. Willie also loved to whittle. He always had his pocket knife with him. When nothing was happening in the Center, he would be on the front step whittling some little figure, or just carving into a stick. There is no memory of any finished figure, just Willie working away.

There was another kid who soon attached himself to me. David Brown was one of the first kids I met at the PAL. David was very dark black, tall for his age, thin likely from an inadequate diet, and VERY street smart. He lived over near the precinct building, so didn't experience the same number of break ins and shootings as the rest of the neighborhood. Still, there were more than enough of both in his building, just not as many as elsewhere in Ft. Apache. His grades were poor. I tried to tutor him, but he had little interest.

"Shit Walter, I still am passing with Ds."

He loved the rap that was given to all the kids. I would tell them to THE MAN (outside middle class white America) they were all a bunch of niggers and spics:

"Your schools are the pits. Your teachers piss poor. Your neighborhoods are shit. All because they don't want you to get the hell out of here. They feel safer if they keep you here in this the hell hole. The only way you are going to beat THE MAN is not by falling into the gang activities, crime, and drugs as they expect, but by getting the hell out of here. The way you do that is by putting up with the shit schools. Get good grades! Then getting into college. That is the only way out of here other than the grave which awaits so many of you if you do crimes or join the gangs."

I used Bill who had a college degree and myself as examples. Charlene, my boss was another good examples:

"All three of us got out of our poverty. We choose to be in the South Bronx to help out the kids!"

This they accepted. Soon there was about a dozen kids, from age 7 to 18 that attached themselves to me in various ways. Many for tutoring. Others to use me as a social worker to discuss their problems, at home, in the street, or in school. Still others as someone they could play basketball, chess, pool, or handball with.

I remember one kid who had decent grades (C's mostly and a few B's) who wanted tutoring on the piano in the study room. I didn't know how to play, but did know where middle C was in the keyboard. We found some sheet music. Together we laid out the notes on the piano keys. Together we would then slowly play the songs. We worked on this together. Finally after a few weeks I said:

"That's as far as I can take you. It is up to you from here."

Soon he was able to play several pieces in the music book. Not well, nor at the proper tempo, but HE COULD PLAY THEM!

Love,
Papa

January 21, 2016

Hello Again:

David Brown was my constant companion during those years at Fox Street. He wasn't legally allowed to come to the shelter, but would occasionally sneak in to see me. Most of the time he would meet me at the PAL. I remember he was part of a group who challenged a former Harlem resident who had moved to the South Bronx as too which was a tougher neighborhood. The new comer's apartment had just been burned out so he was in the shelter. The argument was over which was more dangerous, the South Bronx or Harlem. The conversation ran a little like this:

Kid from Harlem: "Harlem is so bad when they break in they steal everything they can get their hands on."

David: "Hell if they left the pipes and walls they weren't from the South Bronx. Shit we will even steal the stairs!"

This would continue to cover shootings, gang activities, and every other adverse activities in both ghettos. It was actually fun to listen to, and so true in many ways. The welcome to the South Bronx.

There was another incident which was unusual. The PAL got a report that a group of 7th graders had raped their new teacher. The teacher was young, energetic and hopeful. She volunteered to work in the South Bronx despite being warned of the dangers, especially to a young, attractive blond teacher. Bill and I held a counseling session with most of the kids in the class, both boys and girls. We told them it was not nice to rape a teacher who was trying so hard to help them. From what we had heard, she was one of the really good teachers in that school.

"Now after what you had done, do you expect her to stay? Boys you should not gang bang your teachers! Girls, you should not hold her down, strip off her clothes encouraging the boys!"

The teacher did not stay for the second semester!

Bill had an idea. He knew I had training in both ceramics and photography. Why not use the darkroom and ceramics studio in the basement? I got a few of the kids to help me clean up both. Soon they were both in working condition. We had limited supplies so soon used what had been down there for years. The clay was well wrapped and was soon in workable condition. We started with my demonstrating how to use the wheel. There were a number of pots done. I threw 3 matching bowls, in different sizes. They had a dark interior glaze and dark red exterior. Not sure if they still survive, but they were last seen in the Slade Run house.

I taught the kids how to do coil pots and slab constructions. The drying room was not ideal but it worked. Then we had a bisque firing. Everything came out perfect. Next was the glazing. There were a limited number of pre-mixed glazes available. Not the best but usable. So the kids were taught how to glaze their constructions. Again everything came out perfectly. This continued until we ran out of supplies. Bill asked the PAL HQ for more. They refused, lack of funds for such activities. So the ceramics studio was shut down just short of a year.

Next was the photographic darkroom. Again they had all the supplies for developing and printed black and white photos. None of the kids had any cameras. The solution was for me to take picture of what they thought would be good subjects. There were a lot of photos of the back alleys a buildings. Some of the kids felt that was boring.

"What would you like?"

David asked: "Can you take pictures of some of the porn films and development them?"

Well this was totally illegal, but what else was new in the South Bronx. This was when 42nd Street was pure smut. There were a dozen of porn theaters between 6th and 8th Avenues. So to keep the kids interested in photography, I would sneak in my camera into the movies and take pictures from my seat. The boys, and some of the girls loved the subject matter! Can't blame them, I did too. I remember one shot was of a girl going down on a guy. One of the boys asked what she was doing. David answered:

"Sucking on his lollypop."

Well that was one way to give the kids sex education. Considering all that was going on around them, it was appropriate even if unorthodox.

Love,
Papa

January 22, 2016

This being put in mail box on day of blizzard
We'll see when it is picked up! ;-)

Still me:

I stopped the last letter with a story about the darkroom. Several of the boys, mostly, learned the basics of the darkroom. The enlarger was cheap but usable. The sinks small but big enough to handle the baths. We were developing films weekly. A schedule was formulated and kids were asked to sign up. The film I had taken were now developed and pictured printed. Those which were appropriate for the public now posted on the walls of the photo studio. About 6 kids became regulars. They took a great deal of pride in being able to develop and print my photos. But like the ceramics studio, when we ran out of supplies, the request for more came back with the same response: "Sorry no funds available." So photography classes stopped.

Using the same strategy for tutoring as used in the dark room the kids were asked what would they like to read. There were two responses. Comics and porn. So I started collecting comic books. My personal favorites at the time was *Dr. Strange* and *The Justice League*, mostly Dell with a few Marvel comics. The kids did like some of the Marvel comics. Whatever character they wanted, I would try to bring in. The rules were they had to read them in the tutoring sessions. Some wanted porn. I didn't approve of the pure smut that was popular. But exploring what was out there, I discovered the classic Victorian underground English novels. Soon <u>The Romance of Lust</u>, and <u>My Secret Life</u> were included in the reading sessions, but restricted to high schoolers. Here were well written books in proper English, great literature, even if the subject matter was not proper for the everyday audience. Most of those who came to the tutoring sessions started improving their grades. Many even started getting "B's" or better. It was a major success even if inappropriate materials were used. Yet this was the South Bronx.

Can't verify this but here it was communicated to me. One of the 11 years olds was reportedly a major pimp. He must have been a perfect example of possible reincarnation. The kid was a stock market genius. Like any other pimp, he would take 90% of the girls money. But of that 90% he would keep less than half. The other half he invested in mutual funds in the name of the girls. But he maintained control of the investments. They would only get those funds if they graduated from high school and accepted into college. Then they would a nice nest egg to pay for college. There were girls begging to work for him. Some as young as 12. At the time I met him, he had about a dozen in his stable. They were the most attractive girls from the neighborhood. If he needed to take care of business, he would put in a phone call. In a short time his chauffeur would arrive in a Caddie to pick him up. I asked him how did he know about the stock market.

"I don't know. I picked up an old copy of *The Wall Street Journal* in the subway one day and started reading it. It was like it triggered a deep understanding I didn't know I had. So I came up with this idea to make money both for myself and the girls."

He was very successful! As far as the legality of it, better to turn away and pretend it didn't exist. After all he was succeeding in getting the girls out of the South Bronx. As for the young age of the girls, most girls in the South Bronx were sexually active by 12. So this fit into the morays of the area. Don't know how he did it, but he had a lot of mid-town clients. The chauffeur was mostly used to take the girls to midtown Manhattan appointments. He offered me a discount. But I was a good social worker and politely declined the offer. Still considering how beautiful his girls were, that was a hard offer to turn down.

As time progressed I was spending more time at the PAL than in my office on Fox Street. I would meet with Charlene in the office to file weekly reports and timesheet. I was usually the one to take them to HQ downtown. This way I was able to visit the woman who hired me into the Youth Service Agency, Margaret B. She continued to take an interest in what I was doing and would usually set aside any of her normal duties to talk with me whenever I was at Park Row. This would prove valuable sooner than expected.

Love,
Papa

February, 2016

Still me:

In the mean time, I was continuing my studies in anthropology. These were my last few years at The New School. My grades had gradually improved and the classes more comfortable, except for linguistics theory. The days when I was attending night classes where the days I would show up to the Fox Street office in the morning. On those days the briefcase was filled with books! Heavy as anything.

Fat Willie had two close friends, Juan and Kiki. Kiki was a small kid and quite a wise guy. Always getting into minor trouble. Juan was thin and became quite tall, shooting up over 6 inches in a single year. As he grew in height, I would work with him on the B'ball court, teaching how to improve his lay ups and outside shots. All lived in the neighborhood and hung out together on Longwood Avenue when not at the PAL. One day I had just gotten off the Pelham Bay #6 subway IRT line and was walking to the shelter on Fox Street. There on one of the stoops were Kiki, Fat Willie and Juan. Juan just sitting talking to the other two. Willie whittling on a piece of wood. Kiki was his usual animated self walking and jumping back and forth.

They spotted me coming. All of them knew the route I usually took to my office. It was not unusual to see me walking there this time of day. Like most days, I was carrying a very heavy briefcase filled with graduate books as exams were coming the next week. Knowing all the three very well, I was just ready to stop and say hi when Kiki yells:

"Willie your knife."

In the South Bronx, when someone asks a friend for a knife, you don't hesitate, you hand them the knife. In this case Willie threw the knife, butt first to Kiki. What happened next was pure reflect action with no real thought behind it. Kiki caught the knife and lunged at me. The knife was directed at my belly. The second the charge started, I stepped to the side with my right foot, leaving my left in place. As Kiki continued, he now couldn't stop in time to prevent himself from tripping over my left foot. As he fell there was a flick of the briefcase upward, striking him on the wrist. The knife went flying straight up in the air. As Kiki started to fall, my left elbow struck him in the back. With the added force of the briefcase coming down he went sprawling. I spun around, looked up, saw the knife coming down, grabbing it out of the air. By this time Kiki was face down on the sidewalk. Continuing the spin, I dropped the left knee on the middle of his back. Thus pinned, the knife, now in my right hand, was held at his throat.

"Just what the hell do you think you were doing Kiki?" I asked.

He turned his head sideways so he could see me in the eyes. With the knife still held near his throat he replied:

"I just wanted to see if you were as tough as you make yourself out to be."

"Oh, is that all." was my response.

"Did you find out?"

"Yea, sorry Walter, I won't do it again."

I got up releasing Kiki from the knee that was holding him firmly on the ground. When he got up, I handed him back the knife.

"Why don't you let Willie use his knife on the wood he has in his hand and not try a stunt like that again."

Kiki actually looking relieved, while handing the knife back to Willie who just smiled. Juan was almost in shock over what was happened and had a blank stare on his face. As for Kiki, I earned his respect that day. There was never any trouble between us every again. For that matter, when in my presence at the PAL his behavior was exemplarily.

When I got to the office Charlene asked:

"How is it going Walter?"

"Oh just a normal day in the South Bronx. Kiki tried to pull a stunt and almost stabbed me with a knife, but I think he learned a lesson. No big deal."

Charlene who knew Kiki just shook her head and smiled at me. Nothing else was ever done related to the attempted stabbing in my gut. Besides these kids were the ones who liked me. What danger could I have been in??? At least after they learned I could defend myself. There was a number of even closer calls to come.

Love,
Papa

Chapter 12

Progressing in Co-M & the PAL

February, 2016 #2

Hello again:

Now being in NYC the Co-Masons quickly made use of me. Of course I was an officer in Marie Deraismes. During the first election of officers after moving to NYC was selected as the Junior Deacon's (JD), and placed in the southwest part of the Lodge. Alma Olinde, the old Estonian member was sitting on the side lines. She had been the JD for years, mostly because the lodge was short of people. She looked more frail than usual. She was under 5 feet and likely weighted 80 pounds if that. But now she just looked as if she had lost even more weight. Once installed in my seat, she leaned over to me, patted my hand and said with her wonderful smile:

"Now I can rest. You are bringing youth into the lodge. I am very happy."

It was shortly before the next meeting we heard Alma had died. Mom and I were not able to make the funeral. At the next meeting, I was sitting in the JD place in the lodge. When I looked downward, not focusing on anything in particular, I could swear Alma was there sitting in the chair where she had been the previous meeting. If I turned to see if what I was thought was her, nothing was there. When I turned back towards the floor, there just at the peripheral vision was Alma again. Once that impression came to me, the oder of her perfume would drift into my nostrils. I smiled knowing she was still with us. I was very happy she was next to me.

In March of 1973 I was given the 18th Degree in Sovereign Chapter Agape #68. I was admitted into Signet Mark Lodge #9 in April of 1973, both just a little over the year required from receiving the 3rd Degree. By the time both bodies had their next elections I was elected to head both. Mom actually succeeded me in the Mark Lodge. As head of the Mark Lodge taking it over from Myron who had it for many years. Then I was elected Sovereign Master of the Rose Croix Chapter. I encouraged the newly made Master Masons to continue their progressions up the York Rite and Scottish Rite bodies.

We still didn't have a Royal Arch Chapter in New York, so I received that degree in Larkspur Holy Royal Arch #3 which held a special meeting in New York in October of 1973. There were hopes to form a Royal Arch Chapter in NYC sometime in the future. Carol had followed me into the Mark Lodge when she was eligible, then into the 18th Degree the next year.

It was during this time I created a bunch of flyers about Co-Masonry. I would try to post the flyers around the more up scale tea rooms, with no success. They rarely stayed on the bulletin boards for long. I was active in the Arcane School, having completed several levels of their meditation courses. They had Full Moon Meditation meetings in their old headquarters near the United Nations building. Many members and a larger number of non-member/esoteric students attended. Most simply because they were looking for something. Many didn't even know what. It was at these meetings I tried to hand out the flyers. Perry Cole of the School strongly protested. The flyer invited people to Demetria's house for an open discussion and tea party.

The next month I waited outside the School and handed out the same flyers. Perry lost his cool. I told him these were not being handed out inside but on the public sidewalks. He had no right to interfere. That just made him madder. But he realized there was nothing he could do. It made people aware of Marie Deraismes Lodge. Soon I was giving regular talks about Masonry. At Demetria's a number of individuals were curious about Masonry, especially Co-M. One woman, Janet was very interested. Sure enough after my briefing she asked for a petition. There were others there as well. One was Jean. I didn't realize it, but she would change my life in many directions. The point was these were bringing in new members to Co-Masonry. Alice Bailey's dream of bringing Arcane School members closer to Masonry was becoming a reality. Something the current School officers weren't aware of.

I must note the following information related to the Arcane School and Alice Bailey were what my mother told me. They reflect her views and may not be 100 percent accurate but the view of one of Alice's secretaries who felt very close to her. There is other views that exist which may not agree with what may follow here.

Love,
Papa

February, 2016 #3

Hello again:

There were many more adventures at the PAL. Many centered around the pool room. The closest call was one afternoon. Again it was the pool room where the trouble started but this time with the afternoon kids, mostly elementary and middle schoolers. A new kid to the Center was swearing. He was a little short and likely around 7 or 8 years old. It was not in anger, just his normal obnoxious self. I showed him the sign saying: 'No Swearing Allowed.' He gave me the finger and turned away. The next time he swore, I verbally warned him not to do it again. He did. This time I told him, if he doesn't watch his language, he would have to leave the Center. All was relative quiet for a few minutes, then he started cursing when he missed a shot. I came up to him and said:

"You had three warnings. You have to leave now."

He ignored me. So I grabbed the back of his belt and collar, literally picking him up off his feet. I proceeded down the few steps to the main hall, then to the front door and set him down outside. Bill had seen me and smiled, knowing the kid must have violated one of the rules. When the kid was outside he turned to me:

"I'm going to shoot your mother fucking honky head off. Just you wait. I'm going to kill you, you mother fucker."

He turned in tears of embarrassment and left.

This was a normal threat from young kids his age, so it was ignored. Returning to the pool room to continue monitoring the activities there was no thought to anything that had just transpired. About half an hour later I heard a voice behind me.

"OK you mother fucking honky, I'm going to blow you fucking head off."

I turned around. There was the trouble maker. As I turned around there was a .44 revolver pointed right at my head. I could see bullets in the cylinder. The hammer was cocked back. He was holding it with both hands as it was a heavy pistol. I looked down right into his eyes. Instinctively I knew he wanted me to show fear or to plead forgiveness. Instead I said:

"Well are you going to pull that trigger or just talk me to death?"

This was not the response he expected. His attention was diverted from the gun by the unexpected response. This gave me the only chance I had. As quickly as possible I grabbed the gun with the webbing between my thumb and first finger firmly planted between the hammer and the cylinder. Now if the trigger was pulled, the hammer would hit my hand, not the bullet. Quickly the gun was wrenched from his hand. I handed it to one of the other kids. Once again he was picked up by the shirt and pants out of the center. Upon going back to the room, the gun was handed over to me. It was taken to the office. What Bill did with it I don't know. I used to say I threw it in the East River, but that was not the case. Bill likely turned it into the police. The kid must have really gotten into trouble with his older brother who ran drugs in the area and used the gun to threaten those who didn't pay.

The kid did show up the next week. He had bruises from being beaten up. I learned the kids who had witnessed the episode took him aside outside the Center and told him the Walter was OK and not to threaten me ever again. This was reinforced by a good beating. When he did come back to the center, everyone there was watching. He slowly walked up to me and apologized.

I turned to him: "Are you going to behave yourself?"

"Yes sir" came the demure reply.

"So would you like to learn how to pay ping pong?" He nodded.

I took him upstairs and started coaching him in how to play. The next week he came, he asked for tutoring. Within two weeks of the gun threat, he was my shadow. No matter what I was doing or where I was going, he was right there along with some of the kids who must have 'set him straight' as there was a steady group of 6–8 boys between 7 and 10 years old who were really attached to me. He was just one of that group now. Never had any more swearing from him or any kind of misbehaving.

Love,
Papa

March, 2016

Another pool room adventure:

One time a group of boys, in mid to late teens, were playing one evening. One of the boys was pissed about loosing repeatedly to the same other kid. He got mad and threatened him with a pool stick. I stepped in and told him to put it down. He did but then threatened to hit the other boy. As he raised his arm as if strike, the smaller boy, who had been winning all night playing 8 ball, struck the threatening character so fast it was almost impossible to see his defensive punch coming, little less block it. The boy who had tied to cause trouble suddenly moved his hand to his jaw and without saying a word, retreated from the Center.

About 2 weeks later I was called into Juvenile Court. The boy who was hit in the jaw suffered a broken bone and couldn't talk with the jaw wired shut. His mother filed a complaint against the kid who hit her son. I was called as a witness. I told the judge in chambers exactly what happened. How the injured boy had threatened with a cue stick. After I had interceded he had been threatened again, both verbally and as if he was about to be punched. The conclusion was the so called aggressor, was really just defending himself against the real trouble maker, the one with the wired jaw. Case dismissed!

Bill and Pablo were fun outside the PAL. I remember one day seeing Pablo outside Yankee stadium. I had gone to an afternoon game by myself. Pablo spotted me. He came over to say hello.

"What brought you over here? I asked.

"There is a beautiful woman who needed some help. She likes me to come visit when I get the chance. I showed her how I can lick the little man in the boat. Now she wants it as often as possible. I just have to be sure her husband is not around."

I found out why Pablo was not married that afternoon. He had over a dozen women he would visit. As he said:

"Once you get a woman's little man in the boat, she will want you over and over again."

Meanwhile back to Fox Street, Charlene, my supervisor and I used to go to the corner Hispanic deli. Leaving our offices we would turn to the right and walk past our shelter buildings. The next section of the block had a crumbled down building which only had a partially standing wall. The next building was still standing and was occupied as was mentioned before. Then next space was just a pile of rubble. Mostly bricks. It was evident that a building had burned down and crumbled. That was the condition of most on the opposite side of the block. Once you crossed the street all the buildings were in tact and all occupied.

Two delis were across the street from the block our offices were on. It was as if we would take turns as to which we would get our lunch at. They both had a variety of sandwiches. The one on the same side as our office had the best deep re-fried pork, one of my favorite take out meals. The other would have better rice and bean combo platters. Charlene liked getting food from there. So we would patronize both. Likely some of the worse food for you, mostly fried and pork but it sure tasted good.

Another favorite was NewRican *pasteles*. Although similar to those found in Puerto Rico, these were much lower quality! We could get them at one deli. But where I most enjoyed getting them was the food vendors inside the Subway stations. The large stations, especially Times Square, 8th Ave & 34th Street station (Madison Square Garden), and of course 125th Street on the East side. Thin flat bread folded over a mystery meat filling, deep fried to a golden brown. Use to get those for $1.25. Unhealthy as hell, but loved them. The would fill me up.

Love,
Papa

Chapter 13

Breaking up is hard to do

March 24, 2016

Hey T:

Back to Masonry, Carol was progressing. She received the Third Degree (MM) and I even got her to join Signet Mark Lodge. But things were not going well. Once she received the MM Degree our relationship started a down hill slide. At the time I didn't realize what was happening but later pieced together the only logical reason. The karmic debt from our previous lives had been fulfilled. I had led her to a spiritual school. She never accepted what I had been trying to teach her in India as a Hindu priest, but now she was exposed to one of the oldest schools of esoteric philosophy in the Western World. It was completion of what we were brought together in this incarnation for.

At the same time life was moving in a new and unexpected direction. It started when Carol asked me one evening if she could go out with one of her old boy friends. I said OK. But this was followed by another date. In the mean time I had given the talk at Demetria's about Co-Masonry to a group who had picked up the flyers I had passed out as people were leaving the Arcane School meeting. There were about 5 or 6 people who showed up for the luncheon talk. The presentation went very well. One woman showed interest in joining the Lodge. Another was interested as she had been part of the Arcane School correspondence courses. Her name was Jean. Not very attractive but a very up beat personality. Since Carol was seeing her old boy friend, I decided to ask Jean out to dinner.

We met on the East Side and went to a little restaurant. She was wearing a low cut dress with a push up bra that was showing more than was she really had. We had a delightful dinner and fun conversation. I walked her home to her 2nd Avenue apartment. When I got back to the South Bronx, I did a Tarot spread to see what it could tell me about Jean and a possible relationship with her. Unfortunately I wrote down the impressions I had from the reading.

The next day Carol came over. She found the paper on my night table. She was furious. How dare I see someone else. I argued that she was seeing her old bow so I should explore other possible relations This was totally ignored. That was the final straw. She wanted a full break. Over the next few days she demanded she be allowed to keep the engagement ring and the sewing machine.

OUCH! But I agreed. Hate fighting over physical property. Word spread fast at the Settlement House that Carol and I had split. No more volunteer work at Mott Haven.

I called up Jean and told her what had happened. She and I went out for another date. She admitted that the first date she went all out to get my attention. She admitted that her bra was exposing her breasts as best physically possible. She said she had a strong attraction to me both physically and spiritually. So we started dating. I also started looking for another place to move to.

Years later I ran into another Co-M, Sylvia. This was long after I had dropped out of Co-M for regular Masonry and had moved to Washington, D.C. This Sylvia had been a member of Marie Deraismes Lodge and was friendly with both myself and Carol. She told me she had run into Carol a few months before in Yonkers near her home. They had lunch together to catch up with what had happened over the years. Carol had married a Jewish man. But he refused to have any children with 'the mongrel bitch' which is what he called his wife. Real tragedy as Carol would have made a wonderful mother. She was allowed to continue her education and when on to get a Ph.D. Sylvia then told me that after talking with Carol for a while, Carol broke down in tears:

"I wished I had married Walter."

Sylvia told me how successful Carol was professionally but how unhappy she was in her personal life.

Love,
Papa

Want to take you on aside with two meeting of Marie Deraismes when Francoise Gilot, the former lover/wife to Picasso and a feminine Mason, visited 352. She was looking for Masonic activities that included women. Since there were no feminine lodges in NYC our little Co-Masonic lodge was all she found. She first visited at a regular meeting. Of course she was warmly welcomed and encouraged to come back. It may have been the next meeting when she arranged to treat the members to a dinner in Greenwich Village with her current husband Dr. Jonas Salk. Yes, this is the Dr. Salk what invented the Polio vaccine! The couple had a delightful apartment overlooking Washington Square Park.

Since this was primarily Francoise' gathering, Dr. Salk politely introduced himself to the ten or so members of Marie Deraismes that were able to attend the evening's dinner. It was a very pleasant evening. There was a buffet with more than sufficient food, all of which was of exceptional quality. Unfortunately I an unable to recall any of the conversations that occurred between Francoise and the other members, mostly women. I decided to join Dr. Salk on the balcony where we sat for some time just enjoying the evening. Noting how appreciative I was of the vaccine he developed while informing him of one of my mother's friends had a girl which was partly crippled by the disease. After this brief exchange, we just sat enjoying the evening zephyrs cooling off the day's heat. A short time later it was time to depart. After thanking the host and especially Francoise I left with Mom.

Chapter 14

Lenox Hill Hospital and more

March 27, 2016

Happy Easter:

There is a theory that all physical illnesses are caused by psychological stress. One morning after the breakup with Carol started I woke up with a pain in the back at the base of the spine. While at the Concourse Hotel, I was accumulating a lot of annual leave. My job was my vacation. I loved working and playing with the kids. During the last year at the Hotel, I developed a pain in my lower back. The pain got to be pretty bad. I went to Lenox Hill Hospital emergency room. After waiting for over an hour a young intern finally saw me. Poked around the base of my spine on the left side until I let out a cry. His conclusion:

"Just a bruise. Take some aspirin or pain pill and go home."

I went to work the next two days, the pain increasing each day. By the third day the pain was so great that I couldn't walk without being bent over. The next day I stayed home still in the East Side House Settlement House. The next days being in great pain I could no longer walk. A large bump was noticed growing in the place where the pain was worse. Bill S., the head of East Side House, came up from downstairs.

"Walter you OK? No one has seen you for a few days."

"I don't know Bill, something is wrong. Can you take a look?" I showed him the bump.

He turned green. "We have to get you to a hospital."

I used a bamboo stick as a makeshift cane and got dressed as best I could. I called Jean telling her where I was going. Since I had gone to Lenox Hill the week before Bill took me to their emergency room again. I thanked him and said I should be OK now.

"Go home. Don't worry about me, I should be OK now."

As I stumbled into the ER, bent over and in terrible pain. The same intern who had seen me the week before looked up.

"Opps!" was the only word I heard from him.

"You got that right!" I responded.

I was led into an examination room. A regular MD saw me. He took one look and dragged in the intern who saw me before.

"Take a good look. That is a pilonidal cyst." Then looking at me: "You need a surgeon. Who can you call?"

"I don't have a surgeon."

"Well we can't admit you unless you have one."

I was summarily dismissed.

On the way out the intern gave me a name of a surgeon near by. By now it was 4:30 p.m. I didn't know how I would get to any office in time. I decided to struggle to the subway and go home. As I walked out of the ER there was Bill still waiting for me. I told him what had happened and gave him the address of the surgeon I was given. He raced me to Dr. Y's office. The surgeon was an interesting Greek American with a great personality. He took one look at me.

"They dismissed you?" I nodded.

He picked up the phone and call the hospital. "Get me an operating room NOW! I have an emergency."

Back to the hospital. Bill finally when home after I repeatedly thanked him.

It took an hour before I was fully admitted to a room. Then there were a series of tests. My new surgeon Dr. Y came in about 11 p.m. The pain was increasing by the minute. A male nurse prepared me for an operation around midnight. In the middle of the prep Mom called. Jean had called her to tell her I was in the hospital. I struggled wheeling myself on a gurney to the phone:

"Mom, I can't talk to you now. I'm going into surgery."

At about 3 a.m. I was wheeled into the OR. They injected knock out drops into the IV and told me to count backward from 100:

"100, 99, 98, 97–hey this works fast–good night all!" Out I went.

I woke up the next morning. No idea what time it was. All that I could tell was I was in pain. My whole vocabulary was focused on the pain:

"PAIN...PAIN...PAIN." "PLEASE NO PAIN."

The nurse came over: "Sorry we can't give you anything."

I was quite only for a minute if that. Then:

"PAIN, PAIN, MORE PAIN, ACUPUNCTURE! ACUPUNCTURE!"

The nurse just laughed. How I survived that pain I don't know. What's worse was the iodine soaked gauze was pulled out of the wound and then repacked. That hurt so much I swore I bend the iron bars on the hospital bed as they proceeded with the process of providing more PAIN!

I was in the hospital for a week. Charlene told the kids I'd be back and was warmly welcomed when I did return.

Around noon the doctor came in. He said it was the largest pilonidal cyst he had ever seen. The poison was already running through my system which is why the iodine gauze. According to the blood work, he felt I would have died by morning if they had not done the surgery. I only missed one week of work and classes.

At this time I was taking the last class with Dr. Nan Pendrell, one of my favorite anthropology professors at The New School. Also taking an advanced paleoanthropology class with Ralph Holloway, one of the foremost paleoanthropologist in the world.

Ralph developed the method of creating endocasts of the brains of early hominids. His method was to take the reconstructed skull, pour a liquid resin in it and slosh it around the inside of the skull. When the resin hardened, being rubber based, it could be pulled out through the base of the skulls. Then when filled with a liquid, you could make a mold and create plaster casts. These would then be supplied to other institutions and scholars. Ralph also had a good sense of humor.

During my first class with him he was invited to give a lecture at Princeton. That day the *NY Times* reported on the discovery of Lucy. Ralph took the train down. Upon getting to the lecture hall, he noticed several of the graduate students in the audience had copies of the *Times*. Several were snickering. He stood up to the podium, held up the headlines.

"I know many of you have seen the headlines. Here is my talk."

He held it up. Then in one gesture tore it in half.

"So much for my talk! Now let's have an open discussion for this hour."

He said it proved to be a lot more fun and actually more informative than a formal presentation. His was a great class covering the theories on the development of early hominids, his specialty. It occurred at the same time the early reports on Project Washoe were being reported in the professional journals. Project Washoe was the experiment with a chimpanzee by Beatrice and Allen Gardner. The chimpanzee was being taught American Sign Language (ALS). Washoe was reported as learning a large number of signs, thereby capable of symbolic exchange using her elementary vocabulary. I decided to do a paper on a comparison of the forebrains of various hominids, chimpanzees and modern humans. This was the area associated with language evolution. Having been a sub at the Pennsylvania School for the Deaf for a short time, and knowing a little ALS, Washoe captured my interest.

Ralph thought this would be a great research project. He invited me to his lab in Schimmerhorn Hall at Columbia. There in his lab was rows and rows of shelving with endocasts, skulls, and other head bone fragments. The second I walked in, Ralph asked if I would like something to drink. It being a winter day, I wanted a cup of tea. He was delighted. Ralph was a tea drinking himself. There were a collection of cups and two glass pots with hot water.

"What kind of tea would you like?"

"What kind do you have?"

He was waiting for that. He pulled out a small 3x5 card file box. There was a card for each kind of tea he had. There must have been close to 50 maybe more. I picked one and showed him the card.

"Walter go down this row, then bring me the skull at 4:D:15" (*this is not exact but approximate*).

I brought him the skull. He opened it up. There was a bag of loose tea. Great way to store tea, loved it.

While taking the class I ended up with a second operation. The was a follow up on the cyst that had been removed years earlier. The cyst was threatening to come back. A new operation was necessary to clean our the whole area. That stay in the Lenox Hill was an interesting adventure in it self.

Love,
Papa

April 1, 2016

Still me:

It was about a month after the initial surgery the pilonidal cyst began to form again. I talked with Dr. Y. He felt the infected area may not have been complete cleaned out and another operation was necessary. Before going in for another operation I decided to get a second opinion.

Mom got me an appointment with Dr. Jo, her doctor, in Millerton, NY. It was Dr. Jo who got me the scholarship during undergraduate years. I went in to see her. There was a slight bump indicating the possibility of a new cyst forming. I asked her if the second operation was the best choice.

"Only if you don't want a dripping ass for the rest of your life."

We talked seriously for a little while. She was happy I was completing my M.A. After the visit, I scheduled an operation.

Again I would be absent from work. But now from Fox Street. This time I was more prepared, at least mentally. Fully expecting similar pain to the first, it was a pleasant surprise it was not nearly as bad. Still a lot of pain, but not as much. I told Dr. Y the paper I was working on for Ralph. He told me the doctor's lounge was across the hall. There was a model of a brain. If I wanted I could take it out of the lounge and take it apart. Then I would be able to see the areas associated with language, even do drawings. He informed the staff I was permitted to take the model back to my room. What was worse was my roommate was suffering with brain cancer. It was a bit of a morbid scene, he with his head bandaged up and me with a brain on my table.

Like the first operation the new dressing was applied twice a day. I would lay very quietly on my back and try to relax as much as possible. All focus was on the sore. Of course there was a constant taking of blood samples and blood pressure. Sorry no automated hook ups back then. There was one nurse who was in charge of the unit. She was younger than most, but apparently recently completed more graduate work than the usual RNs. She hated the fact I was allowed into the doctor's lounge and was given special privileges by Dr. Y. She would take my blood pressure. It would be very low, I think at one time it was about 50 over 30.

"If it doesn't get higher, I will have to call in your doctor."

"I like keeping it low. If you could take it on the wound it would be higher." was my response.

She kept bothering me about it. Finally I asked:

"What do you want."

"At lease 110 over 70": she announced.

I told her to come back in thirty minutes. During that time Jean was there grinning. I started a series of breathing and arm exercises. Sure enough after half an hour the nurse came back. Taking my blood pressure I asked:

"What is it?" All I could get was a mumble.

"Can you speak clearly?" Another mumble.

"Would you please tell me what my blood pressure it!"

"110 over 70: she yelled.

"Now can I lower it back down?"

She started yelling: "You can't do that! My text books tell me you can't do that!"

She stormed out of the room. I told Dr. Y when he check in. I told him about the whole incident. He actually laughed and told me to ignore her:

"We know better than her books!"

I used my drawings and the diagrams of a host of craniums to do a comparison of early hominid brains (based on Ralph's endocastes) with that of Pan coming to the conclusion that if chimps' brains had so many cc's in language area, then Australopithecines and even earlier hominid with a large brain should have been capable of symbolic language in some form. I got an A+ for the course. What was interesting is that Herb Terrace at Columbia had just started Project Nim. Ralph asked if I would be interested in working with Nim.

"I would love to but just don't have the time."

He thought between my work at the Pennsylvania School for the Deaf and my paper I would be an ideal addition to the volunteers with Nim. The next week I went in to see Ralph:

"You know Ralph, I'll find the time."

I called Herb. There were too few men involved in the project. With the limited experience I had at the Pennsylvania School for the Deaf, doing social work in the South Bronx and having Ralph's strong recommendation, Herb seemed to be very interested. An appointment was made for a formal interview.

Love,
Papa

March 27, 2016

But sent out of order in April

Hello:

The recovery from the first surgery was slow. Dr. Y told me that if I had gone home I would have been dead. The poison from the cyst was seeping into my system and would have likely killed me if he didn't operate when he did. He told me the size of the cyst likely set a record for Lenox Hill.

Having good bed side manner, we would discuss several things. He learned I was into mediation and was a doing social work in the South Bronx. The worse part of the stay was the changing the bandages. To pull the poison out of my system around the open wound, the gauze was soaked in iodine. When placed into the open sore, it would cleanse the area and help promote healing. The problem was that the tissue was beginning to grow back. As a result when the nurse replaced the packing, the gauze was pulled out with a lot of the new tissue which had started to grow back. Those were the worse times and almost equaled the pain experienced in the recovery room. I would grab the bars on the bed. They were iron. I would then squeeze as hard as possible in a vain attempt to take attention away from the procedure. It didn't work. And by the time I was dismissed, several of the bars of the bed were slightly bent.

During my second surgery my roommate was an elder man with a prostate problem. Edgar was originally from Europe. He was very worried about being in the hospital and not being with his wife Hilda. He watched as I was put through the dressing changes, feeling sorry for the evident pain. Soon we were talking. He was a German Jew. He was from a wealthy family and was doing quite well in German until Hitler took over. Hilda's sister was a baroness in Switzerland. Definitely an upper class family. As many others, he couldn't believe that the Third Reich would pick on him:

"After all I was a German just like them!"

But as the 30's progressed it was evident they had to escape. He shipped much of his art work to England for safe keeping after the Nazi's started confiscating the art works of other Jewish families. He told me Hilda and him got out the back door just as the SS was knocking down the front door. He had arranged an escape route and got out just in time.

We would spend hours discussing art and WWII history. He was fascinated that I was related to Edvard Benes the President of Czechoslovakia at the beginning of the war, who he had high regard for. Even after I was dismissed from the hospital I would visit Edgar. One night when visiting their apartment on the upper East Side, Hilda told me if it wasn't for me, she was afraid

Edgar would have likely gone into a deep depression. She felt I helped him through his ordeal, though mine was much more painful. I might add the apartment was on two floors. The walls and much of the furniture were covered with valuable art works, paintings, sculpture, tapestries and other works. We remained close for years.

There were two interesting things that occurred during my second hospital stay. First E. Power Biggs, the great organist, was going to do a concert at Radio City Music Hall. He was the greatest organist alive. He always was asked by those who knew little about organs if he had played the 'Mighty Wurlitzer' to which he would always answer:

"Good God NO!"

Now he was going to do a concert on the very instrument he detested. It took him three days to prep the instrument to get it to sound like a classical organ. I wanted to go to the concert. But was in the hospital. Thank goodness it was broadcast live on WQXR. It was great. Edgar and I both enjoyed it.

The other event was related to my cyst in a strange way. Jean had wondered why I was suffering so and what karma might be in play. We talked about it. Then she asked:

"How old were you when you were killed in WWII?"

I had estimated I was born around 1920. So I would have been about 24. She looked at me:

"Don't you realize, your operation was at almost the exact same age as when you were killed?"

We talked about it. It was the final karmic carry over from my past life. It made since. This was the only kind of cyst that would be close to where the mortar shell had hit me, on the left side of the hip. To bring this to a further closure the two remaining Andrew Sisters were staring in a Broadway show *Over Here*. After being discharged Jean and I saw the show. It was a perfect ending to my WWII connection. It was also wonderful to see Maxine and Patty on stage. LaVerne had died of cancer years ago.

Love,
Papa

The party was over. Nothing exciting happening.

I'll put in a Masonic incident here. Co-Masonry maintains the traditions of regular Masonry in that during the degrees the right, left or both breasts are exposed. In Co-M they try to be a little discrete and only have a flap of a robe exposing part of the breast. This works for most of the older women who may join. They have a tendency to have breasts that sag below the hole in the robe. On one occasion we were giving a degree to a new member.

I was the senior deacon who conducts the candidates. Janet was in her 40's and very attractive. She also had perfectly formed breasts, no sag and glorious. As a result they just protruded from the robe in a most beautiful manner. During the ceremony, her breast being fully exposed a male member became concerned and tried to use a safety pin to cover her a little. This just brought more attention to those beautiful tits. Even pinning the robe up a little, still allowed the nipples to protrude. I must admit, this was the only time when I became distracted during conducting of a candidate. There were many others, but Janet's breasts were the most perfectly formed I have ever seen. This was long before implants were popular.

Not Sent:

It was about this time that Co-M headquarters received permission from France that I was to receive my 32°. I had been a member of the Council Kaddosh (30°) for slightly over two years. Sovereign Chapter Agape the 18° body was under my direction as Wise Master. The turn around for Signet Mark Lodge has occurred mostly due to my efforts and both the Chapter and Council were also beginning to grow due to my pushing those eligible to advance. This concluded with an examination in the Council to qualify for the 32°. I was lucky in one way, the individual conducting the exam was from Baltimore which used a different Chapter ritual. As a result much of what would have been included in open Council exam was open to interpretation due to the differences in the rituals used. After over an hour's exam I was approved and within a few months received the green light from France.

Mother and I went to Larkspur for me to received the 32°. This was an annual gathering of Co-Masons from around the country. All bodies met. Most actually performed the degrees. One woman, Kristen was a tall attractive blond of Finnish heritage and about 9 years older than myself. She and one of her friends quickly found me as a kindred spirit. But with Kristen there was a strong sexual attraction which neither of us understood. Still after two days of conversation she asked me to accompany her to the camper she had arrived in Larkspur from her home in California.

The attraction only grew as we were now in a private setting. Passionate kissing advanced to petting and then removal of clothes. She had never experienced a men who loved cunnilingus as much as I. Soon she experienced the most intense organism of her life. The taste was a bit on the salty side but her reaction was worth it. The next night was much the same with the exception that she has a chance to take a shower in the main building. The salty taste disappeared and the joy of going down on the beautiful pussy was only incensed.

The next day Kristin was to receive her Royal Arch Degree. During the degree you are wearing the apron of a Master Mason. Most don't realize one of the purposes of the masonic apron is to cut the lower kundalini sexual energies from the higher chakras. I was the conductor during Kristin's advancement to the Royal Arch. As she entered the fourth veil of the ceremony I took off the apron. When I untied it and dropped it to the floor, her whole body gave a slight shiver. Later she told me with the dropping of the apron by me, she experienced an intense sexual organism. But it had to be hidden since this was a serious ceremony. She was delighted in receiving the Royal Arch Degree.

That night and the rest of the week at Larkspur repeated the nightly pleasures. At the end of the week Kristin suggested I join her on the drive back to California. My mother was told. She was aware of the strong sexual energy between us. She queried Kristin about her age and just accepted that it was out of her control to resist the relationship that had developed. So off to California we went.

The trip was a true delight. Not only for the casual driving but for the very physical nights. Once in we arrived at her home in Owens Valley. We drove by Manzanar and I was overwhelmed by the negative vibrations of that Japanese concentration camp used to illegally hold Japanese citizens during WWII. After a week Kristin drove me to LAX to take a plane home. It was a sad parting.

The next year I had started a serious relationship. Upon returning to Larkspur with great resistance I had to reject the previous physical attraction with Kristin. It was then she told me that she had gone to a psychic. When asking about our relationship the psychic shouted "Incest, incest." The psychic said in a previous life she had been my father and I a woman. This fit a past life memory when I was an attractive courtesan whose poor Indian farmer sold to a house of prostitution as an attractive young girl. By the time I was an adult woman I had become a very wealthy courtesan. When my father came to visit me to see how I had developed, I seduced my father into having sex with his now adult daughter. Thus the sexual attraction between Kristin and myself spanned centuries and was only reactivated upon us getting together at Larkspur. After all these years I still consider Kristin one of my most beloved memories.

One day while at Larkspur Helen Wycherly, Eugenie Pumphrey and I suddenly felt ill and lost our energy. Helen was the head of Co-M in America while Eugenie later became head of the Theosophical Society Internationally and moved to India. But both were fairly close to me and my mother. I told Kristin that I was not feeling well. She said both Hellen and Eugenie were feeling the same way. Could it be a psychic attack?

I thought for a second and asked who would do such a thing. Kristin mentioned the name of one of the members who was there that she didn't trust. This woman was a known member of Wicca the known witches organization.

When Kristin mentioned the name the face that popped into my head was not who she was thinking of. At first I didn't think the individual I was thinking of would had attacked the three of us. Kristin immediately told me I was thinking of the wrong person. She took me over to the window in the building and pointed to the woman on the patio.

"That's who I'm talking about!

I looked down and realize there was some kind of negative aura about her. Kristin told me to sit and see what I could do to reverse the negative energies. With her sitting by my side, I formed a 'ring pass not' around myself. As that was formed I expanded it to include Helen and Eugenia. Once that was visualized I took the ring to another level. I placed it around the individual who was the individual Kristin and I felt was the cause of the affliction. Upon forming a ring around her the image was 'what you send out will rebound to you.' Within half an hour I felt fine. I asked Helen and Eugenia how they felt. Both said they suddenly felt much better. When dinner came around the woman who I placed the reverse ring pass not around showed up with headache and so weak she could hardly eat. Interesting incident. Also shows if one knows how to do a 'ring-pass-not' they can be really effective. Had to use it many years later when the president and I of the Pentagon Meditation Club were being similarly attacked.

March 28, 2016

Hi T:

Promised to tell you about super rat. I don't know the actual biological history of these rats but was told they came over from Northern Europe in ships that docked in NYC. Rather than the usual grey rats, super rat was a bit smaller and usually brownish in color. They were also exceptionally aggressive. I remember seeing one chasing a cat down the street near Alexander Avenue. One of the kids told me that two super rats attacked a German Shepard and WON the fight. The dog ended up with his tail between his legs running as fast as he could to get away from them.

Another story about the super rats was they were immune to the usual rat poison. There was a story about someone in the neighborhood who put out the usual rat poison. It killed most of the grey American rats. But he went out one morning seeing a super rate eating the poison with no effect. They even told me it looked like after eating the poison, it stood up on it's hind legs as if to beg for more. Eventually a stronger poison was introduced which did kill them, but not until a number of my kids were bitten during the night. It was the second most common bit next to cock roaches in the South Bronx.

There was one Saturday afternoon when I was preparing a light dinner in my apartment on Alexander Ave., for some friends. I was cooking in the kitchen. My friends were in the living room across from my bedroom on the opposite side of the apartment. I heard a series of thuds from what seemed to be across the street. Since my apartment mate was out, I walked to her window and looked towards the noise. There in the Mott Haven project building closest to East Side Settlement House, on about the 7th floor a gang member could be seen in his colors. Then a large boy was thrown against that window. Being plastic and resistant to breaking, the kid just bounced back into his apartment. Now two more gang members became visible. They picked up the boy and slammed him against the window again. The plastic cracked a little. By now the noise was causing attention on the street. The boy who was being tossed against the window as also screaming every time he was thrown. The third throw that I saw happened. The window broke. This time when they picked up the boy again, he flew out and landed on the roof of the entrance way on the first floor. Thud. Seven floor fall. Splat! He was dead instantly. Later I found out he was one of the good kids in the neighborhood who refused to join a gang. I had never met him, as he was about 14 or 15. He was one of those who stayed inside except to go to school. Somehow the gang gained entrance to his home and decided to use him as an example to others who refused to join when asked.

I went into the living room. My friends asked:

"What was all the racket about?"

"Oh, the gangs are just at it again." was my response.

There was no more thought about it. I went back to the kitchen and finished cooking. No feelings about what was witnessed. We sat down and had a great little meal.

It was about a week later that it hit me. I had just witnesses a murder and didn't think anything about it. I HAD TO GET OUT THE SOUTH BRONX!!!! From that point on I was quietly looking for some place to move to out of that environment. It took a while but eventually I moved to an apartment on Britton Street right near Bronx Park East. That was very close to the Botanical Garden. Yet in the year and a half I was there, never bothered to walk over this wonderful garden. Something I should have done. Just another regret. At least I was out of Ft. Apache and had only a few blocks to the subway. It was a nice apartment with its on separate entrance directly on the street. No having to climb stairs or going through a lobby. These were ground floor, behind the front of the building's main entrance. There were about 8 of these ground apartments. We had our own separate little community. We all watched out for each other so there was no trouble, but several interesting things happened. By that time I was no longer working in the South Bronx, but on Park Row in lower Manhattan. But that is getting ahead of myself. More on the move latter.

Love,
Papa

April 1, 2016

Dear T:

You might wonder how so many of the kids in the South Bronx were attached to me, an outsider, while being white. What worked was the rap I gave the kids which was very consistent. It is still true today, if not more so. All one has to do is to look at the current political conversations. Look at the number of minority prisoners in jail. Look at the number of poor single parent homes. Look at the segregated public housing. Look at the gerrymandering of political districts, designed to ensure the minority have minimal representation in state and federal government.

The kids close to me were told my background. It was very similar to theirs. They are poor. I was poor. They came from broken homes. My mom separated from my dad as a result of beating the shit out of me. From then on, I was part of a single parent home. Those in the shelter, be it the Grand Concourse or Fox Street, were there because they are homeless. I was homeless for over a year. The time we lost the apartment in Concord, through the misadventures in Germany until we returned to The Hill is considered homeless. Not without a roof over my head, but no real home. The other major point was I was living in the same shitty ghetto as them. They were in the shelter in the South Bronx. I was living on Alexandria Avenue. I didn't escape to some suburb haven at night. I lived in the same shit as them. I heard the gun shots at night. I heard the police sirens. The gangs. So I was grew up, poor, from a single parent family, considered as poor white trash. They accepted this.

The other thing that was drummed into them was that "The MAN" (always taken to mean the white supremest who control the country) considered them as dumb Spicks and N****s. They have made you live in the worse housing in New York. They have given you the worse schools in the city. They have put up every possible obstacle to keep you in the ghetto. To keep you in the shit. They allow the drugs to come into your neighborhoods and ignore the pushers who are taking your down further. To prevent you from every getting out. You are forced into housing which is terrible or have absentee landlords who refuse to repair or up date you dwellings. This was the rap repeatedly given. One they understood. Then I told them how to escape.

BUT there is a way to beat The MAN! Only one way! You have to put up with the shitty schools. You have to resist joining the gangs. You have to do the best you can in the schools. You have to get good enough grades to get into college. Then get the hell out of the South Bronx. The kids who listen felt I was telling them like it is. They appreciated the frankness from someone who escaped poverty and an education system that tried to keep him down.

Let's face it Salisbury Central Elementary and to a lesser degree, my high school tried to put me into the tracks which would prevent me from getting a college education. From rising above the poverty I was grew up in. But I fought them. I fought the system. I fought The MAN! I did this through the protest marches in Connecticut, at the March on Washington. My mother and I did this by helping the first black family move into my old home town. I fought it when the Italian boys tried to pick on a little black girl on the school bus. I FOUGHT AND FOUGHT! I haven't won yet, but I am getting closer every day!

The fact that I was working on a master's degree proved those sons of bitches were wrong. I was better than the hole they were trying to peg me in. If I did it through all those obstacles,

"YOU CAN DO IT TOO. Yes it would be hard, but it can be done. I am here to help!"

This argument was used from the time I was with Mr. Woods in the case work unit, through all the years in the South Bronx. Even the most die hard racists, once they heard me, began to realize not all whites were part of what was putting them down. I was actually there to help.

Almost all who accepted this asked for help with school work. Many got tutoring from me. Most got their grades up, usually within a few months. I can honestly say that many of the kids who accepted these facts, did better in school. A number of them got started getting Bs and some As. Many started to have aspirations to get into college. I just hope that most of them made it. This was the legacy I was most proud of.

Love,
Papa

Chapter 15

Close call, cats, & leaving the South Bronx

April 18, 2016

T—Flashback time:

When reviewing the previous letters, there were a number of episodes which were omitted in the earlier letters. So this and the next few letters will be bits of flashbacks.

Shortly after moving into the 4th floor of the East Side Settlement House, I was doing some reading for a test coming up. At about 11 p.m. there was a constant THUMP…THUMP…THUMP…THUMP coming from the back. I got up from bed. Parting the curtains I looked out upon 3rd Avenue. On top of the only single floor building in that block was a man with a pickax digging into the roof. This was about 75 feet from my window. Knowing it was a little late for roof repairs I decided to call the police.

You must remember the local precinct was only a few blocks away on 138th and Alexander Avenue. The police were told an attempted break-in occurring on 3rd Avenue. It was easy to see which building was being broken into as it was the only single story building on that block. The only other low building was the Pueblo Market where Alexander and 3rd come together.

After making the call I waited. Turning off all my lights, I sat in a chair next to the window watching. Knowing it was a small family owned store that was being broken into, it was likely he didn't have insurance. The owner had met me on a few occasions which I needed some snack or drink that could not be obtained at Pueblo. So I didn't take kindly to his store being robbed.

In a drawer, I had an antique sling shot. It was originally from Tibet. It had been a gift to me from Marcia my mothers old meditation buddy years before. Just in case I had some round sinkers for fishing in the room. They are perfect ammunition for a sling shot. Sitting in my window, partly covered by the curtains, I started shooting the sinkers at the crook. A number of times, he jerked up. So I must have hit him. He would look all around. He couldn't see me as the street lights from 3rd Avenue made his area brighter than the black windows of the Settlement House. I was perfectly hidden.

This cat and mouse game continued for 30 plus minutes. I heard a ringing of the door bell. I ran to the other side of the building, threw open the common room window. There at the front door was a policeman.

"Are you the one who called in an attempted robbery?"

"Yes, it is still going on."

Despite the description of the building and the street the police couldn't find it. I went down and let them in. Leading this rather rotund cop and 6 other officers through the offices, I opened the second floor's back door. This led to a nice deck, with plants, trees, and lawn furniture. It was often used for casual meetings or for the staff to take a lunch break. It's edge was close to the back of the building being broken into. The building was about eight feet higher and less than 5 feet way from the edge of the deck. I pointed to the building.

"There is where the break in is happening?"

The policemen who seemed to be coordinating the investigation got in contact with the other police. Soon I could see search light beams shining on the surrounding building from the 3rd Avenue side. Plain clothes police were on the roof tops of the buildings to either side of the store. The policeman who I had shown through the offices into the back yard, looked up at the building.

"How do we get up there?"

I pulled out an extension ladder and started moving it towards the building. His flashlight was shining upward. There in the shining beam of light in crook's face. He was staring down at the commotion. The policeman asked:

"So where is this mother fucker?"

"He is in your light." I pointed up.

Sure enough the crook was just standing there. He could now see the place was surrounded. Police on 3rd Avenue, on the buildings around and now in the back side of the Settlement House. When the officer looked up he shouted in an exciting voice he said:

"Get your fucking hands in the air. You're under arrest."

The would be robber, gave him the finger, walked away from the edge of the roof and sat down in the middle. He wanted to make it as hard as possible for the cops to get him.

He turned to me:

"How do we get him down?"

I placed the ladder against the other building bowed with a gesture up the ladder. Some of the more agile police climbed up the ladder. By this time there were ladders in place on the 3rd Avenue side as well.

"Let me know when you are finished so I can lock up and put the ladder away."

I then turned and went back to my bedroom. About 20 minutes later they told me they were finished. I went down put the ladder away and locked up the place. I told Bill S in the morning what had happened. Just another night in the South Bronx.

Love,
Papa

April 28, 2016

T—Another Flashback:

Winter Antiques Show is one of the biggest in New York and very well know among dealers and collectors alike. It is also the major fund raiser for the East Side Settlement House. It is held in the Park Avenue Armory. There are hundreds of dealers who pay fees for having an exhibit from their showrooms to be displayed in the show.

Back then there was a safe which held the checks and CASH which was collected from the dealers. Being Thursday afternoon Bill S and I were helping set up. The grand opening was to be the next evening. The show would last the weekend. We were running lights, carpets and sweeping up wherever necessary. If someone needed help with awnings or other exhibit sets, we were there to help. Rather than the head of the object of charity of the Show, Bill and I were dressed in jeans and grubby shirts. By the late afternoon we were quite dirty.

The coordinator for the show came running up to Bill. He was a stereo typical overweight antique connoisseur. About 6 feet tall, exquisitely dressed in silk shirt, cashmere sweater and shoes which must have cost a fortune by themselves. He was also a bit of a flamer:

"You have to do something about the safe, it is overflowing. I can't fit anything else in there and the actual show opens tomorrow. We need to clean it out before the opening ceremony."

Bill and I went into the office. Sure enough the safe was literally over flowing. All the exhibit fees and the pre-show tickets sales were stuffed in. There was a bag of cash leaning against the safe's open door. The shelves in the safe itself were stuffed. I doubt if you could have fitted more than a dozen rolls of dimes into the safe. As for the door, it would have been impossible to close. Bill looked at me:

"We have to get this to the accountants up at the Settlement House. But I didn't bring my car."

I looked at him: "We could take it up via the subway."

Bill looked at me and himself. Could we pass for a couple of homeless bums on the train? It was worth a try.

We found a number of paper bags with handles. Most looked well used. When possible we doubled them up. The last thing anyone would want would be for the rolled coins to fall through a broken corner. After stuffing four bags, we got on our coats on and walked to the subway. All the way Bill and I were more than a little nervous, but trying exceptionally hard not to show it. Taking two bags each, we went outside to the cold air. We made it to the subway a few blocks away. We got on the #6 IRT line. We rode all the way to Alexander Avenue. Now for the real challenge. Walking the blocks to the Settlement House.

I put on my best South Bronx stride as I could. Bill was next to me. We walked into the Settlement house unnoticed. Up on the second floor we put the bags on the two elderly accounts' desks and plopped down in to a couple of chairs.

"How did you get them up here." one of the women asked.

Bill looked that them:

"We took the subway!"

"What you took all this cash and negotiable checks on the subway?"

Bill nodded. Looking at each other Bill and I burst into laughter. We couldn't believe what we had done. Here was maybe a quarter of million dollars being carried right under the noses of the gangs and penny crooks who would kill for $5. We got away with carrying all that money on what one reporter called the most dangerous blocks in NYC! The two women looked at us as if we were crazy. Maybe we were. But we got the money where it needed to be. Besides the safe in the Armory was ready to receive the receipts from the weekend. I did help out the next two years, but the plans to carry the money was more carefully thought out in those years.

Love,
Papa

May 1, 2016

Time out for a Purrrfect Aside:

In all these letters I have not given enough time to Kali Cat. All this time in the Alexander Avenue she was the perfect companion. She and Carol got along well. When Carol and I split she adopted Jean readily. I told you how she was found as a small wet kitten. Nearly starving to death. How I fed her milk and was expecting to clean up a mess the next morning only to find she held everything in until I shredded some newspapers and put them in a box. Of course that won my heart. So small and yet house broken right off the street.

Kali adapted quickly to her home. After all she knew she was loved. She even got Rose who lived on the other half of the top floor fond of her. There was one game she loved. The apartment was a central hall with two bedrooms, two bathrooms, and two living rooms but a shared kitchen. Rose kept her doors closed. Even if she didn't, Kali instinctively knew those rooms did not belong to me. So they were off limits.

As Kali grew she loved to play games. I would have her chase strings and little balls around the apartment. Kali loved for anyone to chase her. But the way she got attention was unique. As you approached the hall or a room where she was around the corner, Kali would make a jump against the wall, spring even higher, and just as you turned the corner, have her cat eyes at the same level as yours. Then she would run like crazy to hide for you to find her. She loved this trick. I think she liked scaring humans this way.

I remember the first time she played on Rose, Rose was coming out the kitchen carrying some food to her room. Kali jumped up just as Rose turned the corner. Kali ran like crazy to my room, leaving Rose in the middle of a scream of surprise at coming face to face with a little cat. Rose had seen her play this game with me. It surprised her that Kali pulled the same stunt on her. We all laughed about it later.

Kali was maturing and of course was in heat monthly. During this time she exhibited signs of being horny. Carol and I use to masturbate her with her own tale. She would get so excited until she couldn't stand it anymore at which time she would grab our hands and give a sharp love bite. I realized she had to be spaded. I found a vet in Manhattan. I took her there. She was to stay overnight after the operation. I felt sorry for her as this was her first separation from me. When I brought her home the next day she was so happy to be back where she belonged. A week later I was to take her back to get the stitches removed. I looked at the stitches. I asked Kali if she wanted to go back to the vet or would she let me remove them. She rolled over on her back. Taking tweezers and small clippers I removed every stitch. She was happy. So was I.

When I moved out of the South Bronx, Kali came with me. I did take her to visit Nim once. Nim, the chimpanzee I was working with for Columbia University. Nim's introduction to a cat which belonged to one of the classroom volunteers. But Kali didn't trust him. She was never brought to Delafield, Nim's dwelling again.

When I left NYC for Boston University, Mom took Kali. But Mom's cat Carry, was an alpha cat that did NOT want another cat in the household. After a miserable two months Mom told me she had given Kali to a family with 3 small children and one dog. Based upon what mom told me, Kali accepted her new home. The residence was above a gas station.

About a month after moving in with the new family, Kali one night started jumping on the foot of the parents' bed. At first they paid little attention. But Kali was persistent. Finally the man raised up. Kali went to the bedroom door and looked back. She took a step, came back and looked at the man again. He knew she wanted him to follow her. She led him downstairs to the kitchen. There she started scratching the floor. He didn't see anything, but when he got down to her level, he smelled smoke. He raced down to the basement. There near the fusebox a small electrical fire had started. Fortunately he had an extinguisher and put it out. The whole family credited Kali for saving their lives. If the fire had spread, IN A HOUSE WITH A TANK OF GAS UNDERNEATH, the station, the house and all those inside would have been toast–extra dark! As for the dog? He slept through the whole incident.

Love,
Papa

May 3, 2016

Hi T–About Ruth, her daughter and my other favorite cat an:

It was while I was in NYC that Ruth, Mom's closest friend was finally laid off from the Lakeville Journal where she had been a photographer for many years. She was planning to retire but didn't have enough savings. Once out of work she depended on Social Security.

Many years before she had worked on ceramics. She had a potter's wheel in the back porch. It was a very attractive wheel but unlike a normal wheel, the wheel was chest high. It was evidently for constructed on the wheel as coil or slab pots, or or pots that had undergone a bisque firing which demanded balanced decorations. It was not meant for throwing large pots. Ruth was desperate for cash. Mom and I offered a couple of hundred for the wheel. Not what it was worth but certainly more than she could get in NW Connecticut. When her daughter Susie found out, she raced up from New Jersey to rescue the wheel. Aggressively addressing me declared:

"How dare I try to steal my mother's heritage! You have no business trying to buy that wheel."

"OK Susie, are you going to help support your mother?"

I knew the answer to this question **NO**. Susie was an art professor at a small college and had never offered her mother any support. She just glared at me.

"You realize Ruth needs money to say in her home. I was offering a means to obtain a little cash. I'm sure you see the logic in that?"

Susie turned on me: "How dare you tell me what is best for my mother. After all who are you to question me, after all I have my Ph.D."

I knew her doctorate was in fine arts and was only about 64 or 67 credits of graduate work. I had completed my MA at The New School, and at the time was enrolled at Boston so after the first year would have more graduate credits than her. Here was the perfect example of considerable education but little intellect. But I calmly turned to her and said:

"Too bad that in all those classes they never taught you common sense."

She was livid but speechless. Mom was there. She couldn't hold back her laughter. I never spoke to Susie again. Good! Susie took the wheel to her home, but gave Ruth NOTHING!

Ruth had a remarkable cat, Dennis. He hung by his tail from the railing supports on the stairs to the second floor, when a kitten and knock all the Christmas ornaments off the Christmas Tree which had been carefully place on the table out of his reach. Right! No one told him cats didn't have prehensile tails. I didn't believe my eyes when I saw that. He lost that ability by the time he was a year old. I may have told you about Dennis in the earlier letters when you were still in college.

Dennis and I were very close. Whenever I visited Ruth, he would jump into my lap as if to say 'Welcome back.' Ruth, Mom and I would sit around the breakfast bar in the kitchen. If we were talking politics or current events Dennis ignored us. If we talked about Ruth's health, the house or anything that concerned him, his attention was totally focused.

Mom told me of one day when visiting Ruth. Dennis was on the floor watching and listening. By this time he must have been around 18 years old. Ruth had developed a rash around her neck. Dennis would sleep on Ruth's chest with both paws wrapped around her neck. Ruth told mom she was afraid he was causing the rash on her neck. Would mom take Dennis if this was the cause? Of course, Mom loved Dennis too. But when Ruth spoke of her fear, Dennis suddenly jumped into Mom's lap and started nuzzling her on her neck. Mom told me later that Dennis understood the whole conversation. If he was the cause the rash, he was willing to go with Mom. The next few days Dennis refused to sleep on Ruth where he had for over a decade. For the week, Dennis slept on the floor for the first time since he was a kitten–without being asked. The next time my mother visited Ruth, she said the rash was cleared up and she didn't think it was Dennis after all. That night Dennis resumed his favorite sleeping position on top of Ruth's chest.

Thank goodness the rash went away. The rash never reoccurred. I really believe he understood most conversations that were going on around him. Dennis died at the age of 19 1/2. Ruth about a year later. I thought Dennis wanted to hold out as long as Ruth. I pictured them going together. He almost made it. Ruth was depressed from Dennis' death until her own. Ruth was virtuously penniless when she died. It hit Mom hard they were best friends. Yet by the time Ruth died, Mom had already moved down to Virginia. This was where I had settled with Marisol, your mother, after finishing my graduate work at Boston University.

Love,
Papa

May 23, 2016

A flash back about the Adult World of NYC:

Got to tell you one very funny incident. First it is important to tell you this was a time when 42nd Street was known for pornographic movie houses, peep shows and 'Adult' shops where all along 8th Avenue. These 'stores' which would have 'adult' products in the front the usual dildos, pumps, and other 'toys.' You could buy magazines which would be displayed by particular subject matter. Or if you went further back you could simply feed quarters into viewing booths in the back and view about 2 minutes of 8 mm film. Of course to see the whole film would usually take about $5 worth of quarters. Most of the booths had very sticky floors.

Some stores would have 'live models' either upstairs or in a separate the back section of the store. These booths surrounded a room with a sofa which was on a rotating stage. The private viewing booths were where gentlemen could put in their quarters which would lift a window to give them a view of the woman on the stage. They could then see the woman on the sofa in various stages of undress. Once naked the women would often be masturbating or playing with their breasts and other anatomical parts. The stage was surrounded by these men with the exception of one door through which the women could enter and leave. There was a change of women about every 30 minutes. Some of the booths had a little slot for the men to slip additional dollars through if they wanted the girl to do an up close personal presentation.

It was during this time the porn movie *Deep Throat* became front page news, at least in the tabloids. There was an indecency trial in Manhattan. The trial was a zoo. Those supported the film claimed freedom of speech. The churches condemn it as immoral. The case when on for weeks and months in the papers. There was one 'expert' psychologist testifying he wanted to show the movie to all high schools in the city. The film would teach the teens how to have fun without the threat of becoming pregnant. That comment was repeated in all the papers.

While the case was going on, *Deep Throat* moved from 42ⁿᵈ Street to the respectable movie houses. One night Carol and I were walking around after eating dinner in a good German restaurant on 86ᵗʰ Street. On Madison Avenue there was an upscale movie theatre which had *Deep Throat* on the marquee. I looked at Carol. She just nodded. As we walked over to the theater. There was a line to get into the next showing. Likely about 20 people in line. Carol and I got at the end of the line. This was about 10:30 or later at night. *Deep Throat* had become the late night after dinner/theatre treat. This being an upscale East Side theatre the clientele were equally upscale.

As we stood in line, a homeless man came up behind us. It was evident he had been pan handling on Madison for any money he could beg for. He looked at the marquee. His eyes lit up when he saw the 'XXX' rating. He continued towards the line. As he reached into his pocket, he pulled out what cash he had. Then carefully counting out the money his whole demeanor brightened as he realized he had $5 for a ticket. It was only then he looked at the line of couples waiting to get into the movie house. There were women in minks and chinchilla coats. Men in tuxes and suits. Let's face it, Carol and I were nicely dressed but definitely underdressed for this crowd.

The poor man looked at the people. He looked at the marquee again. Then he looked at his hand with the money. Taking another look at the people in the line, he started to shake his head. Slowly he put the money back into his pocket. Taking one last look at all the fancy clothes, he turned and dejectedly walked away. Carol and I felt sorry for the poor guy. But that was the crowd that was seeing *Deep Throat*. A result from all the publicity from the trial. It became the best money making porn movie every. It also opened up porn to the general population.

Love,
Papa

Detroit Trip #1 May, 2016

Hello:

Don't know where to start but feel you need to be brought up to work at The New School. As you know I was taking 2 classes a semester in the evenings. Really enjoyed the classes, well almost all. The class on linguistics drove me up the wall. The first physical anthropology class with Ralph Holloway didn't go well. Only got a C. Two years later I was doing so well in his other class. He asked what I got in the first. I told him and he looked puzzled.

"It was my first graduate course. I wasn't really prepared. It was an appropriate grade." I remarked.

The other class I took that first semester was Prehistoric Archeology with Robert Stigler, also from Columbia. Really enjoyed that class. Did get a B+ so was happy with that grade as a counter to Ralph's. Learned from both. Loved both. Still remember the books and much which was taught in both, even after all these years. Partly helps that keep reading *Archeology* magazine and paleoanthropology books.

Perhaps my favorite teacher was Nan Pendrell. She had actually got her Ph.D at Columbia while Margaret Mead was there. She was not impressed by Margaret. Nan was a perfect fit in the New School's Anthropology Department at that time. You have to know Stanley Diamond was the head of the Anthropology Department. He was also the president of the International Marxist Anthropological Association. Nan was so much of a Marxist, I started calling her grandma Marx. During one of her classes there was a bomb scare in the building. Nan asked everyone to check around the room. Nothing unusual.

"I'm going to continue teaching. Anyone who wants to leave may do so."

Two got up and left. The rest of us remained. She wasn't about to let some fascist stop her class.

There was another young Ph.D who just joined the staff. She taught evolution of cultures and societies. Key reading was Lewis Henry Morgan's <u>Ancient Societies</u>. This was followed by Karl Marx's <u>Pre-Capitalistic Economic Formations</u>, which was largely based on Morgan's work and had been part of Das Capital, his unfinished book. Because Marx adopted Morgan's works most colleges and universities refuse to acknowledge Morgan as the true founder of American Anthropology. Many schools like to say it was Franz Boas as the founder of anthropology in the US. Sorry but in my opinion–WRONG!

Then another course used as a text <u>The Rise of Anthropological Theory</u> by Marvin Harris. It was a tomb of a text, but presented an overview of all the major theories by most of the anthropological theorists around the world. Actually finished it years later. Yes Harris is bias. But after reading all of it I came to the same conclusion the Department was promoting. Marx had it right. Economic modes of production determines how cultures advance. The more and more I've read since has only reaffirmed that conclusion. The only regret is I took Religious Anthropology with Nan rather than Michael Harner. If I had known and understood Michael was doing shamanistic drumming sessions in his version of the same class, I should have taken it with him. But my love of Nan as a professor prevent that. The only class I took with Michael was on current ethnological studies.

In Michael's class was I developed the 'smokey hut hypothesis' for why a highland Papuan culture had stopped all population growth. The tribe brought tobacco into their crops. They already had a high incident of pulmonary disease due to their huts with cooking fires and inadequate ventilation. By adding tobacco it increase the infant mortality and shortened the life expectancy of all tribal members. I had to defend my theory before Mike in his office. Mind you this was in the early 1970s.

Mike, who was overweight at the time, sat back in his chair, smoking an old stogy of a cigar when I came in to defend the theory. It was really funny. Ralph would also smoke cigarettes in class back then. I would describe how tobacco was killing off the tribe's potential for growth as he was blowing smoke towards me while I was presenting my arguments. Might add that Stanley Diamond was on sabbatical at the time. Mike was head of the Department that year. Always loved my experience at The New School! Got an A in the class.

Love,
Papa

Detroit Trip #2 May, 2016

Hello again with another flashback:

Working at Fox Street was an interesting change. It was good to have the other services co-located in the same building. I remember the truant officers in the back room. When there was nothing to do we would play backgammon. While going with her I had taught Carol how to play. We use to play for a penny a game. But with the doubling cube, a penny game came to up to $0.64 or if gammoned, $1.28. If back gammoned $2.56. She started to fall behind. Soon we were playing for nickel a game. That only put her in the hole faster. By the time we broke up, she had run up over $3,000 in Back Gammon debt. Of course it was never paid.

I would play with the other staff in the officers who knew how to play. The lead truant officer once noted a major tournament was happening down town. The entrance fee was $100. He and the other staff would sponsor me. It was a hard decision, but I turned them down. Just didn't like the idea of playing professionals. Also if they sponsored me, they would have liked a return for their investment. But the prizes were only for the very best. Out of several hundred, what would have been my chances? Kind of sorry I turned him down. It would have been interesting to see how I would have stacked up against the best players.

Remember Charlene and I used to get our lunch from the Hispanic deli across the street. One day we had just purchased our lunches from one of the two deli's. I was carrying my lunch in one bag and our drinks in another. As we walked back to the office, we passed the partly collapsed building when there was a 'pizzed' sound and a slight breeze by my right ear. At the same time a bullet entered the windshield of the car I was next to. This was followed by the BANG of the gun shot. Without thinking I pushed Charlene hard, behind the partly standing brick wall of the building on the left. At the same time, my brain calculated that if the bullet passed my ear, entered the car's windshield then the passenger seat, the safest place to take cover would be under the car that had just been hit. I dove under the car. I spun around near the rear wheel. Poking my head out from behind the driver's side rear tire. I looked towards the rooftop of the block we just left. Sure enough, there on the roof was a man with a rifle. He turned away from our direction and pointed his gun in another direction and started shooting in the opposite direction.

I crawled out from under the car, watching the shooter. When it was clear we were no longer the focus of attention I got up. Turning towards Charlene I gave her a hand up from behind the wall where I had pushed her. She thanked me for getting out of the range of the shooter. I helped dust her off. We both picked up the bags with our respective lunches. Then I turned towards the car I dove under when the shot whizzed past my ear. There next to the car was the brown paper bag with our drinks. In all the chaos, I had put the drinks down so gently not a drop was spilled. Grabbing the drinks Charlene and I went back to the office and ate our lunches. We sat back and admitted that was the closest call with a gun we had experienced. Yes, we would hear shots almost weekly, but they were rarely in our direction. Useless calling the police. Unless someone was actually hit, they would rarely respond. We were missed! We never call the cops.

There was one amusing incident. One of the summer employees was told to take our the garbage. He was used to tossing the bags down a garbage shoot in his apartment. So he took the bag to the shoot in the hall rather than out back where the garbage was put in secure receptacles. When he opened the shoot, a pair of super rats jumped out at him. He came back the office shaking.

"Some rats just jumped out of the garbage and jumped at me."

"What do you expect if someone tried to throw garbage on top of you home." was my response.

We told him where to put the garbage in the future. Charlene and I laughed. More about super rat in the next letter.

Love,
Papa

Detroit Trip #3 May, 2016

Hello again:

The New School again. It took three years to complete my M.A. taking 2 classes each semester at night. As I was finishing the anticipating graduates were given a choice. Either they could complete a thesis or take a comprehensive exam. Since I was so busy with work in the South Bronx and with Co-M, and starting to work with Nim, the exam seemed the logical choice. The exam was scheduled for two sessions of 3 hours morning and afternoon. Just on a hunch, I decided to read a couple of additional books. *Argonauts of the South Pacific* was one, then an ethnography on the *Neur of Africa*. Wise choices. When receiving the exam one Saturday morning, as I do with most test, I scanned the questions in each section. The first 3 sections were primarily multiple guess (choice) with some short essays, usually no more than a paragraph or two. The last section was virtually a book report on anthropology books you read outside of class. All the books required in classes, whether finished after the class or in class did not qualify. My intuition paid off. As a result it was an easy exam to complete, at least in the essay section. Never did find out what score I received. It was basically a pass / fail exam.

Upon completion of the exam the Department would notify the students if they qualified for their M.A. The combined effort of the exam, professors' evaluations, and the overall grade point average determined if you would be invited to the Ph.D program. I was awarded my M.A. No invite to continue, slightly disappointing. But realizing there were NO decent jobs in anthropology except for teaching I didn't really want to continue. Receiving several of the journals related to anthro one had just advertised a position exactly in the area I was interested in. Ph.D. with emphasis on cultural anthropology, for an associate professorship in a major state university. Salary $12,000 annually with possible tenure after 5 years. At the time I was earning $12,500 as a youth worker in the South Bronx! So much for a career in anthropology!

All this was going on while still taking one last semester of classes. One of which was with Nan who was mentioned in a previous letter. I received notice that I only qualified for the M.A. After class I told Nan the result. She said I was right on the border. My early grades during the first half pulled me down (two Cs and mostly Bs). Since I was from a white upper middle class background they wanted to make room for more minorities.

"Nan, what ever made you think I was middle class? My mom is dirt poor. We were homeless for some time and I had to drive a cab to earn tuition for my first semester here, before I got a job with the Youth Services Agency."

Nan looked at me with a surprised expression.

"I thought you were at least middle if not upper middle class. I had no idea of your background. I must apologize. I would have changed my vote if I had only known."

"That's OK Nan. It would have been nice to be invited but a career in anthropology is not very practicable. But this should teach you not to stereotype white guys!"

Nan nodded and gave me a hug.

Marisol came down for the graduation ceremony. She was very proud of me. I kept the green and white Master's collar. Later wanted to keep the red one from Boston University. Your mom interfered with that idea. But you will learn more about it and B.U when I start letters about what happened after leaving NYC.

Love,
Papa

Detroit Trip #4 May, 2016

Hello:

I was still working at Fox Street and the PAL around the corner. There was one rainy day when most of the younger kids, most about 7 and 8 years old, were all playing kickball in the up stairs gym. There was one teen up there. In theory he was to help supervise the younger kids but had never worked with me. I suspected he was racist.

After several rounds of kickball, the younger children started a game of keep away with the ball that was being used. During the fun the kids started trying to tackle me. They were pulling me on both arms. They were countering each other perfectly allowing me to stay upright. The teen who was never friendly towards me, saw how my arms will being pulled by numerous kids on either side. Thinking I was helpless he came running towards me and the kids. I suspected he was up to no good. I concentrated and tried to generate some chi energy around myself. Sure enough as he approached, he jumped up and applied a double foot drop kick to my chest. But I was prepared. He just bounced off like a ball. Landing on the floor he looked up at me in horror. He got up and raced out of the gym. The kids who saw what had happened all thought I was some kind of superman. To those not close to me before, now became my friends. This allowed me to bring several into the tutoring sessions.

There was one afternoon when the kids from the shelter came running up to me.

"There's a body in the basement across the street. He's all burnt up."

I when out. But the police had arrived. They blocked the entrance to the mostly burnt out building and the basement window. The kids knew the building next door, only partly standing, had a connecting basement. Soon they led me through the first and into the second basement where the corpse was. The body was on it's back. The legs and hands upraised and the face, partly burned off, was frozen in a perpetual scream of pain.

I warned them to keep quiet or the police outside might catch on that they were in there. Soon there was a steady stream of kids. My kids were charging a nickel each to lead the spectators to the body. One turned to me and asked:

"Can you think of any other way to raise money?"

I turned to him: "Well if you get a carving knife you can slice off pieces of his thighs and sell them as cold cuts."

They laughed. Dark humor is often the only way to handle what was happening in the South Bronx. Soon the police discovered what was going on and shut down that enterprise. What was interesting, that was the only corpse in the South Bronx that caused nightmares. Several nights later I had a dream about how he must have died and the terrible pain experienced. Later it was discovered the body was that of a teenage boy. He apparently was seeing a young girl in the neighborhood. The girl's father didn't like the boy. During a confrontation he knocked the boy out, dragged his body to the basement, doused it with gasoline and lit it. The boy gained consciousness only to experience the painful death of being burning alive. His frozen eyes and mouth in the form of a scream were what got me.

Each summer we would get a number of Neighborhood Youth Corps workers assigned to Fox Street. During the summer we teamed up with Lynch PAL to get the kids out of the South Bronx. If we could get a bus, they would be taken out of the city or at least to a park far away. One day there was a trip to Jone's Beach State Park. Picnic lunches were brought for all the kids. Most went swimming. I took a group into the wood to see what we could find. Not far into the woods were some wild blueberry patches. They were pointed out to the kids who helped themselves. It was an unexpected dessert. After we went swimming.

Charlene and Cynthia were watching the kids in the water close to shore. I wanted to take a longer swim further out. That was OK with them. I went about a hundred yards off shore and started a regular distance swim. As I progressed my hands were constantly hitting something that felt like plastic. I looked. All around me was a huge school of jelly fish. Thank goodness these were small and not particularly dangerous. Still they sting. Carefully only using a half stroke, raising my arms almost straight up, and minimize the kicks, I turned towards shore. By the time I got to shore, my arms and legs were stung in many places.

The I warned everyone not to go out far due to the jellyfish, while rubbing the stings with sand to remove the venom. It was my only encounter with jelly fish. It also taught the kids what to do if you are stung. Overall the trip proved to be very beneficial, despite the stings.

Love,
Papa

Detroit Trip #5 May, 2016

Hi T:

Remember the Jones Beach trip in the last letter. There was another trip to one of the public parks on a bus. It was late July. As at Jones I found a large patch of blackberries. They were almost as large as the one I used to pick on The Hill when I was a kid. The bushes were right off the main path that ran between the beach and the woods. There was an elderly woman who ran up to me:

"Your children are eating those berries."

"So???"

"They might be poisonous. They could get really sick."

I turned to her: "Don't you recognize blackberries when you see them? You don't know what you are missing!"

The poor woman lived in the area all her life and didn't know she was so close to a wonderful patch of edible berries—there for the picking. Others would have paid top money to eat these gorgeous blackberries. That's what too much city life does to you. If you don't buy it in a market, it must be dangerous.

There was one morning when several trips were planned. Charlene was to take one group to one park. Cynthia on another bus out of the city, it may have been to Bear Mountain State Park. One of the Neighborhood Youth Corps Workers was assigned to me. Neighborhood Youth Corps Workers were teens given a job by the city for the summer, hopefully to provide them with positive experienced. We were to take any stragglers who missed the bus trips or didn't have permission slips from their parent to go on the bus. Our limitation it had to be a trip via the subway. It being a Tuesday, and having a membership with the Metropolitan Museum of Modern Art (MOMA), it was their day when guests of members were allowed in for free. There was about 8 kids who joined me around 10 a.m. There was about six girls and I think two boys. Mostly Puerto Ricans. One boy was a black boy who I knew from the PAL. With subway pass for a group could ride for free. I told the Youth Corps we were going to MOMA.

"Ah gee Walter do I have to come. I don't want to go to a dumb museum?"

Of course if he wanted to be paid for the day, he had to help me with the kids. It was explained to him this was his assignment for the day. So off we all went. He was mumbling under his breath the whole subway ride downtown.

The exciting thing that summer was MOMA was doing a series on comedy films in the theater. Most of these kids had never been in a movie theater before. Some had not even see TV. Remember these were children from extremely poor families, who had been burned out and left homeless if not for the shelter. I got tickets for the first film showing. It was a Red Skelton comedy from the early 50's. The film was not for a couple of hours. So I took the kids through the art galleries describing the pieces they were looking at and who the artist was. Then we had lunch in the garden followed by the movie. It was a fantastic day for all of them. Around 3 p.m. I wanted to get back before the rush hour. Gathering the kids around me I said we were going back. The Youth Corp worker came up to me:

"Ah Walter do we really have to go? I want to see the next movie."

There was another short comedy film to be shown around 3:15. Here was the very teen who didn't want to come now not wanting to leave.

"You can stay. If you promise not to jump the gate, I'll get you the ticket. I can take the kids back." That is what I did.

The next day he came up and thanked me for taking him to MOMA. The mother of the young black boy approached me later that day.

"My son Johnny really liked the trip to the museum yesterday. But he told me that he may have seen somethings that he shouldn't. I asked him if they were naked women. He nodded. I smiled and said that's OK if it is art."

We both laughed about his embarrassment. She felt it was one of the best experiences he had every had. She and some of the other mothers were exceedingly grateful for the trip.

Love,
Papa

June 10, 2016 Texas 1

Hi Daughter:

Really need to tell you about Frank Rodrigues. Frank was the boxing coach at the Lynch PAL. I think he was also a coach at another gym. I tried to look him up on the internet but there are just too many Frank Rodrigues associated with boxing to find this particular Frank. Remember I talked about teaching photography and ceramics down in the basement? At the far end in the basement was a gym with a boxing ring. The coach was old Frank. He was well into his 70's when I was there. According to the unofficial records, he had coached more Golden Gloves boxers than any other coach in the city, most likely the country. His record was one of the best with numerous Golden Glove winners in his stable. Frank was a short thin man. Strong Puerto Rican accent. He barely spoke English—and when he did, it was hard to understand. Slightly stooped with age, but tuff as nails. In many ways he was the Puerto Rican equivalent of Burgess Meredith's Mickey Goldmill in the original *Rocky* movie, the old trainer. Frank didn't put up with any nonsense, nor for gang members or trouble makers. Probably responsible for getting more boys off the streets and out of the gangs than anyone else in the South Bronx.

When the gym was open, there was a number of kids in there. Rarely interacting with any one upstairs they focused on their boxing. I don't think I ever interacted with any of Frank's kids. They were all too busy working out in the ring or on the bags.

I remember there was this one kid who was a likely contender for the Golden Gloves championship. Bill had told me this kid had been resistant to joining one of the gangs. According to Bill one night they caught him off guard. They crucified him by tying him up on the side of a building about 10 feet off the ground. Everyone in the neighborhood were told not to touch him. So there he hung for at least 2 days. Bill and Frank had heard about it and cut him down. Frank took him to the gym in the PAL where he stayed for weeks until the gang pressure had cooled. When in a gym, what do you do? You work out. So this Hispanic kid started his training with Frank. After a couple of years he was a top notch boxer. Don't know if he won the Golden Gloves that year, but I do know he won the first round. That was when I was preparing to leave New York.

There was a tribute dinner for Frank. It was celebrating his anniversary in boxing. Likely his 50th though I am not sure. I was not a part of it as the only time I ever spoke to Frank was when passing him in the basement while teaching my art / photography classes. But I heard it was a huge turnout in a fancy hotel. According to what I was told, hundreds turned out. Many were former boxers he trained. Several reigning champion fighters were there. There were other coaches from all over New York and New Jersey. To give you an idea of how many thought well of Frank it was Howard Cosell, the then famous sports announcer who hosted the dinner. Howard was famous in his support of Muhammad Ali in his fight against the draft which went all the way to the Supreme Court (Clay vs. United States) and for being a co-host for Monday Night Football when it started. The plaques and gifts Frank got that evening were hung around the gym.

There was another notable personality I met through the PAL. It was Mrs. Babe Ruth (Clara Mae Merritt Ruth). She was a tiny woman who played off her deceased husband's name for all it was worth. She did see Babe's record of 60 home runs in one year broken by another Yankee, Roger Maris. Then Babe's overall record for most home runs broken by Hank Aaron in 1974. I met her briefly at a fund raiser for the PAL around the same time. She must have been in her late 70's. Feisty and mean spirited. She was not a pleasant person. I know others said she was gracious when talking about Hank Aaron beating the Babe's record, but that graciousness didn't come through the evening I met her.

Love,
Papa

June 2016, Texas 2

Still Me:

I was dating Jean, who was mentioned before. At the talks at Demetria's were three women who would eventually join the lodge. Janet O, Jean C and one of her friends. Jean was not very attractive but was interesting in esoteric studies and had been a member of the Arcane School. During one of her correspondence courses her mentor was Jane Hoppy who was a friend of my mother. I had known Jane Hoppy most of my life. Jean had never met Jane in person. When I told Jean how absent minded Jane was, Jean laughed.

"I always pictured her as slightly scattered brained. What you have told me confirms my impressions from her correspondence."

I asked Jean if she would like to go out to dinner some time. She accepted.

When I went out with Jean I met her downtown on the East Side. She wore a semi-business pink suit with a low cut neckline. I'm sure she would have worn a blouse under it for business, but tonight she was trying to expose the little breast she had to their maximum advantage. Compared to Carol her breasts were tinny. Jean wasn't attractive, actually plain, black glasses, small frame. She a habit of slouching as if she was suffering from osteoporosis prematurely. By the time we split, I had her sitting and walking upright all the time. After the second dinner she invited me back to her place off 2nd Avenue. I'm sure it was for more than a drink, even though by then she knew I didn't drink alcohol. She admitted having former drinking problem, one that would resurface in her future. When we got to the apartment, her roommate was there with a man. So much for after dinner whatever. We politely excused ourselves. We took a long walk by the East River.

Love,
Papa

June 2016, Texas 3

Me again:

After witnessing the killing across the street and breaking up with Carol, finding a new residence was a top priority. Also the break-in where I was almost killed, encourage Bill S to want us out of the Settlement House for fear of another break in which might end up with one or both of us dead. Bad PR for the East Side Settlement House.

About the same time a teen was stabbed, maybe should say sliced, in front of the fire house. His brother while trying to hold his intestines inside, pleaded with the firemen to call an ambulance. None came. A call to the regular police told them that it was the project police department, the fire house being across the street from Mott Haven projects. The project police said if it was across the street it was the regular police. The kid died there in front the of fire house with no one coming to his aid.

I had been dating Jean for a short while when I found a place on Britton Street which I told you a little about earlier. I actually loved the place. I had my own private entrance. As mentioned before the apartments on Britton were really the basements of the buildings facing the other parallel streets. But the 8 or 10 of us who lived there formed our own special little community. We looked out for each other. Being away from the main apartments if a robbery was to take place it would have been on the opposite side of the building as most would hardly notice our little apartments away from the main thoroughfare.

The day of the move was complicated. I had a lot of books from classes packed into multiple boxes. Many trips on the subway to get them to the apartment. Then I had to buy a bed. Decided on a custom made platform bed with drawers underneath. It was the one you used for many years. Next came the only pieces of furniture, two bookshelves. I should have asked Bill if I could have them, but didn't. Instead Jean and I just took them up to Britton Street. Sure enough Bill was pissed. I tried to explain that I needed them and would pay for them. They were not really office style bookcases I just didn't think they were going to be used downstairs.

The first weekend in Britton Street I had planned going out with Jean Friday night. That afternoon there was a torrential rain. As the street was flooded, the drains in the sink and bathtub started a back wash. But this was NOT water. All the sewer was backing up into the apartment. It had no where to go in the sewer pipes which were filled with the run off of rain water. It was a filthy mess.

I called Jean to cancel the date. She volunteered to come up and help with the clean up. Though reluctant to let her, I was grateful for the offer. Together our first date in the new apartment was cleaning up all the shit in bathtub, sink and kitchen floor. I had blocked the flow from getting into the living room or bedroom. It was truly the nastiest job you could imagine. Of course all was cleaned out had to be dumped outside in the drainage ditches, as nothing was going down the pipes yet. We used every kind of disinfectant you can imagine to clean place, then strong cleaner to get rid of the smell.

As for the apartment, it was a large one bedroom. I make some brick and board bookshelves, which survived all the way down to your home in the Slade Run Drive basement. Rather than having the new bed with the storage drawers in the bedroom, I put it in the living room to have a good view of the TV and access to the books. All other items that were collected ended up on the 'guest' room, turning it into a storage space. I didn't help that Mom kept bring stuff from The Hill down to the Bronx once I had my own place.

My immediate neighbor was an Italian woman. Likely in her 70's she was very friendly and on most nice days would sit on the little lawn outside her door. Most of the time she was reading romance novels or growing flowers in the little space she had in front of her apartment. One day she had fixed a 'nice Italian meal with my own special sauce.' She gave me a plate full for dinner when I came home from downtown. I ate it. Didn't care for the sauce. Soon it showed that it didn't care for me either. I was throwing it up all over. Everything in my stomach was emptied that night. Even the breakfast. I was so weak, I had to stay in bed the next day. Never trusted any thing from her again. Always used the excuse I had a dinner date on the evenings she offered something else.

Love,
Papa

June 2016, Texas 4

Still Me:

This may be on the edge of to send or not to send but it is funny. Britton Street apartment didn't have air conditioning so on summer evenings we would lock the screen door and keep the main door open. Then with the window in the living room, it made for a nice cross breeze on hot summer nights.

One Saturday night Jean was staying over. We were just waking up. I had turned on the radio. Then there was the sound of knocking at my neighbor's door. I peeked out around the corner of the living room towards the front entrance. I was a group of black women, carrying Bibles and other leaflets. Looking at the journal title I knew instantly they were Jehovah Witnesses. Now they were coming towards my door. I turned the radio to a rock station and turned up the sound. I told Jean to make a lot of noised as if several people were here. Then when the Jehovah Witnesses knocked on the door I jumped out of bed and ran to the screen door. Of course I sleep totally naked. I had not put on any rob or other clothing. They were talking among themselves when I unlatched the door and opened it wide.

"Look everyone three more for the orgy. Come on in ladies."

The look on their faces seeing a white naked man opening the door was priceless. They let out a thrilling shriek and ran away. I might add, our block was never bothers by any more Jehovah Witnesses again. VICTORY!!!!

That was not my only run in with religious quacks, or at least those religious groups that I consider phooey. One day when walking down Fifth Avenue near Rockefeller Center a group of about 3 Hispanics where proselytizing another one the wacky Christian sects which I have no respect for. Sorry, but just telling it like it is. They were arguing against evolution, the age of the earth and the family structure. Not having anywhere special to go to and being in no hurry I started asking questions about everything they attempted to raise.

Soon a large crowd was surrounding us. Not to hear them, but more to hear me ask questions that were tearing down their positions. It was classically Socratic Methodology. If I got them to agree to one of my points that was raised in a question, then I would lead them on a merry trail defeating whatever position they had just proposed. I was doing this to almost everything they said. They were getting very frustrated. Finally after about 40 minutes of this give and take, I turned to the crowd of almost 30 people around us and said:

"Well now you know their faith is built on shifting sands."

The crowd applauded me as I took a slight bow and left. About 10 minutes later, I notice the group packing up as they could not get anyone else to listen to their garbage.

There was one funny incident when going to a Broadway show. Jean and I wanted to see *Ulysses In Nighttown*. This was a play staring Zero Mostel, the great comic actor who was black listed during the 1950's. It was being directed by Burgess Meredith (remember I referred to him went tell you about Frank R.). The play was based upon Joyce's <u>Ulysses</u>. It was a magnificent performance by the whole caste. The funny thing was it was tourist season.

It was directed by Meredith who played the Penguin in the Batman TV children's show. Staring Mostel who had done several appearances on Sesame Street out of towners thought it was going to be a family performance. Shame on them. The first act ended with Molly's soliloquy. Almost right out of the book's last chapter. This is where she is daydreaming or rather fantasying about past lovers. As she was saying her lines she was lying on a queen size bed, elevated in a way the audience could get a VERY good look at her beautiful red hair, in BOTH places, as she was masturbating. The passionate lines were only matched by the inserting of several fingers in between those moist delicate of lips below the waist. Needless to say there were several mothers with children rushing out of the theatre attempting to cover both the kid's ears and eyes at the same time. That became a secondary show onto itself. Jean and I laughed about it for weeks afterwards.

July 2016, post Texas

I think it's Me:

This would be the appropriate place to add a fun incident with my old hospital buddy Edgar. Edgar called me one evening and said he wanted to drive his car to their summer home, in of all places, Sugar Hill, New Hampshire, very near Franconia College, which I graduated from. The goal was to leave the car there and take public transportation back to NYC. Hilda wanted me to do most of the driving as she didn't really trust Edgar's driving on long trips. A weekend was set up. I met Edgar in his apartment on 72nd near 2nd Avenue. Hilda was delighted that I would be accompanying, not only for the driving but also since we got along so well together I would be good company on the long bus trip back to NYC. Edgar took me down to the garage. We got into the car. I can't remember what make it was, but it was certainly one of the better ones. Off we went.

The drive would be about 7 hours. I did all of it. We got on 95 North and followed it up close to Boston then worked our way to the White Mountains, passing the Old Man in the Mountain on the way towards Franconia Notch. Interesting now The Old Man in the Mountain only exists on the New Hampshire license plates, quarters, and stamps now. On the way up Edgar told me more of his past which I have mentioned impart before. Hilda was part of Jewish royalty. Her sister, a baroness, still lived in Europe. During the war she moved from Austria to Switzerland which remained neutral. Edgar came from an upper class family. When things didn't look good after Hitler took over, he started sending his art work, a collection which must have been considerable, to London. Over 80% of his collection was placed in a storage facility which had some degree of climate control and was considered very secure.

They eventually fled to London. They remained there until the German bombing started. Having money and knowing influential people, unlike the vast major of other Jews who were NOT permitted to immigrate to the USA, they were granted visas to get into our country. As London was suffering from the bombing raids, the warehouse which had their art collection took a direct hit. ALL their art collection that was in storage was destroyed. The only pieces left were those in their apartment in London, now in New York and their other homes.

When Edgar arrived in NYC he realized he would have to find a job. The only thing that he felt comfortable doing was real estate. He got his license and was hired by one of the up scale brokers in NYC. He told me he was waiting to sell one particular apartment, which was listed for over a million dollars (in 1973!!!!). With the commission, together with their savings, he would then retire.

We arrived at their home in New Hampshire late Friday afternoon. What surprised me was we were less than a mile from my former classmate William's house on Sugar Hill. It was on the same road I started walking down the day William refused to let me travel in the car. That was when I had the vision of being broadsided by another car. I called William, he would drive Edgar and myself to Littleton in two days to catch the bus to Boston on Sunday and eventually to New York.

We had a collection of groceries in the car which were unloaded. I took over the kitchen, cooked dinner, and made a cold chocolate soufflé for desert. Edgar was helpless in the kitchen. Hilda did all the cooking in the home, when they didn't go out to eat. He was amazed at the ease I was able to do everything at once. As the meal was cooking, he started to take the sheets off both the furniture and the art works in the house. Like the apartment, the house was filled with art. There was a particularly beautiful bronze sculpture hidden under the grand piano. It was a typical Greek mythological figure. I guessed it was 17th Century Italian. Edgar said it was the most valuable piece in the house, well into the 6 figures if not more. Most of the paintings were larger than those in the NY apartment, many in the same style, late Baroque and Renaissance, as the bronze. Not my style but together easily over a million dollars in value. We had a delightful dinner and went to bed. I was in the guest room. Spacious and comfortable, with interesting art on the walls.

The next day Edgar showed me the way to a friend's house not far away. Elsa was an elderly woman who lived in a little one floor shack. Or so it appeared. She greeted Edgar with a warm hug and big smile. Edgar introduced me and she immediately invited us in for tea. The shack reminded me of the tent in Harry Potter movies. Not that it expanded once you were inside, but the sure amount of art was overwhelming. One every wall, on every table, on every bookcase was ART. The bookcases were filled with art books. We're not talking about minor works, but major pieces from almost all the famous 20th Century artists. Picasso drawing was on one wall, next to a Miro and many other pieces. On the little table where she served the tea was a small version of a Max Ernst sculpture. It was a piece seen in many of the great galleries around the world. Else asked if I like Ernst.

I said: "Yes, the satyrical nature of his works had always appealed to me."

"Pick it up and look at the bottom."

I picked it up. There inscribed into the base was 'To Elsa from Max with love.' It was his original casting for the larger piece. She then showed me one work after another, all dedicated to her. Some on the back, some on the bottom, others right on the front of the canvas. She knew all the great artists of the Century personally.

We sat and talked about art for hours. Elsa's husband was the founder of a major NYC art gallery. He had died about a decade before, and she retired to New Hampshire. She told me the last time she was involved with art was during the famous Rothko trial. The gallery which claimed they owned all the art in Rothko's studio. During the court hearings, the gallery asked Elsa to write a letter to the court explaining Rothko meant for all the works in the studio were to go to the gallery. Elsa grinned as she told me the story.

"I wrote the court. I told them THE ART BELONGS TO THE CHILDREN! The gallery were furious with me. I didn't care. I didn't like the owners and the way they treated my husband when he was trying to retire. I certainly didn't care for their attitude in the trial."

We finally left. It was one of the most delightful afternoons of my life. I just wish I had a camera to take photos of all the art in that little house. About 2 years later I learned that Elsa had died. Her lawyer had a Power of Attorney over her estate. I was told he never processed her will and took all the art works for himself. She had no children, none of her relatives saw a cent.

I introduced William to Edgar when he drove us to Littleton to catch the bus to Boston. We got on the bus. We each took a seat to ourselves. It was not crowded. The trip would take 6+ hours to Boston. It was a local bus with stops in almost every town on the way. There was one scheduled rest stop. It was a bathroom break and a chance to get a dinner from a Burger King. We got out and went into Burger King. I ordered a Whopper.

Edgar looked at the menu and didn't know what to make of it. He was only familiar with ham and swiss on rye from fast food delis in NYC. He asked if they had ham and swiss. No luck. He looked up at the menu again. He was at a total loss as to what to order. I ordered a Whopper for him, along with a coke (he liked coke) and fries (something new to him). We had it put in a bag to bring back on the bus as the driver was ready to get going.

Edgar sat behind me. He looked into the bag. "Where are the knife and fork to eat this with?"

I told him to unwrap it partly and eat it out of his hands along with the fries. His expression was priceless. He was totally bewildered. But as he looked around the bus, everyone was doing exactly as I had suggested, including myself. He gently unwrapped the Whopper and took a bite. Then another. Then some fries. I heard a muttering call of my name:

"Walter, this is really good! I'll have to tell Hilda about Burger King. You know we have never been to one."

I looked back at Edgar. It was all I could do not to burst out in laughter. He had mayo and ketchup all over his face. Here this man in his early 70's looked like a 3 year old just devouring his first burger. I was very glad he liked it.

Edgar and Hilda did retire after he sold that last apartment. They spent their summers in New Hampshire, Autumn and Spring in their apartment in Zurich, and Winter in NYC. When retired, he tried his hand at painting. One evening I got a call from Zurich. It was Edgar. He was very excited. He had his first one man show. The art critic called him a modern impressionist. Now he was making money selling his paintings.

Love,
Papa

Not Sent

Though not in sequential order here may be the place to describe my sexual adventures with Jean. When I first took her out to dinner she wore the best push up bra she had and a suit with advantageous exposure without being slutty.

She shared a small apartment on the East Side with a roommate. This was actually a short distance from Demetria's but a world apart as far as socio-economic status was concerned. On our second date, Jean was wearing a nice dress. We had dinner and went to a movie. During dinner she told me about loosing her virginity. She was having her period and didn't know enough to remove a tampon. The guy who fucked her pushed it so deep inside her she had to see a doctor to have it removed. She blamed it on her Italian parents who told her nothing about sex, menstruation, or anything else. We went back to her apartment. As we walked in, her roommate was riding cowgirl style on the guy she had brought home. Jean and I quietly tiptoed out of the apartment and decided to go for a walk by the East River.

After seeing her roommate fucking her man, Jean was horny as hell. We took the stone stairs by the East River down to the walking paths. The apartment buildings were built on top of the stone walls that separated the walk from the actual buildings. Next to the stone walls were thick shrubs and trees. She said she wanted me! NOW! Looking around I felt the closest thing to privacy would be next to the stone wall and behind the trees.

We made our way through the bushes and I backed her up against the stone wall. She unzipped my pants and took out my erection. Then placing one leg on my hip, she positioned herself so with a bit of stooping down I was able to penetrate her. Once in her, she wrapped both legs around me and started pumping up and down. It was then I realized she was one horny woman. She also could get off quickly, recover fast only to organism again, and again, and again. As she came close to a climax her moans became more and more vocal AND LOUD.

As I was fucking her against the wall, she was letting out little screams of passion. I looked to my right. There at the end of the row of trees was an elderly man walking his dog. But he could care less about the dog. He was enjoying the sight. When I realized he had been watching for some time, I started to stare at him with as much of a threatening expression I could muster. He soon became aware of my gaze and walked away. By that time I was ramming into Jean as fast and hard as I could go. I climaxed with her. We rearranged our clothes and I walked her home. By this time her roommate was finished with her friend. I kissed Jean goodnight at the door.

Some months later she moved into a small apartment on 2nd Avenue around 52nd Street. Friday nights became our fuck nights. But one particular Friday, I had the day off. So off the the 42nd Street porn movie houses. I looked at the various features on the marquees and picked one with 4 feature porn films. I paid the $1.00 and took a seat in the middle of the theater. There was an overweight man sitting two seats away from me. There was a distinct smell of cigar smoke coming from his direction.

"Excuse me, but there is no smoking in here. Would you please put out your cigar?"

He looked at me: "I'm not smoking any cigar, so mind your own business."

I looked next to his leg. There was the red embers of the end of a lit cigar. I quickly leaned over, grabbed the cigar and crumbled it over his lap embers and all. The embers falling on him. He jumped up and quickly exited the theater.

In the meantime I sat back and began to enjoy the films. There was one film right after another. Every erotic scene being watch was accompanied by my hand stroking my erection. Many times I was close to an organism. I would stop, force the erection in the direction of my feet and was able to stop the climax. This was done repeatedly for hours that afternoon. There was a method to this madness. I wanted to be able to get Jean the sexual experience of her life. By getting so close to coming, so often, I thought I would be able to climax with her more than once.

Towards 5 p.m. I left the theater and walked over to her apartment with a carry out dinner from a local Chinese restaurant. We sat at her little dining table and had dinner. Since it was a warm nearly summer day, and not having air conditioning in her apartment we opened the windows to get some circulation. Her window opened to the back side of 2nd Avenue. There was not much of a view except for the back sides of the surrounding buildings and a pathway between the tiny back yards where garbage would be collected once a week.

During the dinner she asked what I had done that afternoon since I had the day off. I told her. Basically getting ready to give her the fucking of her life. Her response was immediate. She started taking off her clothes and then stripped me. Soon I was kissing her breasts. Being small they were very sensitive and very responsive.

With Jean, she was the only woman would could organism in a minute, literally. Moving down from her breast I began to perform cunnilingus. Sure enough, 60 seconds later she came for the first time. She started moaning with pleasure. I quickly mounted her. Not worrying about coming too fast, I got off much quicker than usual. All the time her guttural sounds of pleasure and suppressed screams were becoming louder by the minute. I came deep inside her. She quickly turned around to suck my cock. As predicted it was soon regained its full erection. This time 69 was the selected position which got us both off. Whenever I had an erection, there was never any hesitation in going down on a woman, even if I had just come insider her. As for Jean she never hesitated swallowing. So there was never any need to stop in the middle of post climatic ecstasy to run to the bathroom to spit or clean up. We just kept on going, stroking gently, kissing and petting until I was ready again.

By this time her orgasms were like clockwork. Every 60 seconds another. Each time more intense. Each time louder. Realizing she was now screaming almost at the top of her lungs from the mind blowing realm of ecstasy she had reached she attempted to suppress the screams. Wanting one more fuck, I got on top again with her legs around my shoulders. Now her screams were loud enough for the whole neighborhood to hear. Knowing this, while thrashing around on the bed, she grabbed a pillow and stuffed it in her mouth. She bit down on it. But the thrashing included her arms and hands. She took hold of the pillow and pulled while her teeth held firm. The whole pillow split open. Feathers were flying all over the room. Some even drifting out the screenless window. Then with one last passionate scream from her and one last shove from me as I came for the last time. Jean literally passed out from all the pleasure.

Then from the window came the sound of someone clapping. It was joined by at least two others. Then a woman's voice was heard to say:

"What did you do to her? Can you teach it to my boyfriend?"

We never found out who uttered those words, but sure hope she found someone who could get her off like jean.

June, 2016

There were two presents that Jean gave me which were so appreciated they deserve praise. One day near the Village, we were at the huge Barnes and Noble bookstore. First college section which was on one side of the street, then to the regular bookstore on the opposite side. On the second floor there was special limited editions and discounted books for sale. One that caught my eye was a two volume folio of Picasso's late etchings. The books were oversized and included copies of all of his etchings during his last decades. I really wanted it but couldn't afford it.

At the time Jean was working for a well know analytical company that covers private industry trends and outlooks. Though only a secretary, her salary was better than mine. What I didn't expect was that she returned to Barnes and Noble and got the Picasso folio for me as a present. I loved it! I copied sections of two the etchings and redrew them on the multi-generational proceedings cover while working for Margaret.

Upon moving to Boston, this and all my other books were taken to Connecticut. Many years latter Mom was convinced to sell The Hill and move to Virginia where I had gone after B.U. She got an offer that she liked but really didn't think the sale would go through. It did. She had two weeks to clear out the house. I went up to The Hill to help. We divided the books into two separate boxes. One for donation to the local charity and others to go down to Virginia. But the boxes were all gathered on the breezeway. The Picasso folio was accidentally, along with other valued books, taken by the charity and lost forever. SAD

The other present that Jean gave me was the tickets to Wagner's Ring Cycle. She knew how much I loved those four operas. The MET was presenting the complete cycle. She got the complete set of tickets. They were in excellent side box seats in the first balcony. When seeing *Das Rheingold* I was euphoric. By the time *Götterdämmerung* overture was being played, it hit me that here I was seeing the last of the four operas at the MET. I was so overcome by joy that tears were streaming down my face.

It would be years later I was able to see the complete Ring Cycle again at the Washington National Opera. All four were seen in order and within two weeks. It was one of the most remarkable experiences an opera lover could have. Not only that but the setting was not the Germanic mythical setting but WWII. In the second opera *Die Walküre* the Valkyries were paratroopers descending down to the battle field to raise the deceased warriors to raise them to the upper world, it was a radical reinterpretation of the opera, BUT IT WORKED. Now back to the letters.

Chapter 16

More on Your Grandmother

June, 2016

No Longer Neglecting Grandma:

I have noticed we have been neglecting your grandma's history in this series of letters. The last mention of her was when she made friends with Bonnie Parker. As you can well imagine a lot more happened to her. So the next few letters will catch you up on her life.

The family moved to Houston, Texas shortly after the Bonnie and Clyde episode. She loved school, partly because it got her away from her mother and partly because she was an excellent student. She finished elementary school and was enrolled in high school. There she started participating in track team particularly the high jump also swimming & diving team. She excelled in all sports. According to her, she could jump her own height. I looked up the Olympics for that period. She would have collected a medal if she had participated. There was one major problem her mother didn't see need for girls to get any additional education after elementary school. All girls needed to do was the learn to read and cypher with numbers (as she called math). So Louise was pulled out of high school after what I think was her sophomore year and had to stay home to take care of her younger brother and sister, Forest and Sug.

She would be responsible for fixing the meals. Here is where she would have to stoke the wood stove, change Sug's diapers, watch Forest, who loved getting in trouble, and still cook dinner. She told me the stove would start communicating with her. If something was about to spill over, or get burned, the stove would start making noises. She would rush in and fix what needed to be done to prevent spoiling the meal. Here is where she started thinking all things were alive. Even inanimate objects had some degree of consciousness. She would talk to the stove, asking for help, and thank it whenever she received one of these warnings. She never burned any food, even if she was outside playing with her siblings. Somehow the stove would make enough noise to warn her of impending disaster.

The problem was her father was still trying to make a living as a farmer, elsewhere in Texas. Never successfully. So there was very little money. Soon her mother started 'entertaining' men in the afternoons. This created an influx of additional cash, most of which was spent on clothes and cheap jewelry. The kids got nothing. Your grandmother knew something was going on that was not right. Her mother was very much afraid that if given the chance she would tell her father of what she had seen.

Around the same time, a distant neighbor started driving around the house. He was an older man. Sarsfield was in 50's though you grandmother didn't know it at the time. He was very attracted to this red headed teenager who as very pretty and looked a little older than she was. Soon he would actually stop and talk to Louise. She was attracted to him because he had his own car and money. Their meetings were on the sly so her mother wouldn't know. Besides Carrie (your great grandmother) was too busy 'entertaining' her men in the house. But the threat of Louise telling her father of goings on, Carrie she got an idea. She would put your grandma in a home for delinquent children and be rid of that threat. But when talking it over with a neighbor, your grandma overheard.

Sarsfield expressed his desired to marry Louise. By now she learned he was divorce, had three boys all older than her. He couldn't wait to get this young attractive redhead in bed. But to get married before being 16 needed the permission of a parent. Forget her mother! She went to her father. She explained her fears. She felt that marriage would be to only way to get away from Carrie and a safe distance from home. Her father consented. Thus just before her 16th birthday, Louise married Sarsfield Wilson.

Love,
Papa

June, 2016

More on Grandma:

Being married to Sarsfield started out well. She loved teasing her step sons. Each over 6 foot tall and 200 pounds plus. There was a picture of her surrounded by them. She looked like a small cheerleader between three interior linemen from a football team. But things were not as rosy as they first appeared. Sarsfield wanted no more children. But Louise knew nothing about birth control. Sarsfield never worn a condom. So every few months, Louise's period would be delayed. Sure enough she was pregnant. So off the a back alley abortion provider. She estimated she must have had close to half a dozen during the years with Sarsfield. One of which almost killed her from excessing bleeding. It took her two months to heal.

Soon it was learned, Sarsfield was not loaded with cash. He did invent a form of shorthand which provided some income. Still he was always trying to scheme up ways to make more money. Not only that he was jealous of his brother who had made a small fortune in oil field development expansion. This was 1927. The car industry had now advanced to more than just the Ford Model T. After WWI Ford was on top, but General Motors and the reorganized Maxwell Motor Company which had become Chrysler Corporation, offered customers a number of sizes, varieties, colors, and makes were demanding the production of more and more gas. It was also the era of Prohibition.

The most popular recreational activity was to go to a local speakeasy and get drunk as hell on the bathtub gin, or whatever was provided. This was a popular activity with Sarsfield. It likely opened up the door for your grandmother's alcoholism years later. During one of these forays into the back fields of Texas, Sarsfield's brother joined them. He was totally infatuated with Louise. It was evident he wanted to screw the hell out of her. Sarsfield knew this. While all were drunk as skunks, he leaned over to Louise and suggest she lead his brother down the hall to a bedroom. She grinned and signaled the brother to follow.

Just off the main room was a series of room that local prostitutes would take their customers. One was vacant. Louise and the brother went in. She told me she hardly exposed her breast and lifted up her skirt when he plunged into to her. According to her, he was finished in less than a minute. Rearranging their clothes they went back into the hall. Louise smiled and gave a little nod to Sarsfield, little knowing what was to happen next. Over the next month Sarsfield blackmailed his brother over having sex with his wife. He threatened to expose him to the whole family, including his brother's wife and children. The price—several oil wells.

The effort succeeded. Sarsfield soon had the deeds to a number of producing wells in Texas. All during my early years grandma always told me she made Sarsfield rich. It was not until she moved into the grandma apartment she told me this whole story. Always wondered how a 16 year old would have enough business sense to make her husband rich. When the truth came out it made sense. But there was other important lessons from this venture. She learned all the ins and outs of the oil business. She virtually ran the operations for Sarsfield, learning as she went, but with a skill and common sense that surpassed many others, of any age.

One night Sarsfield came home drunk. Something Louise said or did made him angry. He hit her. This was not the first time, but it would be the last. She got up and grabbed him my the shirt. Not knowing where the strength came from she literally forced him up against the wall and threatened him saying if he ever struck her again she would kill him. Never before had a woman of any kind, young, old, big or small countered his battery with such force. He realized she was more powerful than him when provoked. He backed off. But grandma didn't want to face that again. She filed for divorce using the beating as the charge. Unfortunately back then, if she filed, she would get nothing in the settlement, except her freedom. So after little over two years of marriage she was now 18, divorced and independent. Now the only thought was to get out of Texas!

Love,
Papa

Chapter 17

Different interests including politics

June, 2016

Change of pace–in praise of a deceased hero:

With the recent death of Muhammad Ali it would be appropriate to dedicate a letter to my thoughts and memories about him and his life. When I was young, boxing was one sport that caught my interest. Part of it came from my father Walter A who loved it. Having been a semi-pro wrestler earlier in his life he liked boxing as well. While still part of the family dad would listen to the boxing championship matches on radio. No TV broadcasts yet.

I mention early how Cassius Clay won the gold medal in the 1960s Olympics not as a heavyweight, but as a light heavyweight. He gained weight and became a heavyweight pro. When he won the heavy weight championship many felt Liston took a dive, including me. It wasn't until Ali's death that I finally saw a picture which showed Liston ducking one punch but moving right into Clay's semi-upper cut.

The rematch with Liston proved either Clay was a good boxer or Liston was past his prime. He still didn't have my support. After the fight Clay declared himself as a convert to Islam and legally changed his name from the 'slave name' to Muhammad Ali. I understood his resistance to use the name imposed by white slave owners a century before, but was unsure about his becoming a Muslim.

Then came the fight with Floyd Patterson who came out of retirement to basically shut the kid's mouth. Patterson refused to call him by his new name. I was a long term Patterson fan. Patterson had been one of the youngest heavyweight champs years before, but listening to the fight on radio, it was evident he couldn't couldn't touch Ali. Ali was a serious fighter.

What really changed me my mind was Ali's declaration of being a consciousness observer, refusing to answer to the draft. I was anti-Viet Nam War from the start. Later in college trained as a draft advisor. Ali was part of my inspiration for these actions. Ali ended up having his boxing license revoked, championship stripped and was sentenced to jail. This at the peak of his career as an undefeated champ. Most of the sport announcers turned against him. Only one stood out in his support of Ali, Howard Cosell, whose defense of Ali I found to be inspirational. When Ali's conviction was thrown out by the Supreme Court it was a victory for the anti-draft, anti-war movements. In 1970 Ali come back fight against Jerry Quarry wasn't even close. It was a TKO in the 3rd round. Ultimately this led to the championship fight with Joe Frazier.

By this time I was an Ali fan. Sometimes the fights were broadcast on TV now but in Connecticut, it was mostly radio that kept me in touch with action. Ali lost the first fight against Frazier, his first defeat. But would come and beat him for the title later after fighting Quarry and Patterson both for the second time. Ken Norton broke Ali's jaw for his second loss. Norton lost to him twice later. But the famous 'Rumble in the Jungle' he defeated Gorge Foreman regaining the title. Frazier TKO'ed in the 15th round. In the fight called 'The Thrilla in Manila.' it was one of Ali's most difficult fights. Hooray for Ali!

Howard Cosell continued to support him. I believe Howard helped bring the many of the remaining sports announcers to support Ali as well. Some still hated Ali for his draft resistance, but as the War was winding down, most felt Ali and his position was really the correct stance. As Ali aged, Parkinson's syndrome silenced the voice but not the spirit. His charity work and dedication to others proved his greatness over and over. I shed a tear as he held the London Olympic flame in 2012. If not THE Greatest, he was certainly one of the greatest Americans.

I was fortunate enough to take a photo of Ali while he was campaigning for Humphrey in 1968. I included it in my book's It's Me the Early Years photos.

Love,
Papa

July, 2016

Political Letter:

Flashback–1972 was interesting. Tricky Dick (Nixon) was up for re-elected as President. What was being discovered by *The Washington Post* related to the Watergate break-in was not getting wide coverage. When *The NY Times* finally picked up on the Watergate, most people had made up their minds. It was purely a fictionalized hatchet job against the President. After all Nixon <u>WAS THE PRESIDENT OF THE UNITED STATES OF AMERICA</u>, surely he would not be involved in illegal activities! VP Spiro T. Agnew kept telling everyone it was an attack of lies by the liberal media (an attack used by conservatives ever since–especially when reporting the media is reporting the TRUTH). Of course Agnew had to resign even before Nixon, pleading *no contest* to his corruption case.

At the time I was following the politics as much as I could without purchasing *The Post*. Ed Muskie would have been a better candidate. But he dropped out due to 'dirty tricks' and the 'Kunuck' letter. A letter written by a Nixon staffer to embarrass Muskie and get him to withdraw from he race. I didn't believe the letter. But I did begin to wonder what the hell was going on. Without Muskie, the only Democrat left was George McG. Personally I liked McGovern. He was the Bernie Sanders of that era. But this was at a time too many people still remembered the 'red scare' which Nixon was a major participant in the 1950s. Naturally Nixon was still up to his old tricks (thus the nick name above) and more. But ALMOST everyone (not your father) believed him when he said: "I am not a crook."

I remember talking about this with members of Marie Deraismes Lodge. Demetria kept dismissing the whole affair for the reason stated in caps above. Fred North was a little more willing to accept it may be true. He didn't care for the things being said about the Democrat. I know politics should not be discussed in Masonry, but when we were meeting outside the lodge at Demetria's or elsewhere, I would bring up the latest headlines or breaking news. First that the burglars were former CIA. Then paid for by the re-election committee. That many of Nixon's personal staff were directly involved. I had been begging everyone not to believe the propaganda about George McG and vote Democratic.

"Look at what Nixon is doing!"

But no one was listening. Even life long Democrats like Demetria voted for the SOB Nixon. I couldn't believe it. When suspicions about Attorney Mitchell started to surface, the election was over and Nixon had won in a landslide. So much for the saying: "Dick Nixon before he dicks you."

As the investigation continued. More and more was reveled. After the resignations and convictions started to come in, Demetria turned to me one afternoon:

"Walter, I wished I had listened to you about Nixon. He has to be one of the most corrupt Presidents we have even seen in the country." Little did we realize what would follow in the years to come with Bush junior and the ultimate example of corruption number 45 / 47!

She was right. But the problem was, she and millions of other Americans refused to believe the truth. Instead they accepted the distortions and lies coming from Nixon's staff. So we put up with Nixon. He did do some good. Opening up China. Resolving Viet Nam War (the 1st war we lost). But I never trusted him. By the time the Watergate Committee (which I watch when ever I could) was uncovering all the sh*$ it led to his resignation. But it was too late to do anything about the election. I didn't believe that he came bouncing back AGAIN towards the end of his life. I still hated the bastard! It's strange that now in the 2025+ we are dealing with the same level of corruption and dishonesty in the White House once again.

By the way, the opening up of China started with Ping Pong Diplomacy. The Chinese ping pong team was the 1st official visit by ANY Chinese! They toured parts of the country. They played out at the Nassau Colosseum. I went there to see them play. The US team failed to win a single match. Instead of embarrassing our team, most of their good Chinese players played each other. Only the lesser members of their team played the American team and still clobbered them. Not having a car it was hard to get out there, but I got there via Subway and bus. It was exciting seeing really GREAT players using the pen grip and returning slams standing as far back as 25' from the table. I love it.

Love,
Papa

Chapter 18

Changes In YSA and life

July, 2016

Change in jobs:

A blind YSA social worker had been assigned to Fox Street. Bring an ACSW (Academy of Certified Social Workers) she was to do real case work to any troubled teens in the shelter. Here was an overweight blind woman who had to come to work via the subway and then walk the several blocks to the shelter. I had the impression that management wanted to get rid of her, like they did when transferring me to the Concourse Hotel. I didn't get directly involved with her as Charlene and Cynthia were the ones referring individual children to her for assessments.

It was around this time Margaret B called me up. Margaret was the person who brought me into YSA. She was interested in creating an intergenerational program in YSA. She remembered the interview with me when I was hired to work for the Agency. I had expressed an interest in gerontology and my working with the White House Conferences on Aging. Mr. Woods gave her rave reviews of my work in the short lived social work unit. Now with a M.A. almost completed, she wanted me to be part of a new effort. Somehow she got approval for the creation of the 'Youth/Aging Program' within YSA. I was assigned as the Assistant Director of the program. The youngest in the history of the agency possibly all New York. Only problem, being an experimental program, no raise! Just a nice title.

I talked this over with Charlene and the rest of the S. Bronx staff. I told them this was an opportunity I couldn't pass up. They all knew I had higher aspirations. The PAL was more reluctant to see me go. I promised to continue to come back in the evenings at least 3 nights a week. After some tearful farewells, off I went to my new job.

The new program was located in the headquarters on 60 Park Row. This was across the street from the Major's office and not far from the newly build World Trade Center buildings. It was also walking distance to Wall Street, China Town, and the court house. The once famous Woolworth Building, when built it was the tallest building in the world. It was clearly visible as I emerged from the subway every morning. Great place to work.

The programs first effort was to have a special conference. It was 'The Youth Aging Conference on Intergenerational Cooperation.' Scheduled as a day long conference involving the young people and the elderly to discuss intergenerational problems. Margaret pulled together a number of

119

elderly speakers, some of the more competent speakers within YSA, and had various panels of gang members, elderly and others. One woman opened her talk:

"If you live long enough you will be my age..."

This caught many of the kids in the audience off guard. Many had never considered reaching her age. But it was true. If they lived long enough they would be in their 70's like her. I was taking notes all day long.

The first product from the program was a conference booklet. There were several parts devoted to the speakers who submitted written copies of their talks. The panels were summarized. The woman who had the opening statement didn't have any written notes. Her talk was transcribed from the notes I had taken. To be sure what was going to be printed was accurate I contacted her to review what I had captured. She was shocked anyone was taking notes. She felt what was said not important to be put into a proceedings from the conference. It took some convincing, but she agreed her talk to be published.

Now for the cover. We had to come up with something eye catching. Jean had just given me a wonderful portfolio of Picasso's late etchings. Here was a large collection of his works. Many erotic, but also with both elderly individuals and some young people. I selected three. An elderly man, a young couple, made carbon copies from the three etchings, and transposed them on to the cover. Margaret was delighted. One of the other managers down the hall didn't like it. Too strange looking. Margaret looked at her:

"What don't you like Picasso?"

The woman stopped complaining. The cover was published.

Love,
Papa

July, 2016

Hello:

After the publication of the proceedings of the Youth Aging conference, the Youth Aging Program had something to build upon. Margaret and I worked closely together. It was a pleasure working with her. She was a long time social worker who was a graduate from Boston University School of Social Work. We poured over the panel discussions from the conference. Slowly an idea evolved. Why not try the seniors to open up the senior citizens centers in the worse parts of the city to the youths and gangs in the evenings? If it worked it many reduce tensions between the elderly and the young gang members. But how could be get a dialogue open between the groups?

The first step was to contact the local offices of YSA working in the South Bronx, Harlem and Bedford Stuyvesant neighborhoods. At the time these were recognized as the most gang ridden parts of Bronx, Manhattan and Brooklyn. They were areas where a high rate of crime by teens against the elderly existed. What we proposed was if the elderly opened up their centers in the evenings to the kids, then the kids had to promise to not only leave the elderly alone, but help them take care of the centers, and assist the elderly with groceries and chores. It was a wild idea. Yet a couple of churches who had senior centers joined in.

Soon a dialogue was started between the neighborhood seniors and the kids. The first sessions were full of accusations and name calling. It is important to realize the ethnic disparity between the groups. Most of the elderly in these areas were white, many Jewish or of other ethnic origin. Most of the kids black and Hispanic. The only common element was poverty.

I was traveling to these various locations. First to convince the local YSA unit supervisors to support the effort. Next to get the management of the centers to give it a try. Then to referee the meetings between the kids and seniors. This was quite a challenge. But after a few months, there was to be a trial attempt in each of these selected neighborhoods. At one of the Brooklyn churches, the minister was fully supportive, even more so than the YSA supervisors. That was the group that got started first. Then the South Bronx, finally Harlem.

In each of these locations, the elderly and kids using the centers would have weekly discussions. If the teens didn't clean up, they were instructed to do so. If they needed anything, ping pong tables or a pool table, efforts were made to get them if not already there (pool tables were common, ping pong tables not). In exchange for opening up the centers, the kids were to keep the neighborhood safe during the day. If some of the older women needed help with carrying groceries, the kids using the center in the evening were to help after school. Yes there was a rocky start. Yet after a few months, it was working.

Whenever I was to visit the South Bronx locations if it was a pay period, I would personally take the checks to my old unit. Even if I wasn't to visit the trial locations, I still took the checks to the unit. It was a good way to keep in touch every other week and then go to the PAL those evenings.

Unofficially the police told me that the crime rate against the elderly had dropped 80% in the trial neighborhoods. Margaret and I were elated. The program was a success! Now to promote it elsewhere. That Spring Major Beam announced major cuts in the City's programs. YSA was to be totally abolished. Of course this was not done over night. Each program was to be evaluated. Those which were considered valuable would be transferred to other city agencies. The 'youth walkers' like in my old Harlem unit were to be eliminated all together.

When reviewing our program, the conclusion was it was no longer needed. After all the crime rate had declined. We tried to explain it was only because of intense community organization efforts and group social work that it was working. They didn't want to hear about it. The support of the Youth Aging unit was removed. NONE of the experimental efforts continued more than a few months. By the autumn that year, the crime rates were right back to where they were in the beginning and all the senior centers closed to the kids.

Love,
Papa

July, 2016

T:

Outside of my usual studies, I was reading Lama Govinda's books. He greatly impressed me when I did his introductions at Rockford College. Now in my own way trying I was an attempt to become closer to him through his books. His first book Way of the White Cloud, was basically an autobiography which I loved. He told of how he went to Tibet to study but every time he tried to leave the mountains would not let him. This was confirmed in the book. So he became a Buddhist and eventually a monk. His Foundations of Tibetan Mysticism was also fascinating. Creative Meditation and Multi-Dimensional Consciousness was a little above me, but I really should go back and read it again. Most of my life I have called myself Buddhist/Christian. It was Lama Anagarika Govinda that helped me to gain a better understanding of Buddhism and of myself. While in the South Bronx, his books seemed to quiet me in times of crisis.

Another thing that was a quieting factor was baking bread. This was fun. While I was inventing new recipes Demetria was collecting all her old ones. She had close a hundred recipes. By the time I came up with seventy-five we started putting together a draft of the book. She had approached her publicist / agent and had lined up a possible goal for the book's first draft. Then she suffered a heart attack. Into the hospital! It was a bad heart attack. She remained in the hospital for two weeks, plus.

While she was in the hospital it was announced the famous chef James Beard was coming out with a bread cookbook. Her agent told her, while still in the hospital, the idea of us coming out with a bread cookbook had been cancelled. None of the publishers wanted to compete with James Beard! So the book was cancelled. I was looking for my old recipes but couldn't find them. But I did find the Nim recipes.

It was a few months later, after I moved in with Nim at Delafield. We, Nim and I, started cooking pancakes every Sunday morning. After a few months Nim began to know what went into the batter. After getting him up. Changing his diaper. Having him brush his teeth, I would ask in sign language what he wanted for breakfast. Since I was the Sunday morning caretaker Nim knew it would be pancakes. So he would sign 'pancake' and start his excited grunt-hoots. We then proceeded down to the kitchen. I would lay out our choices of flour, spices and fruit. Nim would carefully smell each of the flours and spices. He would hand me those which he wanted to mix in the batter. After I would add the egg, milk and any liquid flavors or juices we wanted. He tired to mix the batter a few times but would ask me to finish the mixing.

On the wonderful old stove, with six burners and a separate griddle, I would spoon out the mix. Nim, with assistance, would turn over the pancakes. When done, we both sat down in the kitchen for a delightful breakfast. All the time we were creating these pancakes I would be writing down what went into the mix. After a few months, I talked with Demetria. Why not turn the recipes into a pancake cook book. After each recipe would be Nim's rating (grunts, hoots and barks) followed by a little story about Nim and myself.

Demetria thought this was a great idea. She came up with the title: Nim Chimpsky's Pancake Cookbook for Children. It was pitched to her agent. According to Demetria the agent approached some fifty publishers. All rejected the book. Most because didn't fit any of the accepted genera of the time. Was it a cookbook? Was it a children's book? Was it an animal book? If a serious cookbook, it couldn't be a children's book. If it was about an animal, it couldn't be a serious cookbook. It had stories and Nim's rating so it was a children's book, so it could not be an animal nor a cook book. The only positive comment that came back with all the rejections was that *The New York Times* said it was a wonderful idea. But they were afraid Craig Claiborne, their cooking editor would be jealous. So it never got published. Of course you know it was resurrected as an adult book about Nim. But still unpublished.

Love,
Papa

July 25, 2016

NY days:

While in the South Bronx and Fox Street I had run into a black man who was interested in esoteric philosophy. His name escapes me, so will call him Eddie. Whenever we had our chance meetings, we would talk about the Theosophical Society, The Arcane School, Tarot, and other things of mutual interest. One day we met on 149th Street in the Bronx for a lunch. After talking for a while Eddie said he had teamed up with some others and opened an occult bookstore in Harlem. It was right across the river from where we were eating lunch, just off 149th Street but in Manhattan.

One afternoon I decided to visit Eddie's store. I walked across the 145th Street Bridge, something rarely done by any white person. Then turned right up Frederick Douglass Boulevard to 149th. On the block a little way from the intersection was the bookstore. I walked in. Suddenly there were about twenty pairs of eyes all focused on me. All giving me death stares. If they had been from Hogwarts I'm sure there would have been at least a dozen wands casting one if not all the unspeakable spells. I walked to the counter. The individual looked at me as if I was the plague itself.

"Is Eddie here?" I asked.

"You know Eddie?" was the response in a slightly hostel tone.

"Yea from the South Bronx." was my response.

"Hey Eddie there is some strange honkey out here to see you."

Eddie came out. I looked at me: "Hey Walter, it is great to see you."

He came over and gave me a hug. Instantaneously all the negative expressions were neutralized. Soon I was part of a large discussion group all gathered around a table in the store. We spend over two hours discussing meditation, tarot, various mystery schools including Masonry, and exchanging ideas on all sorts of esoteric subjects.

After I moved out of the South Bronx the volunteer work at Mott Haven ceased as did contacts with the Settlement House. But the shelter at Fox Street was keeping me busy. It was also the end of my MA degree at The New School. The interview with Herb Terrace at Columbia about working with Nim went well. He wanted me to start right away. The problem was he was used to having graduate students or former students volunteer. They would be able to work during weekdays in the classroom that had been set up for Nim in Schermerhorn Hall. I was working full time. He was not happy that I was only available on weekends or evenings. He never got it into his head the problems a volunteer who had a real job had which may conflict with his personal desires.

I did take a few afternoons off to work with Nim in the lab. Gave me a chance to chat with Ralph now and again. His lab was right down the hall from Nim's classroom. But the classroom environment didn't fit my personality. I wanted to work with an infant who wanted to look at books, play on a playground, etc. After telling Herb repeatedly I had to work during the weekdays, it finally began to sink into his skull not ask me for classroom duty.

I started to go to Stephanie's townhouse on the West Side to care for Nim on weekends to give the family a break. Of course Nim tested me ever time I showed up. The one big 'no no' was climbing on the bookshelf and jumping on the water mattress. Every time I wasn't watching him, off he went into the library and the bookshelf. After one of his jumps I grabbed both arms as if they were in a straight jacket and just held him until he stopped misbehaving. This taught him who was both the boss and stronger. I must admit it was amazing watching a two year old hang by his fingers from door frames. There is much more about Nim in a possible separate cookbook about our adventures and pancake on Sunday mornings.

Love,
Papa

Chapter 19

Nim and Boston

August 23, 2016

Hi T–a little bit on Nim:

Stephanie's townhouse was getting to be a bit uncomfortable for Nim to live in. The two primary reasons were he was getting bigger and stronger, also Stephanie's husband and Nim did not get along! Herb wanted tighter controls on the experiment as Nim was learning more signs. It took a while but he found a new location.

A Columbia University benefactor who had moved to Florida, donated his home to Columbia. It was to be the President's home. But it was in the Bronx. The President lived not far from campus in Manhattan. Somehow Herb got the University to allow the estate to be used as the residence for Nim. Efforts were made to turn the exquisite Delafield estate into a chimp proof home for Nim and his human companions. The goal was to divide the house into a separate chimp and human areas.

The front foyer was totally off limits to Nim. As you entered the main door, you would be struck by a panorama painting of a Civil War scene which encircled the whole entrance. There was to the right of the foyer a library. One that I envy to this day. Wall too wall, floor to ceiling hardwood bookshelves surrounding a double sided hardwood desk where two individuals would work facing each other. Each side had file drawers and storage. Past the library was the main living room, or rather a ballroom, as it was almost large enough to be considered a ballroom. The doorway to the left of the foyer was locked tight as it led to the Nim's part of the downstairs. What was once a dining room, now playroom, next to a solarium. On the opposite side of the dining room was the kitchen. Huge kitchen with a large center island. Plenty of cabinet space and a stove with six burners, two ovens, with a grill which I loved.

Nim and I would soon be cooking pancakes on it every Sunday morning. Opposite the kitchen was the laundry room, and a small stair to a very small cook/maid's room on the second floor which in theory was to be another room for Nim to work in, but rarely used.

At the left of the entrance was a circular stairway proceeded to the second floor. If you turned to the right at the top of the stairs, it led to the master bedroom suite. There were other bedrooms on both left and right of the landing. One modest size. Another over the large kitchen and laundry room. Every major room in the estate had a unique marble fireplace. Each with various forms of marble, imported from around the world. The only rooms that did not have fireplaces were those designed as servants' quarters.

At the end of the hallway on the second floor was the back stairs next to the kitchen. Originally for the servants, it was to be Nim's access to his third floor rooms. One was a mini playroom with a small wooden ladder against the wall for him to climb on. Next to that room was his bedroom with a loft bed platform. Of course he has his own bathroom.

Herb had a challenge. Who would move in with Nim and take care of him weekends and the evenings? By this time Laura had become the head signing teacher. The second individual chosen was Amy. Amy was a small young woman who had been doing volunteer work with the gorillas in the Bronx zoo. Knowing a little sign language and having worked in the classroom with Nim made her a priority. She would move into the only third floor bedroom over the main part of the house, closed off from Nim's rooms.

Herb wanted a male in the house. I was the logical choice. Physically and with experience in the Bronx gave a level of assurance the women would have some level of protection if needed. Besides having learned a little sign language at the Pennsylvania School for the Deaf and having worked well with Nim on weekend at Stephanie's it was a logical choice. Andrea was the final choice. An audiologist by profession she knew sign language and was very motherly towards Nim.

I had met Laura before the move. We had attended several professional conferences related to psychology and anthropology, especially if they included panels or presentations on language development or acquisition. Each of us who were to move in were notified by Herb.

About two weeks before the move, the four of us got together for the first time. It was my first meeting with Amy and Andrea (who delayed moving in by about a month). We were told which rooms would be ours and the rules of the house. Also where Nim was and was not allowed, both inside and out. Laura would move into the master bedroom. One reason because it was far from the other bedrooms and therefore offered the most privacy. Perfect when Herb had his nocturnal visits. I would be the only male in the house in the bedroom over the kitchen. Offered with good view of both the east and west sides of the property. Andrea's room on the second floor next to mine. Amy had a room on the third floor, closest to Laura's and the only person to access the that floor through the main staircase.

Love,
Papa

August 24, 2016

Hello:

After the announcement that YSA was to be closed, the next step was to find new jobs for its workers. Those with tenure were found jobs in other city agencies. Few of the youth workers had the tenure necessary to be retained elsewhere. There was to be a union meeting. Almost all of us were union members as it was a closed shop. There was one meeting where workers' concerns were to be discussed. Basically discussion those who were senior enough obtain new jobs. Those under 10 years of civil service were going to loose their jobs. When appealing to the Union President to find jobs for my old workers in the South Bronx and myself, he turned to me and with his Jamaican accent said:

"Fuck you, I save my own job!" while giving me the finger.

So much for union support. Did join a union later in life, but never had much confidence in them, despite being aware of the need of good unions.

I remember taking the last pay checks up to the unit at Fox Street. In each envelope was the traditional pink slip notifying them of their termination of employment. We all just sat in the office not even wanting to look at each other. The two Viet Nam vets who were part of the unit for the previous two years took it very bad. I remember when talking to NewRican after he was first hired asking how many times he had been shot at. Only a couple. He was in logistics and in charge of unloading supplies on the docks and seeing that they got to the appropriate field units. I use to tease him. First that I have been shot at in the South Bronx more than he had in Nam. Also taking the last course with Ralph at The New School the names of many of the early hominids were rattling around my mind. If he did something he shouldn't have I would called him an Australopithecine. One day I asked if he was related to a Neanderthal. He said I finally gave him a complement.

"Sorry to disappoint you, but that wasn't a complement either." We were close enough so he never took these little slights seriously.

The other vet was a black combat vet. Some of the action he was in included intense fighting. It took a while for him to adjust to civilian life. We would have long talks in the evenings working out his issues. He was very good with the kids and especially the gangs. Having seen a lot of action, he was encouraging them to go to college so if drafted at least try to get to ROTC pr OCS (Officer Candidate School). This just reinforced what I had been saying for years. We were a good team.

I remember when one of the very young Hispanic mothers was leaving the shelter, she came down to say goodbye to all of us. He gave her a kiss good bye. Just a peck on the lips. I had been talking for months with her about what would be best for her infant son, including suggesting playing classical music to him, as it would help him in school later. She came over to me and gave me a hug. I was fond of her and gave her a kiss on the lips too. The positive energy in the kiss took her breath away.

"A little tongue actions there!": is what I heard from the side.

"No tongue, was there?" was my response as I turned to the woman.

She just shook her head, still a little weak kneed from the kiss. I smiled.

When I handed this combat hardened vet his last check, he couldn't speak. I gave him a hug. The next day I got a phone call from one of the workers in the unit. He had gone home and shot himself in the head. As one of the kids at the PAL who had caught on to my morbid humor said:

"Well at least he doesn't have to look for another job."

That was perhaps the hardest day, and week in the Bronx. We lost a great individual. Others lost their jobs with little prospects for getting another in the near future. Tough times.

Love,
Papa

August 25, 2016

Hello T:

With the anticipated move to Delafield and having recently moved into my new apartment, I had to decide if I wanted to keep the apartment or reside in Delafield alone. The latter choice would not allow for any escape from Nim and the other caretakers. I had to keep the apartment. At this time Jean wanted to cut back on her job and go back to undergraduate work full time. She had helped me move in. She knew Kali cat and could take care of Kali if I was not around. Perfect solution, she was to sub-let the apartment.

I was to take care of Nim on Saturdays afternoons, alternative weekday evenings and Sunday Mornings. When I was allowed to escape, it was great having a place to go to. Usually at least one weekend a month there was no Nim duty. As long as Andrea, and Amy were in Delafield, I would have two nights in a row when they were taking care of Nim. So on some nights off, I went back to the apartment. This would change when Andrea left.

Kali cat was just as happy, if not happier than Jean to see me. Now Jean was certainly happy too as that meant a nice evening at home as a couple or a movie night out in Manhattan. All this worked out perfectly. By this time I had an old VW hatchback that mom had bought for me. Did make it up to The Hill a few times, but with work, Co-M, and Nim those visits were rare.

I do remember one time when Mom came down to Delafield to meet Nim. He took an immediate fancy to her. Nim always respected older adults. Mom with her gray hair and personality were just the type of person Nim loved to meet. This past weekend I was able to find the old Polaroid photo of her holding Nim in her arms.

It was shortly after mom's visit to Delafield that YSA was abolished as mentioned in a previous letter. In the month between the announcement and the laying off of all the workers, especially the younger workers. The last two week of YSA's existence were hard on all of us. Mrs. Bebek tried to help me find work, unsuccessfully. When another agency picked her up, I applied but was told:

"You can't do what you were doing you don't have your MSW."

So had to consider going back to graduate work as a MA in anthropology didn't work. In the meantime I tried to find work, still doing volunteer work at Lynch PAL. A private firm was coming in to help. They had a job opening. I applied.

I was interviewed at Lynch by their manager, a young black man who was trying to create this new social service private company. Of course all those at Lynch including the kids wanted me to get the job. The interviewer told me that they wanted a black, someone who the kids could identify with. I went downstairs and told Bill Rainey. He exploded! Running upstairs and letting out every word he never let the kids use. He pleaded for me to be hired. No luck. He came back down totally dejected. Still I was there every night not taking care of Nim until I left New York. Just another case of prejudice, black against white this time.

Love,
Papa

September 1, 2016

T:

Now came a time which your sister has experienced. Unemployment! Within a few days of being RIF'ed (Reduction in Force as government calls it) from YSA I applied for unemployment. What was interesting was the office was in one of the World Trade Center towers, 55th floor. After being accepted, every week I had to report down there in person, report all that had been done the previous week in terms of a job search. I did consider driving a cab again, but really wanted to continue working in the social work or related fields. The checks would cover rent and some expenses so with Jean helping out for the apartment I was doing alright, not great, but OK financially.

Of course most of my time was being spent with Nim on evenings and weekends. So the intensive look for a job was not quite as intensive as it may have been. Also it was about the same time I got an acceptance letter from Boston University. Funny it occurred about 2 weeks after I told Margaret B about being on a waiting list. As mentioned I'm sure she must have called them as the turn around was much faster than most waiting list students.

Attempts were made to keep my unemployment a secret from Herb Terrace so he would not ask me to take on extra work at Columbia with Nim. Besides the fact I was constantly in the South Bronx gave him the feeling I was still working. He just didn't know it was volunteer. It must have been a weekday likely while Columbia's normal routines were closed for finals or some other reason as Nim was home all day. Laura and the other volunteers were not around. I volunteered to take him for the whole day. One of the things we like to do was to ride around the yard in my old VW. When at Delafield Nim loved to sit in my lap and try to drive the old wreck. We got into the seat and I started the engine. But this day would be different. I buckled him into the seat belt.

Now Nim knew were were going somewhere and NOT to the college. When I drove the old VW to the Lynch PAL. No worry about that clunker being stolen. Doubt if they could have gotten more than $20 from the junk dealers. What was unique this time driving to the PAL was Nim was with me. Most of the kids knew of my work with Nim and had seen pictures. Now Nim was there in person. You have to realize Nim loved kids. And there were kids with black skin which he has seldom seen in Riverdale or Columbia. The kids were excited. Nim was excited. Even Bill was delighted. Nim had come for a visit.

Of all the kids that Nim took to the fastest was David B. Maybe Nim sensed a special attachment between myself and David. Maybe it was David's height and being thin. He was almost as tall as me. In any case Nim signed "up" with David who took him around the Center. All the kids were following us. At the basketball court, some kids were shooting hoops. Nim wanted to play with the ball. He didn't want to shoot it, just roll it around and try to bite it. Then came a game of catch, not the ball but each other. The kids would run with Nim chasing them. Then they would make a 180 and charge Nim. Nim would try to run away, at least as far as I or David would let him considering one of us had a hold of his lease at all times.

I was a little fearful of possible tantrum or biting, but nothing even came close. One time Nim opened his mouth in a play bite expression. That proved disastrous for one of the teachers. But when I told the kid just to match Nim's open mouth with his own. Everyone followed those instructions. When this happened even Nim would laugh. I wanted to get Nim back before dinner. I signed to him we had to go home. Nim must have hugged a dozen kids good-bye. But after a few hours with all the attention, he was getting tired. Waving good-bye we started off to the opposite side of the Bronx. A different country entirely, in appearance and socio-economic stratification.

We got home in plenty of time for the hand off to the evening volunteer. Likely Amy or Bill T. who had started working on some evenings. When I moved out in September Bill moved in as the male of the house. By that time all four of the initial Delafield residents had moved out sending Nim into a major fit of depression. This is seen in the rate of learning new signs. Andrea left first. No major drop. Laura and Amy left close together. A drop in learning can be seen. I was the last to leave for Boston. That was the beginning of a significant drop in learning new signs until I came back for the Christmas holidays.

The week before I left for Boston, the City Government called. They owed me almost half a year worth of annual leave. I had taken sick days for the operations, but only one annual leave day in all the years with YSA The asked if would I like to receive a lump sum check or proportioned out like regular pay. I chose the latter. That way I would be getting a pay check just as the unemployment ceased and just as I was starting grad school.

Love,
Papa

Sent from BALPEX September, 2016

Hi T–how about a little musical fun:

While dating Jean she and I discovered the PDQ Bach. I had heard selections on the radio and realized they were satirical variations on Classical music themes. I believe the first concert I attended was the 1974 concert at Avery Fisher Hall in Lincoln Center. Many of these were around the Christmas season, so they were perfect gifts to myself. But to understand what was so amusing is to get a picture of what a live performance was like.

Peter Schickele who '*discovered*' the works of PDQ Bach. According to the descriptions Schickele was a professor at the University of Southern North Dakota at Hoople. Of course the school doesn't exist. If you ever read the PDQ Bach book you will see photos of the campus, basically the same same old barn taken from different positions. PDQ was the 20th odd child of JS Bach 19 children. Love his dates as he died before he was born. What Schickele was doing was working on variations of the old Baroque and Classical modes of musical structure, taking them into different directions and turning the result into comical musical compositions.

The concerts usually started with the stage manager, a younger bearded blondish man, coming out just before the concert began and was always looking around. Most of the time he was looking for Professor Schickele. At each concert it was always a mystery how Peter Schickele would enter the auditorium. During one concert he swung in on a rope from the nearest balcony seats. He repeated that style of entry at Wolf Trap years later. At the time, your mother and I were sitting in the front row of the balcony. On the end was a man with a newspaper covering his face, with combat boots resting on the railing. Sure enough it was Schickele. Another year the stage manager was looking all around, suddenly a rope dropped down from the ceiling of Avery Fisher Hall. The spot light and everyone attention was focused on the source of the rope, upward. Then what few noticed was the stage was covered with a large brown paper covering. As everyone was looking up, the paper broke with Schickele also looking up at the rope as he and his piano came through the floor.

One year at another Avery Fisher Hall there were three characters running around that looked like Harpo, Chico and Grocho Marx. To add to the confusion those three there was a man in a gorilla costume running around. They would appear randomly during the concert, on stage, down the aisles, basically all over. Not only the music was great, but the side humor was just as much fun. Another concert Schickele was looking for the sheet music for the orchestra. None were to be found. He announced that 'someone', looking at the stage manager, placed the music by the intake vent of the HVAC system. So the music was somewhere in the ventilation system. Then during the first piece, sheets of music started to float down from various parts of the ceiling. There were hundreds of sheets. I got one, it was the score for the 'triangle.'

The last concert I attended in NYC Sheickele asked how many had been to a PDQ concert before, most raised their hands. Then how many attended 2. Still many hands up. How many had attended 5? I raised my hand, but one man stood up in the audience and started yelling out all the concerts he had attended. As he was shouting all the locations of concerts he had attended. Schickele signaled the stage manager over and whispered something into his ear. In a few moments two men in white coats carrying straight jackets appeared with a third carrying an oversized butterfly net. Schickele pointed to the man and all three started towards the man in the audience. He saw them coming and ran. For the rest of the concert, they would appear at different times. Sometimes they would grab his shirt, only for him to slip out. Then his pants. Same result. By the time the concert was over he appeared on stage in only his underwear with two the psychiatric attendants in the straight jackets and the third in his own net. Plus there was the music. Still love PDQ Bach, even after all these years.

Love
Papa

Chapter 20

BU challenges and relationships

Hi T:

Mom drove me up to BU. The graduate dorm was on Buswell Street, just two blocks from Beacon Street and the finish line for the Boston Marathon. It was a short walk to the BU campus, just across the Mass Turnpike bridge. The dorm was a converted brownstone which likely had two apartments on each floor. They were now converted into about 8 rooms per floor. The graduate residents had a choice of single or double rooms. My room was double on the second floor facing the street. There was a shared bathroom down the hall. Men and women shared the same dorm. Most of the women on the opposite side of the dorm sharing a different bathroom. A second graduate dorm was next door.

As I was moving in, after saying good-bye to mom, Tom M introduced himself as my roommate. He had moved in the day before. Tom was an interesting character. He was conservative but likable. Sharing the same first name as my undergraduate roommate at Rockford, in every other way he was different. He had completed his law degree and was attending BU Law School for his graduated tax law degree. Having dual residence in Colorado and NYC and had taken both Bar Exams. But didn't think he would be able to pass NY because it was recognized by many as the most difficult bar exam in the United States.

He decided to call me Bennie, rather than by my real name. Talkative when having something to share or say, but not overly so. We got along well. Unlike Tom F from Rockford, Tom M was very athletic. A Marathon runner having completed a couple while at Cornell. He was widely read, not limiting his interests to law alone. Qualities I liked. I might add he was easily embarrassed which was evident when one of the other graduate students came by with a copy of the soft core porn *Screw Magazine*. *Screw* was in competition with *Hustler*. They usually had a poster size center fold which was double the size of *Hustler* center spreads, four times larger than *Playboy*. The center fold was a life size girl legs spread as openly as possible, showing every bit of her shaved sex organ. Tom's reaction was:

"That's disgusting. There must be something wrong with that girl."

I took a look at the picture. "She looks normal to me."

131

I responded with a snicker coming from the owner of the magazine. Tom did make it clear if we were to have a female guest in the room, to use the old custom of placing a tie on outside of the door. If either of us saw a tie, we would simply retreat for at an hour.

After Tom's introduction he was off to the library as his classes had already started. Mine were to start the next day. Now was the time to unpack my boxes. As I was carrying one of my last boxes up to my room when a blond grad student came up and asked if she could hold the door open for me. This was gratefully received and I thanked her. She was very friendly, little overweight, lively and likable. She followed me up to the room. She watched me unpack and put everything away. She even helped me make my bed. She asked what I liked to do or play. I mentioned my love of backgammon.

"I would love to learn how to play backgammon."

I suggested she come back in an hour and I would teach her. She excused herself to her 4th floor room.

An hour later she came down for me to teach her the game. I broke out my leather board and pieces. As I started to set up the pieces. She asked if I would like to see pictures of her family. Wanting to be polite, I nodded. She pulled out a photo album with pictures of her parents who were:

"*Happily* married. This is my brother hand his wife. They are *happily* married. Here are my cousins and their spouses. They are all *happily* married!"

It was evident she had no interest in playing backgammon. After 30 minutes, I said I had to check in with the college about my classes and excused myself. Later I found out she was pursuing a M.A. in education. But what she really wanted was her MRS degree. Her father sent her to BU to find a mate, he didn't approve of his Brooklyn daughter being past the age of 25 not being married. Not finding a husband while an undergraduate this was her second chance.

Love,
Papa

September vacation 7, 2016

Hi T:

Remember the girl who's family were all "Happily Married?" Later I learned she had pulled the same routine with Tom and half the men in the dorm. Tom and I felt sorry for her. We agreed she was just too desperate. We talked about her and her efforts to hook up. Yet to all the men in the dorm she was a pariah. It was her last semester having spent all of the previous year in the dorm. She never hooked up, graduating in December, but with the wrong "M" degree. I might add none of the men even had sex with her. No one dared!

The next day there was a girl who was also outgoing. Jane tall, glasses, and appeared to be a very talented pianist. She was going after an MA piano performance. BU was one of the hardest music departments to get into for a graduate degree so it verified her abilities on the keyboard. I would soon learn she was a wonderful pianist. We met in the TV room just to the right as you entered the dorm. I started talk about my love of music but not having any training in it. She was telling me that she had accompanied a major violist during his tour that summer.

Jane was from SW Virginia. Her father was a dentist. She was fluent in Russian and with her talent on the piano the CIA had expressed an interest in her as an operative. She turned them down, though I think deep inside she would have been a very good spy. I asked her out. It was the start of a wonderful relationship.

The Music and Social Work graduate departments were near the Charles River but in opposite directions, a long way from the dorm. When I was finished I would go to the library where Jane would meet me after practice for dinner. I would often study at the BU Library because your could rent headphones and listen to their extensive music collection. Studying for hours listening to classical music was wonderful. This actually help expand my knowledge of composers and their music.

I started to play a game with Jane. I would put the least popular musical compositions on, especially 20th Century composers. Time and time again when Jane showed up, I would ask her if she knew the piece being listened to. She guessed it every time. Over the next year there must have been a hundred pieces I attempted to stump her with. I failed each time. She had phonographic ears! Even the most remote pieces she knew.

One afternoon we returned to the dorm. I was putting away my books when she heard Tom coming in the front door.

"Lets scare Tom" she suggested.

"How?" I asked.

"Come over here in bed with me. You can get on top and pretend we are really going at it when he comes in."

We covered our fully dressed selves. I was on top of Jane, kissing her passionately while pretended to be going at it in full force. Tom came in.

"Oh Jesus. Oh Shit. Oh God." all came out of his mouth instantly.

He quickly ducked out the door.

"Bennie–There is no tie on the g.d. door!"

Jane and I jumped up and pulled open the door. He looked and realized it had been a joke. There was no way we could have dressed so quickly. His face was red as could be. Jane and I were in hysterics. Later when he cooled down he had to admit we really pulled a good one on him. It was a good laugh all around. But it also shows you how easy it was to get Tom embarrassed. After depositing his books and helping carrying Jane's upstairs, we all went to the graduate dining room, back over at the main campus.

I might add, upon leaving the smaller dining room one evening, I stepped out the door and right on the back of a rat that was crossing the doorstep. I looked down when it squealed. Raising my foot he ran off, followed by two more, one of which almost ran over that same foot. Made you feel good about the cleanliness of the kitchen where the food was prepared.

Love,
Papa

Not sent

Jane and I were really beginning to develop a serious relationship after a few weeks of dating. She telephoned her mother asking for a renewal of her birth control prescription. Her mother didn't approved, but knowing Jane was already sexually active sent it.

Jane wanted to have sex with me after just a few dates. For the first few times we had sex, it was usually taking turns orally or 69. She desired to have me inside her. But it was uncomfortable. It was as if she had a huge hang up about normal intercourse. She enjoyed it, but never got really excited. I wanted to please her. I took time with foreplay and willingly went down on her as long as she liked. But no matter how much I tried, she always fell short of a strong organism. Little ones yes. <u>Big one</u> NO! Penetration failed to get her off even after prolonged oral stimulation.

One evening I asked if there was something bothering her. After all I was training to be a social worker and wanted to help if at all possible. She opened up. Jane had been having sex since high school. Some of which was satisfying. But the previous summer she wanted a special job. She learned one of the teachers at the Juilliard School of Music in NYC was looking for a pianist accompanist for his summer tour. He had just been named the violist teacher of the year and was going to do a nation wide tour. He needed a pianist.

It appeared he couldn't get anyone at Juilliard to accompany him for what would become obvious reasons. Jane applied for the position. She was interviewed and performed for Dr. D. He asked her back for a second interview at his apartment. This time it was to be a horizontal interview. The condition for the job was sex. Jane really wanted the job. It would look great on any resume and would be fantastic experience. She just accepted that putting out physically was just part of the job for most female pianists in the 1970's. She said he fucked the hell out of her, but didn't know an additional requirement would follow. She got the job.

Then as they began to tour he was not happy with normal sex. Jane going down on him wasn't enough either. He had to have anal. He didn't like using a condom, and didn't want her to get pregnant. So for the remainder of the summer he fucked her in the ass several times a week during the tour. It was rarely with any foreplay or even a lube. Being painful and exceptionally displeasurable by the end of the summer she was no longer turned on by any kind of sex.

Now that she was going with me, she wanted to find a way to enjoy it again. We tried talking it out for a week or more. It released some of the tension. Yet full enjoyment was still not coming through.

One day Jane accompanied me to tour the Grand Lodge of Massachusetts on Tremont Street downtown. She knew I was involved in Co-M and loved Masonry. We both enjoyed the tour. On the way back to the dorm we walked past what was then the Red Light section of Boston.

This was a time when the red light district was clean, well kept and not at all slimy, unlike 42nd Street in NYC. She had never been exposed to hard core porn before and was looking in all the window displays. We went into one of the store. She picked up some of the magazines taking careful look at the huge erections and penetration shots. She saw the variety of dildos for the first time. All these visual sights made her giggle. I could tell she was getting a little excited.

We started back toward the subway station. A block before we the station there was a X-Rated movie theater. I asked her if she wanted to see a hard core movie. She giggled, squeezed my hand but enthusiastically nodded yes. She almost dragged me to the box office where we purchased our tickets. We went in. Sitting in a back corner so as not be to become obvious to the other patrons, mostly men. There were two other couples both on opposite sides of the theater by themselves. It was obvious that they were enjoying themselves kissing, then manually and sometimes orally as their heads disappeared or would be bobbing up and down. We were in the back and separated all the other viewers, with about three rows between us and the nearest other patrons.

As with most porn, it didn't really matter if the film had started or not. In our case, it was already about 20 minutes into the first of a double feature. As we started to focus on the movie Jane was getting excited. Her attention was really focused on the screen. I held her hand. She had never seen an erect penis on a movie screen. And the erections being shown on the screens were of the major porn stars at the time. Most of the cocks were at least 8 inches, many 10 inches plus. The girls were mostly large breasted and appeared to be very wet prior to any penetration. Of course the actor going down on the women helped. It was fun seeing what actually happened with a man went down on a woman. This was visibly something very new to Jane. She had experienced it but never had seen it done before. I had done it to her but a woman can't see herself as someone is going down on her. The visions of cunnilingus on the movie screen was exciting and stimulating.

As the scenes began to show action, she was twitching in her seat. Seeing the huge erection of the actor was exciting for her. She had seen only a few cocks, and had admitted mine was the biggest she had seen. Yet my erection is only slightly above average at the time. Here was some of the great stars of the 1970's porn movies, rarely short of eight inches when fully erect. When the first penetration occurred in the movie Jane squeezed my hand. When a man went down on one of the women, she moved my hand to her crotch. I stroked it gently through her panties. They were getting wet. Then one of the men withdrew and ejaculated all over the woman's breasts. Jane had a spasms. Little shivers ran through her body. She began to twitch and do little jerks upward to meet my hand every time a man on the screen shot a load anywhere on or in his partner.

Soon she was having full blown climaxes every time a man came on the screen. She loved seeing the thick globules of sperm coming out of the penises. We stayed for the whole movie and part of the next. Her panties were soaked. She loved every action scene. Every money shot (when an ejaculation is shown) she would have another mini organism. I tried to kiss her, but she wanted all her attention on the screen. I did get her to stroke my erection, which had been taken out of my pants. This just excited her all the more. Now when an ejaculation occurred on the screen, the pressure of her squeezing my cock was painful. After all a pianist, especially a classical pianist had STRONG hands.

After being in the theater more than two hours, she couldn't take it any longer. Not wanting to watch the movies any more she said she wanted my cock in her. We took the subway back to the dorm. She led me directly to her room and almost tore off my clothes. We did everything you can imagine, except anal. She had one massive organism after another. Thank goodness for youth. I must have cum at least twice, maybe more. Hang ups and any inhibitions were totally gone. From that point on, we had a fantastic sex life.

A short time after this one afternoon one of the grad students from Hawaii gave her a persimmon. She took one bite. Jane said it tasted like my sperm. What was funny she said it right in front of him. He turned red, but liked the response. I called her cinnamon as she has a slight taste of it when she got excited and where juices flowed all over my tongue. From that point on we gave each other nick names for our personal juices.

Soon those words were as good as foreplay when spoken, usually with a giggle no one else understood. What was funny any time she wanted to perform oral she would say 'persimmon.' If I said 'cinnamon' in response it was all we could do to race back to the dorm and have a wonderful session of 69. She really loved the taste and swallowed every drop. So did I. I must admit it was some of the greatest sex I ever had. After the first round, she had not hesitation on going down on me after I had cum in her, to try to get me erect again. Then sometime she liked it back in her pussy. Sometimes she shifted back into a 69 position.

Jean back in NYC may have been a nympho and great in bed. She would pass out from having too many organism. Sometimes when I had yet to come. It was almost like fucking a passed out drunk. Fun yes, but not really great. Also Jean's breasts were small and saggy. Not exciting and surprising not as sensitive as would be expected. Not the same with Jane. Jane was enthusiastic and willing to do anything. She had classic ice cream cone breasts, large and pointing straight out. Not large nipples but sensitive. She also like being tit fucked like Carol which would allow me to cum in her mouth. Unlike many women, she loved to swallow it.

I didn't impose anal on her due to her prior experiences. We would fuck almost all night on Fridays or Saturdays and in as many positions as possible, usually in her single room. The other advantage to her room was it was right next to the bathroom. More than once we quickly ran into the bathroom to take a shower after sex. Of course cleaning ourselves would only get us excited again, which would lead to more sex. More than once we fell asleep with her hand on my flaccid, diminished penis. Great times for sex. After all this was graduate school. No more inexperienced sexual encounters, but fully mature sexually active adults who loved it.

September vacation 8, 2016

Hello Again:

There were an interesting collection on other graduate students in the dorm. A former Green Beret roomed with an oboe musician directly downstairs from my room. Can't remember his name but he was an interesting character. When discussing the war he would tell of narrow escapes and a lot of hand to hand combat he experienced. One of his missions was considered top secret. He and a platoon of other soldiers were parachuted into south China at the beginning of the Ho Chi Minh trail. This was the supply route by which the Chinese supplied the North Viet Nam troops with weapons and food. They carried nothing but their weapons and explosives. The assignment was to blow up as many bridges over the various rivers as they ran back to South Viet Nam. Of course this would take them through parts of Cambodia as well as North Viet Nam before the trail ended in the South.

They lived totally off the land. This was to eat and drink what they could find. This included insects, plants, and any animal they could catch. They did not want to use their guns as it would lead to them being discovered. If one was injured or killed, they were told to dispose of any recognizable identifying marks. Luckily they all made it back. That alone was remarkable. Every time they blew up a bridge, the Viet Cong (the term for the North Viet Nam supported troops we were fighting) would be after them. It was those days they would be running for 24 hours without stopping or until they lost their pursuers.

Every now and again, this vet would wake up screaming. I asked him if it was a result of the unofficial mission on the Ho Chi Minh trail. He said: 'No.' One day he finally told me the nightmare that he couldn't shake. His platoon was in close combat with Viet Cong, He told me a kid about 13 or 14 years old came at him with a rifle. At the time he had a Browning Automatic rifle, which was a powerful weapon. He shot the kid in the stomach. It blew a hole right through his mid section. But the kid wasn't dead. He kept trying to get up and continue the charge. Our Green Beret yelled:

"You're dead, you're dead! Don't you know it."

It was the vision of the kid with a hole through his midsection trying to get up to kill him that was the reoccurring nightmare he couldn't shake. He said for some reason the nightmare came back often after making love to a woman, thereby scaring her half to death when in the middle of the night he would start screaming. Not good for trying to form a relationship.

This vet's roommate was also interesting. Kirk was an oboe player. He was considered to be a gifted oboist. It being a small instrument, he would often practice in the dorm. Yes he was a very good. But there was one problem with his style. When he took a breath he had a very loud inhaling sound that distracted you from the actual music begin played. I could never seeing him making it in a major orchestra for that reason.

It was also funny when he would bring back a women into his room at night. He had an attraction towards the undergraduate girls. He liked them young as possible. If they were blond and stacked, they fit his ideal. Still there were times when various other would be brought back who were brunette or red headed. Never saw a female graduate student. Being both a musician and fairly good looking he was able to bring back many girls to the dorm. I don't remember ever seeing the same girl twice.

During the love making sessions, from my room above, one could hear his moans and grunts as he approached his climax. Then when he actually came, he would let out a loud scream / grunt that could be heard over most of the first floor of the dorm and part of the second. This included the TV room.

As he was about to graduate, his ideal of finding a job in an orchestra had been crushed. He ended up as a high school music teacher. Don't know where, but hoped he learned not to take on the high school girls who would be considered jail bate.

Love,
Papa

Philadelphia Oct. 1, 2016

Hi T:

I soon got busy with classes. The most important year long class was a general developmental psychology class taught by Debbie M. She was a middle aged social worker who had given up private practice to teach at BU. Entertaining and lively she kept even the most boring subject interesting. The week that was most memorable was the weeks on sex.

The first day of sessions on sexuality Debbie admitted it got her horny every time she discussed the subject. She said her husband always knew what week it was because she would almost strip off his clothes as he came into the house. She would suck him to an erection and fuck the hell out of him on the living room sofa, table, bed, anywhere as long as he was screwing her. This was repeated each day of the week that sex ed classes were held. It was a pleasant surprise for him as she never told him which week was sex ed week. He knew it was in the spring time but never exactly which week. This made the episodes all the more exciting to him. Debby felt her husband loved that annual session as much as she did. All this she admitted, in class!

One afternoon the class met in a large auditorium during the sex ed week. Debbie noted there were more students in the showing than in the whole school of social work. Looking around there were students I had never seen before. Some from the medical school, some psychology majors, but a lot others. It was a special film shown in one of the auditoriums along with other Masters and Johnson movies about the physiology of sex. One film was on the female organism filmed from inside. It showed the tenting effect during organism and how it pulled the deposited sperm into the tubes where fertilization was most likely.

The special film was called *The Frogs*. It was an animated film of two bean bag frogs having every kind of sex you can imagine. Missionary, side, rear entry, standing, sitting, and almost every other position you could imagine placing the frogs in was shown. The female would suck him to organism, as seen not by the fluid but by her bulging cheeks and a large gulping motion was shown not by the fluid but by her bulging cheeks and a large gulping motion plus the drops dripping out of her mouth.

He would go down on her, until her juices were all over his face, which he would clean with a typical long frog tongue, wiping all her secretions off and drinking them with a wonderfully excited expression on his face along with a rolling of his eyes. It was a classic beanbag porn movie, but at the same time very information as to how to satisfy each other.

The whole audience was laughing. It was a great short film, about 15 minutes long. Looking around you could tell who in the audience were likely undergraduates, as many of the younger girls were turning red as some of the scenes on the screen. More so with *The Frogs* film than any other. I have tried but have been unable to find. This was all part of the sex education week. Certainly one of the most enjoyable weeks in grad school.

Back in class Debbie would hint at her very active sex life prior to marriage. She described the races in terms of the male members.

"Blacks you see what you'll get. The only difference is whether it is hanging down or sticking out. There is no way around it Asians are small. I prefer white men. Their cocks are like Jack in the Box. You can never tell what will pop out. It might be small or it could surprise you and be huge. I like to be surprised. That's why I married a white man."

It was an interesting lecture. Not sure if it would be acceptable with the extreme political correctness which hates to discuss anything racial now. Even if it is reporting basic facts.

About half way through the semester my roommate Tom M got notice he passed The Bar in Colorado. This was great news as it would assure him of a job upon graduation. But he was really waiting to hear from New York. About three weeks later he got the letter he didn't expect, but hoped for. He pass the NY Bar Exam, the first try! Now he had to make a decision. Was he to be a NY lawyer and work for the big firms, or go back to Denver where there was less pressure and a nicer natural environment, perfect for running and getting in shape.

"What the hell am I to do Bennie? I have promised jobs in New York and Denver if I passed. Now I have in both. I just don't know what to do."

When he did make up his mind, it shocked the whole dorm.

I might add there were about 5 other graduate law students in the dorm. All men. No women. One rooming with another musician. Then there were two others on an upper floor rooming together. The tall thin one was from NYC but born with a silver spoon in his mouth. The other shorting and pudgy. But the latter was the more intelligent and would soon be writing for the law journal. Both were snobs. More on them in the next letter and when we move to the next year as they were there for two years like myself, while Tom was finishing his second year.

Love,
Papa

November 18, 2016

Hi T:

One of the most important credits needed for an MSW is the internships. During the first year, it was a two day a week placement. The second year it would be three days a week. Not knowing what was available my advisor placed me with the South End Settlement house which was on the Boston South End / Roxbury border. It was a neighborhood that reminded me of the South

Bronx. Not Ft. Apache as it didn't have the burned out wreaks of former buildings, but it was anything but a desirable neighborhood.

My supervisor was named Tamara. She had graduated from the BU School of Social Work a few years before and was happy to be in a position of becoming a mentor of graduate student. She was a nice person approximately my age. In our opening interview she asked me about my experience. I told her about my work in Harlem as a case worker and then as a group worker in Ft. Apache. I told her about the intergenerational effort which was a city wide experimental program. During the discussion she asked me what was my salary when I left New York. When I told her she admitted she was making less that what I was in S. Bronx. This disturbed her, more than I realized. But it would not manifest it until after the school year.

Since South End Settlement was both a day care center and a senior citizens center, this would be an ideal place to try something new. We brained stormed some ideas. Speaking to the day care staff their most challenging problem was what to do during nap time when the hyper active children just didn't want to take a nap. After some discussion it was decided to create a program where the elderly could help with the hyper active pre-schoolers.

This would work perfectly into the schedule of the Settlement House. The senior citizens' lunch was from 11 a.m. to noon. The pre-schoolers nap time was around 12:15 and usually lasted an hour. It was decided to get some senior volunteers to set aside time after their lunch to read and do activities with those half dozen hyper active kids. The children would be taken out of the general child care area into the lunch room area, after the tables were cleaned. There there would be a one on one activity, a child with a senior. Most seniors would be reading to the child. Others might be using coloring books or other on hands activities with the pre-schoolers.

After getting about half a dozen older women from the senior citizens to volunteer the program started. Tamara and I would have weekly reviews to look at the comments from the day care staff and my interviews with the senior volunteers. It was working wonderfully. The biggest problem occurred when the day care workers complained about one of the volunteers who couldn't control her bladder during the session with the child. This was NOT a good example when these children where going through toilet training. Tamara told me I had to bring it up with the volunteer.

When I did, she felt very uncomfortable talking to a man about the problem. As the creator of the program it was explained I had to discuss it with her. We discussed her wearing an adult diaper. It was a difficult conversation, but necessary. Tamara insisted I had to have it with her. I didn't want to loose her as she was benefiting as much as her child.

Admittedly there were some interesting interactions with some of the other staff in the Settlement House. Tarmara's boss was a black woman who I had very little interaction with. There was a white receptionist, likely in her 40's. One morning I said "Good morning." She smiled at me. "You know Walter, you look great. I would love to tear off your shirt and pants so I could jump on you."

I turned to her with a smile: "I don't look as great as you think, but thanks for the complement."

Nothing every happened. There was another young woman who did work part-time. Never was sure what her job was as she was part of the day care staff. She was about 5'4" a little overweight, and VERY well endowed. She also was giving me the eye more than once. But I rarely paid any attention. Should have kept it that way. That is something to come up latter.

Love,
Papa

November 20, 2016

Hi T casework time:

After Christmas break Tamara said she felt I needed some one-on-one case work. Counseling is a key element in social work. I'm sure the school encouraged this. She suggested I get to know three men and see if they needed help with any issues. One was a gentleman who came for the senior citizens $0.50 lunch each day, but never interacted with any of the others. The others were a pair of shut ins; men who seldom left their apartments due to mobility or mental issues. You couldn't have had three more different types of individuals if you tried. I will tell you about the one which was in the Center almost daily. The other two will be in the next letter.

The senior I was asked to get to know was John. He was in his mid to late 70's, tall, thin and appeared to be an extreme introvert as he never interacted with the other seniors. He would come in at 11:30 pay $0.50 for the senior citizen's lunch and then leave. When eating he usually sat alone and never conversed with any of the other seniors. After one lunch I asked him if he had some extra time to talk. Being introduced as a social worker intern, he agreed. We sat in a little lounge near the offices. After a couple of after lunch conversations, it was evident first impressions were all wrong.

His daily routine was to get up at 10:30, shower and dress, come to the lunch and then leave. The reason he didn't talk to any of the other seniors was he felt they were beneath him. He was a retired lawyer, well educated and quite an intellectual. Had been married at least three times and had 17 children, or so he said. All his extra funds when to alimony and support to those children still under 18. His youngest was under 10. One afternoon when leaving the lunch, one of the characters across the street decided he was an easy target. He tried to rob him, but John ran into the traffic. Then running between the cars and putting on some speed, he out ran the would be mugger who was likely under 35. Just shows he was in good shape.

What the rest of his normal day proved more interesting. After the senior's lunch he would jog down to his private club on the bay. This was about a 2+ mile jog. There he would catch up with the other upper class lawyers, judges, and investment brokers, often playing cards and read the periodicals in the reading room. During winter, he was a member of the Polar Bears, and would join the plunge into the Boston Bay in sub freezing weather. If not doing the polar splash, he would swim about 20 laps in the Club's pool, shower and get dressed for the evenings. He loved to go to college theater productions or if there was a special show in the theater district he was go to that show.

Remember this was during the 1970's. Many of the popular plays would have a scene with nudity thanks to *Hair*. He asked me if it was normal for someone his age to get an erection watching these naked young women on stage. My response was it shows he is still alive and normal man. It was then I found out the rest of a typical day. Dinner as a nice restaurant, if not attending a theater production he would then go to a dance club. He loved to dance. These were not the senior dance clubs but modern rock clubs with lots of young women. He loved the clubs near Harvard and MIT.

"You know Walter, the young women are surprised how well I move on the dance floor. About 3 times a week they are curious if I have equally good moves in the bedroom. So I'm getting laid several times a week."

Then he returned home and to bed around 3 a.m. That is if he did not spend the night in a young woman's apartment. Depending on where he was during the night he would rise just in time for the senior lunch, his only money saving endeavor. This was his typical daily routine. It was evident he was a modern day Don Juan! When I was asked about my assessment of John by Tmara my response was:

"A woman may not agree, but he is living a man's dream life. There is nothing wrong with, but don't share his routine with the other women social workers, I don't think they would agree."

Tarmara when told the details agreed, with a big smile on her face.

Love,
Papa

Nov. 29, 2016

Case work with shut-ins:

Case work on 2 senior shut-ins was totally different from my discussions with John. These two gentlemen were in small apartments. There was one senior black councilor who visited them. He introduced me to both. Appointments were made for me to do individual visits. Tamara wanted me to work up a psycho-social assessment on both.

The first shut in was a short little elderly man. He had trouble walking up and down stairs. He remained in a wheel chair most of the time. His apartment was his solitary refuse. The senior's meals on wheels was his single meal for the day. Since he was under 5' and likely less than 100 pounds, but physically strong above the waist. He was a former Sargent from WWII. He may have joined the Army before the war as indicated he rose through the ranks during the war early. He loved to talk. Likely because he had no relatives nor friends he could converse with. His favorite subject was his war experience.

He saw action in Europe. Not sure if he was involved in the Battle of the Bulge but he did see a lot of combat in France and Germany. He got a Purple Heart for a non-life threatening injury, he once showed me some of his metals, there may have been a Bronze Star, but I'm no longer sure. Your grandmother certainly had an equal number of metals which we had framed.

But what he liked to talk about was one particular USO show that came to entertain the troops. It was likely early Spring 1945 as the war was winding down after the Bulge. May West was the female star of the show. She was the great star of the 1930's and 1940's. She was arrested for obscenity when a show opened on Broadway which she wrote, directed and starred in. The obscenity was the title of the show: *SEX*. She had many quotes including: "Come up and see me sometime." Another: "I speak two languages, English and Body." May was not very tall, but with her high heels she always appeared taller than she actually was. During the USO show, she spotted this little Sargent in the first row. He was invited up on stage.

She gave him a big hug. Being shorter that May in heels, his face was smothered between her breasts. He loved telling me that he would have been willing to die right there suffocated by some of the biggest breasts in Hollywood. I can assure this was a story often repeated when I visited him. After multiple visits I felt this was the highlight of his life. He had been married, but the former wife was long gone and no children were mentioned. It is rather sad that this one event was the only happy memory in his life.

The other man I was assigned to was an extreme introvert. He had a lovely apartment with a nice window looking out to one of the better streets in the South End. Up until a few weeks before, there had been no radio or TV. He seldom read. All day long he would stare out the window.

The only person he every talked was the other councilor who would visit 3 times a week. It was the councilor who convinced him to purchase a TV. The man had plenty of money in the bank. According to the councilor his bank statement was well over $100,000. He never want to spend his savings! The meals on wheels program fed him. If he wanted something from the store he would venture out, but seldom. Then he only bought what he wanted which never exceeded $10. Not newspapers, no magazines, no communication with anyone. Never married. No family. He was totally alone.

It was hard to get him to talk. His speech was slow and difficult to follow at times. When I visited him I asked him why he didn't watch TV when I came in. He told me he didn't know how to turn on a TV. I told the black councilor that he needed help to learn how to turn on the TV and change the channels. This was towards the end of my internship. I didn't find out if he ever learned how to operate it.

There was one visit which had a significantly impact on me. I wanted to start a normal conversation. I asked his if there was anyone he liked in history or currently. He said he loved Joseph McCarthy. This is the McCarthy of the House Un-American Activities Committee and the leading force behind the Black Listing of the 1950's. This response surprised me. I was shocked and disgusted! It was almost impossible to control my emotional response.

The only thing I said was: "He committed suicide didn't he?"

Actually McCarthy drank himself to death after Edward R. Morrow took him down. I told Tmara, this was perhaps the first time in my life, my negative emotional reaction came out. She understood said I would learn to gain control with practice. Not sure! Event now if I see something in politics I don't like, I speak up. Did it in Toastmasters and may have cost me a contest win.

Love,
Papa

Dec. 1, 2016

Hi T–follow up on grandma:

We left your grandmother in LA caring for her sister Sug. When Sug graduated from high school, she wanted to go back to Texas. It was shortly thereafter she met and married a man down there and in no time gave birth to Nikki, her oldest child. Mom would still stay in touch but Sug was largely out of her life.

In the mean time you likely remember Hollywood party totally turned her off the acting and actors. She knew there was something out there more than what was in her life. After the negative experiences she started exploring different churches and other spiritual schools. She soon rejected the normal churches. Some where in her travels around LA she heard about Manly P. Hall lectures. Manly P. Hall was one of the most prolific esoteric authors of the last century. He was a Mason and author of a large number of books. His most famous was <u>The Secret Teachings of All Ages</u>. I have read a number of his books, as a Mason I know says: 'you have to take what he says with a cup of salt.' Many of his theories just do not hold up, but raise a lot of questions and issues.

Mom started attending M.P. Hall's lectures regularly. She soon was reading his books, but also other esoteric authors as well. Now here is where the details must be speculated as we never discussed much past the Hollywood party.

It was about this time she met, possibly at the lectures, Bernard Morrow. Bernard was an interesting. Bernard had been studying a host of esoteric teachings. They started dating. He taught her photography, philosophy, and meditation. She also learned the basic secretarial skills of typing and shorthand. Her exposure to a form of esoteric Christianity was a philosophy she could accept. Bernard gave her some of his books to read including those complied by Alice A. Bailey. I mentioned her in the previous book. Here is a brief review and some additional information.

Alice had been a member of the Theosophical Society (TS). There had been a number of TS groups in the 1800's but the dominate one was the he TS founded by Helena Petrovna Blavatsky (HPB), a Colonel Henry Steel Olcott, and William Judge. They brought a mix of Eastern and esoteric philosophy with modern science to the Western world. HPB claimed to have been in contact with a disincarnate spirit referred to as 'The Tibetan.' He had given HPB a lot of the materials found in her books, especially <u>Isis Unveiled</u> and <u>The Secret Doctrine</u>.

After HPB's death and some struggles, Annie Besant became the TS's President. There were many famous members, including the artist Wassily Kandinsky (who you know well from the painting in your room), Nicholas Roerich, the composer Alexander Scriabin, C.W. Leadbeater and the young Indian boy Krishnamurti who was promoted as the possible as next great incarnation of Maitreya (another variation of the Christ incarnate). Not all remained in the TS but it shows the great influence. From HPB's death through the first half of the 20th Century many were attracted to its philosophy. Alice Bailey was a member.

Alice was approached by The Tibetan to continue the dictations. When Alice informed Annie, the latter became jealous and demanded Alice to reject the responsibility. Annie insisted since she was the head of the TS. It should be she taking the next series of dictations. Of course that kind of ego would never be approached by one of The Masters. The Tibetan continue to approach Alice. Finally Alice separated herself from the TS and formed The Arcane School in the LA area. Bernard was trying to help Alice and her husband Foster develop this new esoteric school which was incorporated under the name The Lucis Trust in 1922.

Grandma became fascinated by the Alice and her books. She also became more attached to Bernard. Soon they were married. She once hinted that he was great in bed.

When Alice was told to move the Lucis Trust to NYC. Bernard and Louise followed. Thus ended her life in California. New York was to become her new home. So grandma became Mrs. Bernard Morrow and moved to a small apartment in NYC. She became one of Alice's secretaries. This began a new phase in her life. One that continues to influence your father and many of the directions I have taken over the years.

Love,
Papa

Dec. 3, 2016

Dorm experience

Need to fill you in on some of the other graduate students in the graduate dorm. We had another musician by the name of Kirk downstairs. His roommate was another law student who was occasionally referred to as Jim the virgin. It was an appropriate title as he was a virgin at the age of 24 and had never seen a naked woman, except in pictures. More on him later.

There were two other graduate law students who roomed together on one of the other floors. Their names were Richard and Lewis (I think). Both from NYC and both from upper class families. As mentioned before Richard was born with the proverbial silver spoon in his mouth. He was rich, his family was rich, all those without money were beneath him. As for his roommate, Lewis was the more intelligent, but also a bit of a Jewish snob. The second year he did make the BU Law Review, so he must have had some talent. Those two were constantly together for both years I was there.

There were a number of women, mostly education majors. Then there was Ann G who was a business major but also an exceptional artist. Some of her paintings were in her room. They were so close to Edward Hopper's style and technique it would have been hard to tell them apart. It was later I learned she was interested in esoteric philosophy. Part of it came from her background in the Armenian Apostolic Catholic Church which she grew up in.

There were at least two additional music majors in the dorm. Had very little contact with them, except through Jane as they spent most of their time in the practice studios on the main campus. One was a pianist who would come into the picture in the second year in the dorm.

One of the things that upset me was Richard's constant putting down of those not in professional degree programs or from any lower class. As graduate students, we often ate in the smaller graduate cafeteria. I remember one evening I was describing how I observed a very expensive car stopping across the street from the Settlement House. A exceptionally well dressed man got out with two others carrying a briefcase. They all went into the pool hall. A few minutes later they came out with a different briefcase, got into the double parked car and drove off. I told Jane and the others at our table I suspected there was drug sale. Richard overheard:

"Well you of course reported it to the police?"

I turned to Richard: "Report what? That a man went into the pool hall carrying one briefcase and came out with a different one. I have no idea what was in them. What can I report. There was nothing illegal about their activities that I could tell. It is only my speculation that a drug deal was going on. I'm certainly not going to report that to the police. Besides I have to work down there. Wouldn't be good for me if I did report something like that."

Everyone agreed with me and told Richard as a law student he should have come to the same conclusion. Even Louis his friend had to agree I was right. This just made Richard mad. He didn't speak to me for a couple of days after. Glad to be relieved of his patronizing ways for a while.

Another occasion I had worn a beautify green shirt that resembled silk. It wasn't but it looked like it. Richard noticed it that evening in the dining room.

"Is that silk? It looks like it. I didn't expect a social work student to be wearing such a nice shirt."

"No Richard it is not silk" I responded, "but thanks for the complement. I don't think it would be appropriate for me to wear silk when working with the poor in the South End."

Richard just turned away and didn't say anything else. Of course you can tell I was getting tired of Richard's snobbish attitude. But my favorite revenge for his ways would come a few week later in the graduate dorm TV room. But you will have to wait for the next letter to find out what happen.

Love,
Papa

Dec. 5, 2016

HAPPY BIRTHDAY -as this will likely be delivered close!

But you can't wait to hear about the next run in with Richard the snobbish law student. It happened one evening when the TV room was crowded. Everyone wanted to watch *The Muppets Show*. Jane was sitting on my lap. The sofa had 4 to 6 sitting on it. Richard was in one chair by himself. The Show's guest for the evening was Edgar Bergen. Edgar Bergen and Charlie McCarthy were two of the most famous characters in the 1930's though the early 1950's. Edgar was a ventriloquist. Charlie was his puppet. They were a great act.

Charlie was a wise cracking, slightly insulting puppet, opposite Edgar who was the calm soft spoken gentleman. Perfect opposites. It was as if Charlie was the alter ego to his handler. Just as famous guests wanted to be on the Muppet Show in the 1970's ever star in Hollywood wanted to be on the Edgar Bergen and Charlie McCarthy show some 30 years earlier. I remember the sexy bomb shell Mae West on their program once. The sexual endow-endows between Mae and Charlie were flying fast and furiously. After a series of exchanges Mae said to Charlie:

"Be careful little wooden boy or I'll turn into a Pinochlio."

That just floored Edgar and for the only time in their career Charlie didn't have a come back.

Well on this evening, Edgar and Charlie were performing on *The Muppet Show* as the guest stars. Edgar must have been in his late 70's by then. During one of the ads Richard started making fun of Edgar.

"Look did you see that old fool. You can see his mouth and lips move. This has to be one of the worse guest ever. Who would every want to see this idiot."

I turned to Richard:

"Richard, if it was not for Edgar Bergen and Charlie McCarthy there wouldn't be a *Muppet Show*. They were the ground breaking puppet act. Their show was the top comedy shows for over ten years. Every week millions of Americans would tune into the Edgar Bergen and Charlie McCarthy Show. If it was not for them there would have been no puppets on TV or anywhere else. They made puppetry popular!"

Richard: "Well I don't see how anyone would have wanted to watch their show. He is not even a good ventriloquist" was his response.

"Well Richard, it may be because the Edgar Bergen and Charlie McCarthy Show as on the radio and no one cared if Edgar's lips moved."

The whole room bust into laughter. A couple turned to Richard:

"Walter sure put you in your place."

Richard just sank deeper into his chair and didn't say another word. Jane still on my lap was laughing so hard she had to burry her face in my shoulder. Tom later congratulated me in putting that snob in his place. It was then Richard realized, though not a law student, I was smarter and sharper than he was. Never again did he dare to put anyone or anything down when I was present.

As the year progressed Tom couldn't make up his mind if he wanted to join a law firm in New York or Colorado. He struggled over this for weeks. Then in April, having finished most of his exams he wanted to take a break. He took a few days off. After the weekend he came back to the dorm.

"Bennie you won't believe what I've done. I can't picture myself chained to a desk for the next 30 years of my life. I don't want to be a tax lawyer! So I've joined the Marine Corps over weekend. They promised I could become a JAG lawyer and do real trial work."

I was shocked. Still being part of the anti Viet Nam generation I couldn't believe my ears. But Tom was more conservative. I could see he was happy about his choice. I congratulated him and wished him all the best.

Love,
Papa

Dec. 7, 2016

Grandma in NYC:

The last I spoke about your grandmother was when she married Bernard and moved to NYC. Bernard immediately started working for The Lucis Trust Company, Alice Bailey's corporate name for The Arcane School. As mentioned he taught Louise how to do black and white photography. They had set up a little darkroom in the bathroom of their apartment in NYC.

Grandma pickup up on it really quickly. She took photos of Bernard, some really good. Hopefully I will be able to pull them out of the boxes one of these days. She also entered an amateur photo contest. One early morning she had photographed a man walking on Wall Street. She told me the photo won her first prize as the best amateur photographer for that year, which must have been around 1938.

Grandma really loved Bernard. She was also getting involved with the meditations in The Arcane School. But to make ends meet, she took a job in a fashion house. Sounds familiar? Seems like some else in the family is following her footsteps, your sister, hopefully to a better end. She was working as a secretary and receptionist for one for one of the house on 6th Avenue. One day her boss started making a play for her. He wanted to have sex with her once the rest of the staff left the office.

"I'm a married woman!"

"So what, I'm a married man. All I want to do is to fuck you. Come on you'll like it."

She quit the next day. There were a number of other jobs, none of which she spoke about. The next job she related to me was with Merrill Lynch, when it was just *Merrill Lynch*.

In the mean time she was advancing in The Arcane School's inner circle. Marcia Moore, remember her from my years in Concord, Massachusetts? Was also a part of this inner circle, along with Wei Tat, Marion and Rhoe Walters, my god parents, Homer Carrinege. What many people don't know was Alice was active in Co-Masonry. She was a member of the Brooklyn lodge.

One 4th of July there was to be a major parade. The Masons were a part of it. Alice and other members of the Brooklyn Lodge wanted to March in the parade as women Masons, wearing their full regalia. They didn't ask permission from the HQ in Larkspur, they just did it. By this time one of the Theosophical Society members had taken over as the American head of La Droit Humain. The fact that one of the lodges was participating in the parade made HQ furious.

Now the conflict didn't happen all at once. The end result was HQ pulled the charter of the lodge and reprimanded all of those who participated. Alice was still taking the dictations from D.K. wanted to keep active in Masonry. She felt, as does your father, the Masonic lodge was one of the best places for spiritual advancement to those who take the Masonic ceremonies seriously. All the symbolism and teachings of the ancient initiatory schools can be found hidden in the Masonic rituals. Alice approached some of the member of The Arcane School to see if they wanted to form a new Masonic obedience.

Grace Petral, Alice and a number of others formed Ancient Universal Mysteries (AUM) as the Masonic off-shoot of the Arcane School. Somewhere in my collection of papers I have the list of original members of one of the AUM Lodges. Shortly after the first lodge was formed a second followed. But by now 1940 was approaching and the world was deep in a WWII. Grandma took her Entered Apprentice (1st) Degree in AUM sometime before 1940. In that lodge, you had to work and study before you would be advanced to the Degree of Fellowcraft (2nd). But then Pearl Harbor was attacked.

On the home front, Bernard was refusing to have children. Louise couldn't accept this. Also Bernard was a micro manager of the money, even that which she brought in. This led to fights and finally a divorce.

Love,
Papa

Feb. 20, 2017

Hello T:

I should clarify the program at BU. Most schools of social work offer the standard M.S.W. (Masters in Social Work). The special program I was in offered a M.S.S.S., a Masters of Science in Social Services which combined the standard MSW with a supplemental concentration on Social Service Administration. It was a unique degree and required an addition 10–12 semester hours of credit over the usual two years of a MSW study. But the time I graduated I had collected 72 hours of credit.

The one nice think about this program was it involved joint seminars at other college. There were sessions at different institutions. I think they included Tufts, Smith College (a major college for Social Work), Boston College, but the best sessions were in Brandeis University. These sessions were usually an afternoon or occasionally a Sunday. Brandeis was a Jewish college so Sundays were normal for special studies. Most focused on social service administration problems. In a lot of ways you could call it project management for social service agencies and not for profit organizations devoted to social services.

I may provide additional information about these programs if I can only find my old notebooks. But one of the last sessions during my second year, I had been making a lot of suggestions and raising major issues which had not been originally considered.

After the session one of the professors from Brandeis came up to me. "

"Walter, what are you going to do next year? If you want I'm pretty sure we could get into our DSW here."

I told him I had no support available and couldn't pay for the extra two or three years of study. Always regretted not accepting that offer, but there was just no way to find a way to reimburse the loans I would have to take during those years. If a straight grant was found, maybe, but with the studies at BU taking up so much time, there was no way to devote time to search for scholarships and grants. I just didn't want to take out loans. The $7,000 I had to take out for the second year was hard enough to pay back on a social worker's salary.

In the mean time I was taking classes which would enhance my experience and desire to promote inter-generational programming. Of course the program I had started at United South End Settlement was a major effort in this initiative. Debbie's classes had a large concentration on early childhood development. I remember doing one paper on the roll of classical music had in the development of the young child. This was years before tests showed that classical music helped develop the cranial pathways which are required for learning math.

I also took a basic class on geriatrics. The problem was I didn't take a class with Louis (Louie is what he was known by his students) Lowy who was the cornerstone of BU School of Social Work's gerontology program. In reality he was one of the major drawing points to BU.

Louie Lowy was a brilliant little man. I don't think he could have been much over 5' tall. He was very thin and with an interesting tattoo on his wrist. These were the numbers on the wrist of every Auschwitz inmate who was sent there during WWII. There is even a book about his life: The Life and Thought of Louis Lowy: Social Work through the Holocaust. Maybe one of these incarnations I might ready that book.

All those who were fortunately enough to take his classes were in ahh of his mind and ability as a professor. After he died BU School of Social Work created The Lowy-GEM (Geriatric Education Model) Program in Aging. The program is a comprehensive, master's-level social work training program preparing MSW students to meet the 'unique needs of older adults, their families, and the organizations that serve them.' The fact he is still remembered by the program named after him gives me a warn feeling about the school where there are so few such feelings.

Love,
Papa

March 10, 2017

Hello T:

At BU one of the most popular study areas in warm weather was the green area between the Law School's nice building and the School of Social Work's old converted run down town house. The lawn was bounded by the school's main entrance on Commonwealth Avenue and the Charles river on the other side. There were a number of other buildings next to the School of Social Work but most were offices and other administration buildings. It is interesting that most of the social work actual classes were held elsewhere. The only real classes held in the building were small seminars.

It was a warm April day. I was studying for finals on the lawn. The lawn was shielded from the sound of the traffic on the highway next to the Charles River by an earthen mound. A stone bridge connected a pathway next to the mound and the bike path next to the river. The bridge went over the 4 lane divided highway which ran into downtown Boston. The bridge was a classic old stone bridge supported in the middle by a stone support which was build up from the medium strip separating the lanes of the highway. For the most part, those studying on the lawn couldn't hear the traffic or activities on the highway thanks to the mound which separated the two areas.

As I was studying faint sounds out of the normal came from the bridge area. I got up and walked over the bridge. As I climbed up the stairs of the bridge the flashing lights of emergency vehicles became visible. Crossing the bridge you could see the cause of the commotion. A car had jumped the center strip and hit full force the bridge's stone support in the median strip. The front end was mangled. The engine appeared to have been thrown into the front seat. The fire department attempting to cut the driver away with the 'jaws of death' which is a tool used to pry steel apart. The driver was caught in the car. Much of the frame was pinning him in. Frantic attempts were being made to get him out by the firemen. What was interesting was there was only one other student on the bridge watching this, about 10 feet way from myself. Bikers on the bike path had stopped to see what was going on from the Charles River path. A few cars were stopped as the emergency equipment were blocking the lanes.

I starred down at the car. The driver did not appear to be conscious. Suddenly I felt his presences in front of me. But it was not his physical self. His body was still in the car. I closed my eyes and did a quick centering exercise. I felt his spirit/astral form was floating there in front of me. It was so close, if I stretched forth my arm, my hand would have touched him. I couldn't see him but could feel him looking down at what was going on. The mixture of confusion, fear and total disorientation were all strong. He could see himself below. Yet he didn't understand what had happened or how he was able to see his lifeless body below.

Focusing strongly on the disincarnate soul in front of me, in my mind I said:

"Listen to me. I know you are there in front of me."

Somehow the realization his attention was now drawn to me more than the image below.

Softly I spoke to the spirit in front of me.

"Hear me. I know you are confused. You have died. You will see a tunnel with a light beyond. On the other side of the tunnel you will find old friends and family that will take care of you once you have passed through. Look for the tunnel and the light. Leave this place. Don't be afraid. You have passed beyond this realm."

I felt he heard every word and was starting to pass through the tunnel. His fear and confusion faded. Suddenly as if he was next to me in a physical form I clearly heard: "**Thank you!**" loud and clear in my head.

I smiled and walked back to the green to continue studying for the upcoming exams.

Love,
Papa

May 2017, New Orleans #1

Flashback—Grandma at joins the Army!:

After divorcing Bernard, Grandma was working full time at Merrill Lynch. She reverted to her maiden name, Powers. When December 7, 1941 happened the US entered the war officially. Many of the draft age men in Merrill Lynch ended up in the Armed Services. Grandma may have started out in a clerical position but she moved through the ranks to becoming an investment analyst. Taking over many of the accounts from the men who were now in training camp, she proved she could manage a portfolio as well as any of the men. Her experiences with her first husband helped her become a petroleum analysis.

As the war progressed, the men in the offices were being shipped out all over the world. Louise was taking on more and more responsibilities at Merrill Lynch. One day she saw the pay stub her male counterparts. Her salary was less than half what the men were getting. Yet her portfolios were doing as well if not better than most of those who remained in the office. She went into the boss' office and demanded equal pay for equal work. She had more than proved her worth in the accounts she was managing. Now they should recognize her talents by giving her at least the same salary. Then next day she had a pink slip. She was fired!

This was 1944. There were other options open to her. She once told me there was an ad for women volunteers in the Army and Navy. One ad said: 'Join the WAC and free up a fighter.' She bought it and signed up.

Grandma joined the Women's Army Corp (WAC). When she volunteered for the WAC the first problem was proving her citizenship. She had been born in New Mexico. No hospital. No birth certificate. No records. She had to put an ad in the newspaper which was closest to where she was born. In it she asked if anyone remembered a girl born to the Powers family on April 10, 1912. The WAC recognized many of their recruits from the country often did not have birth certificates. Receiving confirmation letters from witnesses or neighbors who knew of the recruit's birth would often suffice. Then with that in hand they could accept the volunteer. It took some time but several women remembered a baby girl being born to Carrie Powers. This was sufficient for the Army.

After a basic physical there was a batter of tests given to all the recruits to determine their talents and what duty would be appropriate. Grandma was only a non-com (non commissioned officer) in other words low rank. With what would be considered a GED and no records of courses she took in the community college in LA. They assumed she would only be fit for the secretarial pool. Until she took the aptitude test. After taking one of the tests a Sargent came up to her and accused her of cheating.

"No dumb bitch from no where could possibly score as high as you did. Where did you get the answers?"

"How could I have gotten the answered, I didn't even know what tests would be given."

Still the Sargent couldn't believe that a woman of her background could score a 167 on an IQ test. So ended the first week in the WAC. She was shipped off to Pensacola, Florida for basic training.

She took advantage of being in Pensacola. When not in training she learned of a flight school outside the base. By now she was assigned to a secretarial pool on the base, but was bored with the daily routine. Emilia Earhart was always an hero in her eyes. The idea of getting a pilot's license had a very strong appeal. She signed up for the flight school. The interesting thing about the school was all the planes were pontoon planes. In other words planes that took off and landed in the water. This just added to the challenge. She soon mastered all the basics.

Then came her first solo flight. She took off and started a climb. Suddenly the plane was hard to control. It started to dive. The dive took it into an uncontrollable spin. She couldn't pull out. About 20 feet above the water she finally was able to pull up. She regained control, as she said:

"Just a few feet from crashing into the bay."

When she got back to the dock, she told the instructor there was something wrong with either the controls or the balance.

"I'm sure it is just your inexperience. I can guarantee the plane is in perfect condition."

She told him it was not but left. The next day when she arrived at the school, her instructor was white as a sheet. He had taken up the plane to test it. Sure enough he lost control and almost crashed. He told her she was going to make one hell of a pilot pulling out of the spinning dive on the day before. When they both inspected the plane, there was an excessive amount of water in one of the pontoons, making the plane off balance, but only when doing climbs and other arial maneuvers. She was always listened to from then on.

Love,
Papa

May 2017, New Orleans #2

During winter break in that first year, I went back to stay with Nim for a few weeks. Herb wanted me as Laura, Amy, and Andrea had all left the project before I left for BU. Being Christmas many of the new volunteers wanted to travel or take a break from the baby sitting. The new group of volunteer had moved into Delafield. I had to take Andrea's old room on the second floor as my old room was now taken by Bill T.

I was told about how Laura and the other volunteers would give Nim cigarettes, alcohol, even pot. Here was an effort to raise a chimpanzee in something resembling a human home, as an infant who is learning sign language! But being given all the negative addictive elements which would never be given a child of his age. Right there was the evidence that Project Nim was a phony effort. I was disgusted by what I was told.

Bill was bringing Nim from Columbia Friday afternoon. I was in the downstairs playroom. As Bill was carrying Nim in his arms through the kitchen towards the playroom, he started signing:

"Who is in the play room? Walter is in the playroom."

As he repeated this a second time, I heard Nim start hooting in excitement. As Bill came into view, there was Nim leaning as far as he could out of Bill's arms to get a glimpse into the room. The second he saw me, he let out a massive shout, jumped out of Bill's arms, and jumped into mine. Thank goodness my stance was such that I was prepared, or at least mostly, to be hit by a 40 pound flying chimpanzee. From that moment one, no matter what we did, Nim would sign my name over and over again. What is interesting is that though my name sign was reported early in the study as part of his vocabulary, he had refused to sign it in front of me all the time I was working with him.

I was told they tried to keep up the tradition of making pancakes for Nim on weekends. But no one had watch how Nim and I worked together in creating different recipes. Those who tried to take over, failed miserably. I was told that Nim would throw the boring pancakes at the volunteers rather than eat them. The problem was simple. With me we created pancakes with spices and fruit. Also different kinds of flour. As a result no two were the same. Unless there was a recipe that Nim really liked, then we might try to repeat it. But since I never did exact measurements, even when we attempted to come up with the same pancake, it was always a slight variation on a theme.

I quickly discovered the problem. They tried to use standard pancake mixes and did nothing to the recipes on the box. When I came back over Christmas, we resumed our Sunday morning pancakes. But now just for the two of us as Laura and the others were no long living in the house.

As those four weeks were coming to an end, this time I told Nim I would have to leave again. When I told him this he seemed sad. But based upon his learning rate, it did not seem to impact him as badly as the summer before. I did tell him, verbally I would try to come back when the weather got warm again.

It seems strange but the second half of my first year at BU is a bit of a blur. Nothing stands out except for the sex education class and the thanatology class. I know the schedule was full, and the work at South End Settlement was going well. Jane and I were still a steady couple, at least for the first semester.

Love,
Papa

May 2017, New Orleans Trip #4

Greetings T:

I'll get back to Grandma in the next letter. But for now back to the BU studies but now in the 2nd Year. There were winds of change happening in the school. Not all students were in favor of the changes and of course your father was one of those, but with reason.

There was a new Dean of School of Social Work. A DSW black man from a very traditional social work background. His vision for social workers were they should be case workers, or group workers, occasionally community organizers. This was far more narrow than those of us in the special MSSS program. He wanted to drop the MSSS (MS in Social Services) program as: 'it's not real social work.'

The six of us in the program quickly objected. We were all grouped as community organizers, but in reality focused on management of social services as the 'SS' in the degree inferred. As a group we quickly opposed the dropping of the degree. One of us threatened a law suite against the school if it was dropped. Obviously one of the students with more money than I.

After a few weeks of discussions, mostly in the form or editorial comments in the School's newsletter and with the threat of court action the decision was the degree was not be be dropped until after the June graduation. But there were to be no new students admitted into the MSSS program.

The problem was those going for the MSSS were focusing on community organization, a recognized track in social work, but also management, political organization, and government administration of socials programs. Areas usually not popular with social workers. The other great thing about the program was it led to the consortium sessions at Brandis, Smith, and other schools in the Boston area. Great experience.

My long term plans were to work in government at the city, state or Federal level. I would have loved to return to NYC, but felt it was unlikely. In an attempt to get a placement which would help these long term goals, I knew the school with the change in focus would not be of much help.

Before summer break contact had been made with the local Federal Offices in downtown Boston. I lined up a possible new internship at AoA (Administration on Aging). There was a secret to AoA considering me. When I was at Franconia College in my senior year I worked with the White House Conferences on Aging. First on the local level. Then for the state of New Hampshire. Both times as the recorder for the committee on 'Spiritual Concerns.'

During the state conference there was an AoA observer. A short thin man, likely in his late 40's with greying hair. When I did the summary of the findings of the committee, I submitted the draft notes to him, followed up with a written report. He met me a few weeks after the State Conference in 1971. He said if I ever wanted to work with the elderly in New England, to contact him. Well–6 years later it was time to contact him.

I arranged a visit to his office. He remembered me. We talked for a little while. He asked me to come back in a few days to see what might be done. The next visit I sat down with the Director of the office along with him and another AoA Administrator. The little man did most of the talking about how he was impressed with me years ago and thought AoA would benefit if I was placed in the office. The other administrator said he could use a graduate student who could help with putting together guidelines for the state and local areas on aging programs. Most of the work would be developing an administrative and legal reference guideline for local offices to use.

Currently the CFR (Code of Federal Regulations) and other guidelines were almost unusable. They needed a simple guideline and some kind of implementation instruction. Would I be interested in developing such a guideline? Of course I would. They agreed to accept me as an intern and drafted a letter for my counselor. Now came the bigger challenge.

Love,
Papa

May 2017, New Orleans #5

Hi T:

Remember in the last letter about my planning an internship placement at AoA Federal Office in Boston? For my objectives and goals it was perfect fit. My councilor accepted the placement. After talking with him, he agreed it was perfect for me. But the only problem was it was the School of Social Work that wanted to select the internships. This was typical of the new dean. He wanted the graduate councilors to have complete control over the internship placements. He did not approve students to create their own placements, especially those outside of his focus. He didn't care if it was a perfect fit for the student. After all the 'school knew best.'

I realized if the placement was to be a reality it had to be fought for. This would put me in direct conflict with the new dean. There were a series of new guidelines for internships issued by the Dean in the School's news letter. I immediately wrote a reply. It basically stated that most of the graduate students in the School were adults who had been working in the field for a number of years. We were mature and not like undergraduates. If the individual student lines up a placement which is in perfect alignment with their individual goals and objectives, it should be accepted. Then I threw in the really dangerous phrase:

"The School needs to remember, we are purchasing their services. We are the School's customer and should be treated with both respect and recognition that occasionally the customer is right."

The shit hit the fan. The Dean was furious over my editorial. I was called into his office. It felt like Rockford College all over again. Was I to be expelled? Should I defend my position? Rage, fear, and determination were just a few of the emotions running through my veins as I walked into his office.

The Dean went into a long harangue about how the graduate faculty needed to be in charge of placement. The dean argued the school knew better. He wanted to direct all the graduate students into his vision of social work. He had no idea of my vision or objectives, nor of my experience in the South Bronx. During the heated 'discussion' while he was still angry, I asked:

"Are you going to expel me?"

He said "No."

So it was my turn every point he brought up I was able to counter.

"OK then, here are my points."

I laid out how most of the graduate students were mature with an average age of 30+. Many of us had already been in the field for years. Some of us had specific career goals which did not fit the traditional case work or group work objectives. This was why we applied for the MSSS program.

I explained how my goal was to work for the AoA or other government agency on gerontological issues and not be in the field. I had been the Assistant Director for a NYC program. Yes small but it was a city-wide government program. He had no idea. Mind you I didn't tell him how small it really was, just two, Margaret and myself. Not only that but my placement, if successful, would open up a whole new arena of possible placements in the future. As far as I could tell no other student had been placed with the Federal Government from the School of Social Work.

At least he listened. After what felt like hours of debate, which may have actually taken only 15 minutes, he reluctantly conceded that AoA was the correct placement for me. But that was the final straw in killing the MSSS program. The six of us in the program were the last ever to receive that degree!

I walked out of the office with a feeling like a victorious general coming out of a war. There were at least two other MSSS students who later said my fight led them to find their own placements over the objections of their counselors. Placements like mine would fit their long term objectives better than the traditional internships.

It was then summer break. I said good-bye to Jane who was off to southern Virginia. While I was off to The Hill in Connecticut for the summer. I contacted Herb me to see if they needed me to be with Nim again. He did.

Love,
Papa

May 2017, New Orleans #6

Hello there:

Back to the mundane. The second year in the dorm resulted with my having a Texan roommate. A physically large white man striving for a MBA. In many ways he was the very kind of Texan that reminded me of my cousin Gary who I felt was an insult to mankind. This guy was arrogant, egotistical, and a know it all. Gee, like me in a lot of ways. But as I fell on one side of the political spectrum, he was definitely on the opposite.

He loved to have a beer in the dorm (against the rules) and loved going to the sports bars to watch the various games on their TV. The TV in the common room rarely was tuned to sports and since that set was dominated by the graduate education majors, most of the time it was turned to what would be called now 'Chick' programming. This may have contributed to his extreme sexist views occasionally expressed. I could not imagine how any woman would put up with him, but occasionally he would bring to the dorm a stereotypical blond bimbo with a subpar IQ based on my limited conversations with them. NONE were graduate students.

As the days progressed we realized a conversation between the two of us was almost impossible. No matter that the subject, we would take opposite sides. I would point out the logical flaws in his position and pose an alternative view. He would fume at my arguments. Rarely could he counter my points.

The final straw came with his playing his radio, a common occurrence, but this was different. He listened to rock music, usually louder that what I would tolerate. So I would turn the radio down. He didn't like my touching it but didn't say anything. One afternoon there was a rock piece playing. The strains of Prokofiev's *Lieutenant Kije Suite* in the rock piece.

"I can tell that was heavily borrowed from Prokofiev." I noted.

Apparently he liked the piece and became exceptionally defensive.

154

"What do you mean? This is an original piece by this *band*" (can't remember the name of the group).

"It clearly the theme of Lieutenant Kije." Was my response: "A piece I love. I have to give them credit for choosing such a nice piece to work into their music."

"How dare you accuse them of plagiarism." was his last words as he stormed out of the room.

The next day I checked out the recording from the library. When he came in, I hit the play button. There was the same theme. He listened. He realized he was wrong. He didn't talk to me for a week and then only reluctantly.

After that we rarely spoke. He spent most evenings elsewhere. This was fine as it allowed me to study and allowed Jane and I more time together.

He moved out after the Fall Semester. I was glad to see him go and really didn't care where he moved. About into a month of the new semester he came by the dorm.

"Sorry Walter I was such a jerk. I probably could have learned a lot from you. But I just didn't want to listen."

Have no idea what turned him around but it was a surprising comment. I thanked him. He turned and left. I never ran into him again.

Love,
Papa

May 2017, New Orleans #6

Grandma goes to war!–almost:

By the end of 1944 after the Battle of the Bulge, where you read about my experiences in the early letters, it was apparent the war in Europe would soon be over. Yet your grandmother had proven her self while in Pensacola.

During one of her leaves she when back to New York. Before leaving she had been accepted in AUM, remember the Masonic obedience for Arcane School members. She wanted to catch up with Alice and attended the lodge meeting. It was at the meeting she received her Fellow Craft Degree. What no one could have expected, it was to be the last degree to be conferred by the original AUM. There is a photo of her and the other advanced members of the Arcane School, she is the only one in uniform. Many of her closest friends are also in the photo. Remember all of these were individuals of unique talents when it came to meditation and other psychic abilities. Mom took me to Alice for her blessing when I was just a few months old. Alice died less than a year later.

In the WAC she made it through the ranks quickly. She was recognized for her intelligence and her ability to adapt and serve in whatever capacity needed. Her commanding officer suggested she take the test for Officer's Candidate School (OCS). She wanted to become an officer. OCS was in Florida so it was be an easy transfer. By the way there is a photo of her diving off a diving board which was taken during her stay in Pensacola. But she was a little indecisive about what to do.

She wanted to get to Europe before the end of the war. When she took the OCS test the results showed she was the top candidate. But now came the tough choice. There was a troupe ship leaving Florida about the same time as OCS was to start. She often told me this was the hardest decision she every had to make. OCS or give up on ever becoming an officer and get into the war.

Her decision was to go to Europe. The ship took off around the first of May, 1945. While in transit came an announcement over the ship's speaker.

"The war in Europe is over. The Allies have won and Germany had surrendered."

There was a great celebration on board that night. When the ship landed in Le Havre, France, the whole city was in a celebratory mood. So was most of Europe. But for a secretarial pool the real work was just beginning. There were tens of thousands of soldiers to ship back to the States. Many were going to be sent back from La Havre. But the officers and particularly the Generals assigned to discharge the troops didn't want to be stuck at a desk when all the celebration was going on.

Shortly after arriving the 2 (or 3) Star General in charge of signing the discharge papers had a contest. Which of the members of the Secretarial Pool could forge his signature the best. Of course Grandma won. Soon she was discharging soldiers as fast as the paper work could be filled out and spaces on the transports found to send them back to the States. She told me she likely discharged over 10,000 soldiers. She would giggle when she thought about how many thought that General X had signed their discharge papers and awarded them the WWII victory medal when it was really a woman Sargent!

What did the General do? To say nothing of the other high ranking officers? They wanted to party. Especially in Paris and the other capitals such as London, Brussels and Amsterdam. Officially they could not use an official pilot to fly them to these cities. But Louise was a licensed pilot! She was not an official WAC pilot. They could ask her *unofficially* to fly them to Paris or Brussels 'off the record.' Now no one is going to stop a Colonel or General. If the guards wanted to get home they couldn't tell the brass they couldn't take a plane. So grandma was the unofficial chauffeur for big brass in most of France.

Of course she took advantage of these trips and got to see a lot of France and some parts of Belgium. She felt it was some of the most fun she ever had. She also met a lot of soldiers going home. Every now and then there was one who was in a questionable mental state. She was warned to keep away from them, but never told why. Now we know it as Post Traumatic Stress Syndrome (PTSD). But at the time there was no such term for their condition. She also met some prisoners of war who were being released from prisons, as the war was over. She tried to help them as much as she could. One made her a wooden art box, which I still have. One of the officers she got home gave her a German Mauser (32 caliber) pistol. She was a fantastic shot with it. Eventually it was sold to an antique dealer as I had no real use for it.

Love,
Papa

London #1, 2017

Hi T:

Still at BU. In the mean time Jane and I were still steady. She would practice in the school of music in one of the many piano practice rooms. Sometime without her knowing I would go to the practice rooms and sit outside the door where she was playing. She was really a wonderful pianist and getting better all the time.

Besides the performance classes she had to take music theory and composition. I remember when she was taking a course on counterpoint. Though counterpoint can be found in the Middle Ages and the early canons, the composer who Jane had to study as developing counterpoint in the Renaissance was Giovanni Pierluigi da Palestrina. One of her assignments was to compose a piece of music which emulated Palestrina. Though familiar with Palestrina previously, her coming to me and demonstrating her composition gave me a greater appreciation. To this day I love Palestrina and of course for the Baroque, Bach and Fux as great counterpoint composers. The next assignment was totally different and was to be part of an orchestral composition. Jane had no desire to become a composer, but all her assignments proved that she had the capability if she wanted to apply herself.

I do remember one day when she was practicing in the actual theater where she was to perform her solo for her MA in Piano Performance exam. She had chosen a number of Debussy short etudes for piano along with a number of preludes. What most people didn't know Debussy was interested in the occult and esoteric study. He may have been interested in Theosophy but definitely was into a number of mystical concepts. I was sitting in the first row of the auditorium listening to Jane practice her pieces. Piano performance are traditionally memorized. This suited Jane as she didn't like to wear her thick glasses when playing. She would often put them on the side of the piano.

This afternoon she was playing some of the rare etudes. I had my eyes partly closes, as I like to do with in concerts. The theory is to devote all my attention to the music and not the performer. As I was looking downward, there in the peripheral sight was what appeared to be slightly transparent yellowish images dancing around the piano as Jane played. I later read that Debussy did write compositions meant to invoke elemental beings. Those dancing around the piano were some type of etherial creatures. If looked at directly, there was nothing there. It was only when looking downward or in another direction did the vague images appear at the outer edge of my range of vision.

After the practice I asked Jane:

"Have you ever seen anything around your piano when you play these pieces?"

She looked at me. "I thought I was going crazy, but whenever I practice these pieces, I see little yellow creators dancing all around me. "

I described what I thought I had seen. She was relieved. She had always thought it was her imagination or that her poor vision was playing tricks on her. What I had described was exactly what she had seen many times with playing Debussy. A few weeks later, her performance requirement for her Master's in Performance came off beautifully. She still had to complete additional classes but the performance requirements has been met.

In the mean time, I was thinking about developing a more permanent relationship with Jane. I started trying to figure out budgets and places where we could live if we were married. Knowing I would need a decent salary. A pianist can not depend on a steady income unless they are teaching. I didn't tell Jane, but in the back of my mind I was thinking about proposing to her after the winter break.

In the mean time she started working on duets with another pianist who also lived in the graduate dorm. This was a little man with almost no personality. I thought him boring. He was also a strict Catholic, didn't believe in sex outside of marriage, and had very conservative ideas. I never thought that Jane would take him seriously. So I encouraged her work with this other pianist.

At the same time, I was still visiting the South End Settlement House to see the program I created would still in existence the next year. It was, though not with the same amount of enthusiasm as when I was running it. There was one woman working there who I rarely paid attention to but she came on to me very strongly. I told her I was not interested as I was in a committed relationship. No more thought when into her advances.

Love,
Papa

London #2, 2017

Hello Again:

I need to back flash for this letter to the summer between the two years at BU. Jane needed a job before coming to BU for graduate work. I was unable to get job between my two years at BU so contact Herb Terrace to see if you wanted me to come back to Delafield for the summer and work with Nim. Of course he did.

It was evident from the reports that Nim's rate of acquiring new signs had greatly decrease after I had left, first at the end of the previous summer, and again when I left after being with him during Christmas break. At least at the end of Christmas break I told Nim verbally that I had to leave again, but would try to come back when the weather got warm.

Meanwhile Jane continued her tour with the violist who she had accompanied the summer before. But this time, when she went to NYC to meeting with him. She wanted me to come along. The violist invited us to dinner which we gratefully accepted. We met him at his apartment near Julliard, were he taught. He was about my height, but slender and must have been approaching 60 by appearance. I shook his hand. Though his hands were strong, the rest of him was very much the opposite. While I was trim, for me, at about 210 lbs but strong. That was one of the reasons Herb wanted me back with Nim. I was one of the only individuals who could out muscle Nim. Dr. D took notice. Jane meanwhile draped herself affectionately around me.

It was rather a funny dinner. It was evident that he wanted Jane not only for her ability to accompany him when he was performing, but also for the extra circular activities he had demanded the summer before. My presence changed those thoughts real quick. I didn't say anything directly, but just notified him that Jane and I were a serious couple. I would never want anything to happen to her that would upset her. He got the message. They had a few gigs around the country. Every time they came back to NYC Jane would call me up and we would get together. I even met with the violist and Jane for a casual trip to one of the museums to see an exhibit and have a lunch. This was pure strategy on Jane's part to be sure he would keep his 'hands' off of Jane while on tour. It worked. By the end of the summer, Jane had done about a dozen performances with him and not once did he try to pull any of the sexual assaults which he was guilty of the previous summer.

Meanwhile, Nim's learning rate with my return to Delafield began to increase. But it was nothing like what it had been when I was there the previous year. They also started filming him in the classroom. This time Nim was in a permanently bad mood. It seemed to me he would be looking at the 'teacher' as if to say: "What do you want me to sign?" The teacher would go through the usual routine of asking what something was. Eventually Nim would give the appropriate sign. My interpretation was that all those who Nim had become close to, deserted him. When first in Delafield, there were 4 of us. By the end of the summer when I left for BU all four of us were gone, with Nim never understanding, or even told why. At this stage I felt we were working with a mentally disturbed chimp.

When Nim was with me at his home, he was much more at ease. We began to have the same relationship we had when I was with him before BU. We continued our walks through the neighborhood, particularly on Sundays. He always loved meeting new people and seeing the crowd coming out one of the many churches in Riverdale. He never cause any trouble and was always very nice to everyone, with one exception. He saw a young baby in a stroller. He didn't like being strapped in. So he started trying to unstrap the child. The father came up to stop him.

Nim hunched up as if ready to attack the father. I had to call off the father. Nim thought the dad was about to attack the child. Nim would have torn him apart. But I explained Nim's aggressive reaction. The father backed off. All went well after that with Nim giving the baby a kiss as we said good-bye.

Love,
Papa

London #3, 2017

It's me again:

By the end of summer break of the first year at BU there was not much to do. I had to come back a couple of weeks early to establish my internship. Jane was at her home after the tour with the violist.

Mom was still working with Adm. Hart's widow. They had completed <u>From Frigate to Dreadnaught</u> the biography of Missy's father. Now a professional writer was hired to work on Adm. Hart's biography. It would eventually be called <u>A Different Kind of Victory</u> but much of the controversial information didn't make it into the final edition. Mom was the 'research editor' like the earlier book. But this time she didn't get credit.

The Admiral's intense dislike of Gen. MacArthur, and FDR were white washed. The fact that Hart had warned Washington in the spring and summer of 1941 of a possible attack by the Japanese on American installations were omitted. All of this and more of what the Admiral would tell me when I would talk with on those high school and college days when I would pick up mom from King House in Sharon were omitted from the book. When I finally read it, thought it left out anything which might be controversial. The problem was the book was put together after the Admiral's death.

Challenge to Placement

Due to my internship at the Administration on Aging in Boston I wanted to return to Boston before school. There were some ideas my advisor and I wanted to discuss in focusing on the year. Part of it would be to develop a legal reference handbook for aging programs based upon Federal guidelines. I would be attending a paralegal training programs for individuals working with the elderly. The advantage was since I would monitor it as part of AoA. Unknown at the beginning I would be credited with having completed the course and become a certified paralegal for the aging.

The graduate dorm was open so I moved back in. Jane was not scheduled to come back for a week plus. I decided to visit Southend Settlement to talk to my previous internship advisor. Tamara told me in confidence she was unhappy as a social worker. She felt there were some racial problems with her supervisor, she being white and the supervisor being black. The straw that broke the camel's back was her intern (me) had a salary in NYC greater than her's. She was applying to law schools, and had been accepted to one. If she was ever to earn a decent salary, it wouldn't be in social work. I had to agree with her. She left before the end of the year.

After talking with Tamara, I did my usual flirting with the receptionist. She was the one who wanted to tear the shirt off of me and jump on my bones. Of course this was our standing tease from the previous year. Another worker best described as a Rubenisk woman who had come on to me the year before came on to me again. As busty as ever, wearing glasses and hippy jewelry. I still didn't find her attractive and not interest in her. But after a few minutes of talking she literally asked me out to dinner. Since Jane was not due back for a week and most of the dorm empty, the idea of having company for the evening was a welcomed invitation. That was my first mistake.

We met downtown for dinner. We talked. Don't remember any of the conversation. She was mildly intelligent but we had little in common. When dinner was over she invited me up to her place which was a short distance away. Again not having anything planned for the evening. I accepted. Second mistake. What happened next is not for this letter. Staying was the third and fatal mistake. At least when it came to Jane. By the time I left in the morning I was glad there was mutual agreement that we would not see each other again.

Love,
Papa

London #4, 2017

Still me loss of relationship:

Jane returned a few days later. I was very glad to see her and the welcome by her was mutual. She was everything I enjoyed in a woman, a nice, intelligent, talented and interesting person to be with. Someone who I really loved. But there was a veil between us, that had been created by my indiscretion the few evenings before.

The problem all my life is those close to me can read me like a book. Almost immediately Jane sensed my disloyalty during the break. At first she though I had screwed Jean, my old girlfriend from NYC. I assured her that I had not even seen Jean over the break. But Jane was sure I screwed someone. I had to confess. I told her there was no attachment associated with the dalliance. I apologized profusely. But a wedge had been planted between us. We continued as a couple.

She started working with another graduate pianist again on a duet. He lived upstairs. As said previously I considered him exceptionally boring. He was thin, very much a Walter Mitty type personality and physically. I could feel her attraction towards me decreasing each day. I did everything in my power to make up to her, but nothing really worked. We still enjoyed our dates, but there was never the strong emotions that were experienced the first year.

It was late October when Jane came up to me and said she wanted to break up. She liked this other pianist. Their practice sessions had become more frequent and the after practice sessions included dinner. They had been planning a program together as part of their graduate requirements. Being Catholic he didn't want to have intercourse until he was married. This would mean she would be able to stop taking the pill. Her parents encouraged the split, though they had never met me. She admitted the practice sessions were turning into make out sessions and she liked his company.

I was distraught. There was nothing I could do. I tried to send her notes to try to get back with me. No response. The notes got more intense, insulting her new bow. Finally she agreed to talk with me. I told her how devastated I was by us breaking up. She didn't know, but I had been budgeting how we could be together AND married after graduation. She was not aware I was on the verge of proposing to her. Still she was unmoved. Still that meeting was the closure that I needed. I gave her a little kiss and we never were together again. I would still try appealing to her in the way I looked at her whenever she and I passed in the street or saw each other in the dorm. But she paid not attention to me.

A good month afterwards I thought about it. Once the emotions had died down a little, I realized I had supported her in everything she was doing. But there was little or no reciprocal attention. I always asked about her classes, accompanied her to all her performances, even would listen to her practices. She never came to any of my activities and never asked about my studies. It took months to come to the realization it was very much a one way relationship. As heartbroken as I was, it was likely the best thing that could happen.

Not like being alone and the fact the education major who's family were all 'happily married' had moved out (frankly a disguised blessing), there was no one on the horizon who I felt I could be attracted to. Except Ann G., the business major upstairs. Ann was an exceptional student and artist. She felt sorry for me and was concerned about my depressed mood after the break up with Jane. But she was uncomfortable dating someone who had dated another woman in the dorm. Still she would sit and talk to me when she had the chance.

Love,
Papa

Aug. 1, 2018

Visit From the Past

Hello—long time since last letter (missed sending some from Arizona):

Long time no letters. Back to BU. Jean from NYC came up to Boston. I was able to get her a bed in the graduate dorm, one of the women in the dorm had a roommate out of town for the weekend, and let Jean sleep in the spare bed. She was very frank. She came to Boston to ask me to marry her, especially since she discovered I had broken up with Jane. We had a long discussion but I told her:

"Sorry but I feel coming to BU was telling me to move on."

Actually, even in NYC I was getting a little tired of Jean. Yes she was a nice person and very passionate. We were both familiar with the Arcane School (Lucis Trust) and the Alice Bailey books. Both interested in the esoteric side of life and strong reincarnationists. But she never stopped talking, except when practicing her mediations. Her continuous chatter was tiring. So when trying to decide between Fordham in the Bronx, or B.U. I was happy to move to Boston, not only because it was a superior programs, but it allowed me to break ties with those in NYC who had been close to me.

Unfortunately this included leaving Dementia. She changed her will. Somehow she felt me going to BU was a form of abandoning her. It had been rumored the former will left me almost everything. Since she had moved from her former residence to move in with Grace P., the other cooking editor, there could not have been much, but anything would have been welcomed. Being in Boston, her will left everything to Grace who's apartment she had moved into, and to her partner Annette. Appropriate, but with an increasing graduate loan to shoulder after graduation, any assistance from her would have been greatly appreciated. Of course I was hoping she would remain alive for years to come. She was the one thing that would have led me back to Manhattan, provided I could find a job.

Jean stayed for the weekend. She accepted my rejection with no emotion or anger. As a matter of fact she and I and two other women from the Social Work program had breakfast Sunday morning together in the large cafeteria. I spotted Ann and asked her to join me. She later said:

"I didn't want to be seen part of Walter's female collection."

Jean left that afternoon. We parted as friends. You actually met her many years later, when she was planning to move from the East Coast to the Mid West. She just stayed overnight wanting to meet you and your sister, though I was thinking she really wanted to see how was my relationship with your mother Marisol was going, perhaps to renew old ties again.

After parting Jean actually went to Unity Church's divinity school. She became a minister in the Unity Church. Of all things they sent her to a parish in Baltimore. She changed how individuals addressed her. Jean was her middle name which she used in NYC, not she wanted to go by her first name. That was part of the change during while going to the divinity school. But there was another problem.

All the time while she was going with me, she never drank much. What I learned later, was that she had been a heavy drinker before we started going together and after we broke up, she took it up again. Not as much, but once she got to Baltimore, the drinking became more heavy. She initiated an Alcohol Anonymous group as part of her church. 'To address the needs of the congregation.' But later she told me it was really so she could try to get sober again. She also started Transcendental Meditation (TM). I found this interesting in that she had gone much further than me in the mediation classes associated with the Lucis Trust. I felt that TM was a far inferior form of meditation. She felt it was what she needed and fully supported it.

She later told me over the phone her parish deeply divided between two camps. She was sent to attempt to rebuild the church and smooth out the congregation. She tried, but failed. After a number of years in Unity, she left the ministry and went back into secretarial work. Later she hooked up with another couple, got a real estate license and tried to make it in that profession. But that too failed. The last I heard she was in Iowa. Not sure doing what, but we still exchange Christmas cards.

Love,
Papa

Oct., 2018

New relationships

Still me:

By the beginning of October, having broken up with Jane it became evident that I was deeply depressed. It was evident in my daily life. I was taking additional psychology classes. This was also a time when mom was keeping exceptionally quiet. She refused to tell me what was going on in Connecticut. Yet it was evident something was wrong. I just couldn't get anything out of her. Later I found out she had quit working with Missy and was now totally dependent upon Social Security for an income. Also there were added pressures at my internship. Nothing I usually couldn't handle, but with everything else, the added work just added the pressure.

In the class I was taking they had all the students take a mental stability test. The scores would indicate the likelihood of serious depression and possible suicide. The higher the score, the more sever the depression. Any score over 700 was a warning signal of imminent suicide. I scored in the 800s. The professor told Debbie my professor from the previous year. Debbie suggested I get therapy and consider getting on anti-depression medications after seeing a psychiatrist. I laughed and dismissed her suggestions saying all this would pass.

Remember my mentioning Ann. It was at this time Ann who I was very friendly with became concerned. She was aware of how fond I was of Jane and the break up. She started walking with me from the dorm to the cafeteria. As the weeks progressed she became less concerned about Jane and others seeing us together, and actually accepted my offer of going out with me. We had several dates.

I remember one was the Boston Symphony concert. The main part of the program was Strauss' *Thus Spoke Zarathustra* which was used in the movie *2001 a Space Odyssey*. When we go the the concert hall she looked at the program. She was a little familiar with the Mozart and Beethoven minor pieces but said she had never heard of the Strauss. I assured her that she was very familiar with it.

"No I've never even heard of it. How could I know it, if I don't even know the name."

I still assured her she would recognize it once it was started. Now being discount student tickets we were in the first row of the concert hall, RIGHT behind the podium for the conductor. This evening it was not Seiji Ozawa conducting but a friend of his from Japan. Even as he bowed to the audience, Ann was denying she had ever hear *Thus Spoke Zarathustra*. Then came the opening 4 chords. Ann turned excitedly to me and said in a loud voice:

"I know this piece!"

She said it so loud the guest conductor was thrown off at least one beat. After the performance I teased her about it. We had a good laugh about the concert.

Ann was Armenian Apoplectic Catholic. This is the oldest continuous Christian Catholic church in existence, having been founded in the 3rd Century, even before the Roman Catholic church, though they would love to debate that fact. After a few dates she asked if I would accompany her to the Sunday service. Off we went to the 11 a.m. portion of the service. Being an anthropologist, the whole service was a fascinating exposure to a branch of Christianity not previously experienced. She told me the actual service starts at 9 a.m. but the first two hours are only for the most devout and for the priests themselves.

A lot was learned that Sunday. So much so, a couple of weeks later I went by myself to see the whole service. It was a unique service. I could see parts were adopted from Judaism, parts from Eastern religions, including Hinduism. There was a major censing of the whole room, with a procession of the priest. One was carrying a large staff with a circular disk on top which when shaken would make a sound. In Hindu and other Eastern services, the incense and sounds were to scare away demons and negative evil spirits. I was totally inthralled by the whole service.

Love,
Papa

Nov., 2018

More with Ann:

When I told Ann I went to her church by myself for the whole service, she was very impressed. Her feelings towards me grew three fold that week. Rather than simple dates between friends, it was quickly becoming a more serious relationship. She was aware of the type of relationship I had had with Jane. She made it clear from the beginning that she would not have sex until marriage. I accepted that.

I used to visit her in her room. We would talk for hours. She was very interested in mediation and esoteric studies. I shared what I could and told her about Co-Masonry. Sometimes we would play a game, board games mostly, backgammon definitely as it is the national game of Armenia. I won most of the games.

There besides all the MBA books were her collections of smaller paintings she had completed. All of the works reminded me of Edward Hopper. One of a diner and the stools to sit at the counter reminded me of Hopper's *Nighthawks*, minus the people. When she had time she would do sketches and small paintings, but since the graduate work was so intense she didn't have time to develop her artistic talents. The more I got to know her, the more I began to think: '*Maybe this the woman I was meant to marry.*'

In November she took me to her grandmother's home. Her grandmother was a delightful elderly woman, who looked every day of her 70+ years. White hair, wrinkled and walking with a cane, she tried hard to make me comfortable. We had a delightful lunch, after which Ann wanted to study. She proposed to her grandmother and she and I should play backgammon. Her grandmother was excited. She considered herself as an expert in the game. I would be a delight to play someone else who loved the game. Ann warned me that she was really good.

While Ann was looking for some books she had stored in the apartment, her grandmother and I sat down for some serious backgammon. We were to play a match to 15 using the doubling cube. I think the first game was won by her. But then mentally I said to myself: '*What if I'm playing for the hand of your granddaughter?*' I may have taken it easy on her in that first game, but from the moment I said that to myself it was gloves off. That was the last game grandma won. From then on it was all out effort to beat her. Soon even the old woman looked at me as if to say *I can't beat this man*. Ann was very impressed. I didn't mention the mental thought that turned my playing around. Maybe I should have.

As Christmas was approaching, I decided to make up Christmas cards for the 12 days of Christmas. But since we would be on vacation during the time between Christmas and Three Kings' Day, it would be the 12 days before Christmas that I would give her the cards. Each day I would slide one under the door. The problem was, after the first 6 days I couldn't remember the order of the other gifts. A search in the library didn't help. I couldn't find any book with Christmas music and the 12 Days of Christmas lyrics. Remember this is LONG before the internet. All we had were books and libraries. So I continued to make and send the cards. The last card was the most beautiful. I said to myself this has to be special. Rather than sliding it under her door, I sent it though the transom. Meditating on where I wanted to it to land, in it went. When Ann came back from studying, she came right down to my room:

"Do you have a key to my room?"

I told her I didn't.

"Well the card was perfectly placed on the corner of my bed as if you had come in and placed it there."

I took it as a good omen.

Love,
Papa

Nov., 2018

Hi T:

Thanatology and BU.

I was taking the usual classes for 2nd year social work student, having my internship three days a week. It was going well. On one evening there was a course on thanatology from a professor from the School of Nursing. I strongly felt in fit into my gerontology concentration. My advisor agreed. So it was being taken for credit.

The professor was called Jo. She was very much out of the box style professor. She reviewed the usual 5 stages of death from Kubler-Ross' <u>Death the Final Stage of Growth</u>. But she went beyond the clinical aspects of death. It was about this time near death experiences were first being reported. Months before Jane and I attended an evening program in town by Raymond Moody. He had just published his ground breaking book <u>Life After Life</u>. It had been published by Mockingbird Press, a small alternative press. This was before it was picked up by a major publisher, which only occurred after the Mockingbird Press edition was sold out. Jane and I got an autographed copy of this first edition. Of course I devoured it the next week.

Jo picked up on Moody's findings. She had experienced some of the same NDEs in her practice. She also rejected the official agnostic position of the graduate school and accepted the concept of a soul.

That was something I could never convince my old social work professor to acknowledge, even after she confessed seeing her decease father, a few days after his death. I tried to explain it was likely his astral form trying to say good-bye.

"No that's impossible. I was have hallucinations from grief."

She could not accept any concept of continued consciousness after death. I felt sorry for her.

A paper was required for Jo's class. I wrote the first edition of my past life experience in WWII which was one of your early letters. It involved all the details from the Battle of the Bulge, how I was killed. Then taking my platoon which had been wiped out into the light. Jo was so impressed with the paper she asked me to present it at the next class. I don't remember what happened at AoA that day but I showed up exceptionally fatigued at the class. My mind was just not working as usual. I was drained. Not sharp.

After presenting the paper there was a question and answer period. There were several very polite question and good comments. Then one of the students really laid into me. It was one attack after another. I found myself unable to counter his barrage of comments. Even Jo was shocked by his aggressive manner. Suddenly one of the women in the class told his to stop his attack.

"Walter is only expressing what he experienced. You shouldn't attack him for sharing his experiences."

The man sat down. Most of the students applauded me. I felt ill. After the class the man came up to me to apologize. We talked briefly. He came from a conservative fundamentalist Christian sect that totally rejected reincarnation. Then he said something I didn't expect:

"You talk triggered memories I have suppressed all these years. That scared me. I think I have been reincarnated but never wanted to acknowledge it."

A few sessions after we had a Rabbi come in to present the Jewish view of death. When questioned about the afterlife he said that reincarnation was the ultimate teaching for Judaism but rarely discussed. It was a further validation for my paper.

Soon after a number of post class discussions Jo asked if I would continue to attend the class the next semester as the unofficial co-teacher. The next semester I was the unpaid teaching assistant in subsequent classes

Love,
Papa

Dec., 2018

The MSSS Program

Hello:

The classes in the second year was focusing more on your concentration. As one of the 6 in the MSSS program our concentration was community organization. For most schools of social work the three areas of concentration are case work. Case work was what I was involved in when I was working with Mr. Woods in Harlem. The second most popular area is group work. This is when you work with groups to resolve issues or conduct a semi-group therapy session. This is what Alcohol Anonymous does. You could also apply it to Weight Watchers, one of the reasons I don't want to consider it. Family therapy is a little in between. It is one on one for individual members of the family, but can include the whole family. This is what we were undergoing with "E" and the social worker where your sister, mother and I would go once a week.

The third concentration was on community organization (CO). This where you become an activist for a cause, or organize a group for a specific purpose. Cesar Chavez would be considered a classic community organizer when he created the farm workers' union in California. There are many other examples but that is a good one. It also fit into my work at The New School. A lot of the work associated with applied anthropology is very similar too CO but on an international focus.

I had joined the Society for Applied Anthropology along with the American Anthropological Association after graduating from The New School. The journals for both were still being received. As a matter of fact many were retained in the basement while you were growing up. Your mom asked me to throw them out. So I had gone through all of the issues from about 5 years, and saved only those which had articles I was interested. However, never got back to them so when I moved out, they were all thrown out. Ah well! An example of today's CO efforts to keep the Affordable Health Care is a major CO effort.

You can imagine I was very comfortable with a CO major. The supplemental courses, mostly as part of a consortium with Brandeis University. The 6 of us in the MSSS program would carpool to Brandeis for seminars and special sessions. These were often thought provoking and covered a lot of critical issues which were a part of the late 1970's civil and women's rights, the environment (yes the environment) and of course the political corruption, nationally, in the various states, and even locally in Boston. An aside which I mentioned previously, at the end of year, one of the professors at Brandeis told me if I applied there for a Ph.D. program he would see I was accepted. The problem was a graduate loan which needed to repaid. At the time I was considering marrying your mother. So with a sadden heart, I told him unless they offered a full scholarship, I would not be able to attend.

CO had mandatory classes. What was interesting was it was being taught by a professor who had just received her DSW. She knew the name Eugene Debs due to his labor activities and involvement in the Pullman Strike. But those were focused labor activities. She didn't know any details. She did mention several social workers including Jane Adams, but as local organizers. [My connection to Jane Adams was we were both kicked out of Rockford College, Jane for smoking and I for 'arrogance as you know from earlier letters]. I asked about Norman Thomas. She had never heard of him.

Part of the problem was that BU, unlike The New School, it didn't like to consider any socialist. Norman Thomas took over the American Socialist Party when Debs retired. He ran for US President in 1928, 1932, and 1936. Some historians feel Franklyn Roosevelt was fearful of Thomas' gaining in popularity. Especially after the Wall Street Crash. This helped The New Deal to get through Congress.

Thomas was an early supporter of Margaret Sanger and birth control. He opposed internment of Japanese Americans during WWII, citing the ACLU of 'dereliction of duty' when they refused to support the Japanese Americans. Quite a man! A major CO leader. In follow on classes, I brought up other early CO leaders which social worker emulate, mostly socialists. The professor ended up being fearful of me.

She always recognized me when I raised my hand, and gave me straight 'A's' because it was evident early on, I knew more about CO and its history than she did. I did tone it down as the year progressed.

Love,
Papa

Dec., 2018

Back to Jo's classes:

I was a regular in Jo's thanatology class second semester. Not up front, but still there to give comments and exchange ideas with the class. It was not being attended for credit. Jo looked at me as the unofficial assistant professor. If homework or thesis deadlines demanded greater focus, she would be told and she always understood if I didn't attend. I did deliver the paper given the previous semester to the class. No one attacked me this time. Many were really excited by it and several came up later saying they had strange memories of things that could not have happen in this life.

One day Jo told me she wanted me to do a presentation to her normal nursing geriatrics class. Many of the sessions were on end of life care. This particular evening I was to do one of my talks in the second half of the class. For the first half, one of her colleagues suggested a documentary movie called *A Wrinkle in Time*. She had not prescreened it. She was just taking the other professors word that it was a good film for her class. So the film started interviewing two senior citizens. Both the male and female were over sixty. Both of average bodies considering their age, the man with a slight pot belly, she with a slim waist but sagging breasts and big hips. Soon these external observations became validated. As they were being interviewed, they began talking about sex past the age of 60. Both agreed it was more exciting, especially since there was no worries about becoming pregnant. They stood up and announced they wanted to show the viewers how much fun sex can be at their age. Soon both were naked. They climbed on a bed and proceeded to have first with foreplay, then oral sex, finally intercourse in various position. Jo was VERY embarrassed. The woman had multiple organisms. The man came with one tremendous thrust and a grunt of exceptional pleasure. By this time Jo was almost hiding her face and couldn't look at anyone directly. Slowly she got up and came to the front of the room.

She apologized to the class and to me when the film was completed. She swore she would never show a film without previewing it first. She then introduced me as the guest speaker. I got up and said since we were all in the health care profession there was nothing to apologize for. Then I looked at her and the class and said:

"Besides it certainly showed one of my favorite positions. You can always see a lot more on Tremont Street downtown. In the Red Light section."

The location of the red light district at the time. The whole class, of mostly women, all laughed. Several turned a little red. But Jo turned redder than the whole class put together. After I told her there was no harm in seeing the film. After all the sex education film shown to the social work graduate class had a lot more details, just not the evident pleasure being experienced by the elderly couple.

An aside–Tremont Street was the location of the Grand Lodge of Massachusetts at one end at the edge of the financial district. Then on the other end was the Red Light District with the 'adult' stores Each well stocked with with the usual variety of toys, magazines, ointments, and the individual quarter viewing booths in the back. Of course a couple of movie houses were there too. Remember me taking Jane to see a movie there. The theaters usually had double features (or more) of 75 +/- minute films with John Holmes, Kay Parker, Marilyn Chambers, Vanessa Del Rio (the first major Puerto Rican porn star), Seka, and Ron Jeremy, who stared in *Bad Girls* which the undergrad dorm wanted to show on movie night. But they ended up having to cancel due to a threat from John Silber the President of BU. Yes, I know all those porn stars and like a number of them. Now with the internet and DVDs all those old movie houses have all but disappeared.

After the film, it was hard to talk about reincarnation. The talk brought out those examples of possible kids who likely had past life memories. I used several of the kids in the South Bronx as examples. Also the little girl in Rhodes Island who remembered being a boy who would go for a ride in the family surrey which I have mentioned in an earlier letter which is presented in the previous book. The talk was well received and most were very interested.

Love,
Papa

This ended the regular sent letters. What follows is a narrative of continued life adventures.

PART II

Unsent narratives

This continues the autobiography of myself and the biography of my mother. Also included are some of the episodes which were not sent in letters to my daughter mostly due to their sexual nature. Still they are part of life and some may be considered amusing starting with the first incident back in NYC.

Chapter 21

Flashback aggressive hookers

THIS PART WILL BE further NYC incidents and more details while in Boston. Some of which will be sexually explicit but only in terms of what actually happened. This will begin with a flashback to when Carol and I were still a couple and living in the South Bronx.

I believe it was this occurred on one day when I either was not working or before I obtained my job with the Youth Serices Agency. I had been near the Times Square area off Broadway and 7th Avenue. It must have been after having dinner in one of the restaurants as I was walking eastward on 49th Street. This was shortly after the rather silly soft core film *Cry Uncle* came out which stared an actor named Allen Garfield playing a second rate detective. There were a number of soft core shots with various women and our (anti-?) hero.

As I was walking east from a Broadway across the street I noticed Garfield and one of his friends walking on the opposite side of the street going towards Broadway. As I progressed past where I would have been directly across from him, two of the local hookers also noticed him.

Both went running up to him begging for a part in the next movie. He told them he was not in casting. He buddy just stepped back and watched the two women begging him for a roll. Not being satisfied with his answer one of them said something akin too:

"We can show you how good we are!"

As she was saying this, she got on her knees unbuckled his belt and proceeded to pull down his pants. The other stripped off her top and was pushing her tits towards his mouth, just as the first was taking his cock into hers. Garfield appealed to his friend:

"Help me get them off of me."

His buddy just laughed and said they looked like they were doing a great audition. I watch for a few minutes. Despite being taken advantage of, the effects of the oral ministrations where having the appropriate effect. Soon both hookers where on their knees taking turns between sucking his cock and his balls. By now his friend was in near hysterics watching the whole episode with great amusement. Soon, despite his resistance the climate of the assault was apparent as poor Garfield needed help to remain standing after shooting a load into their awaiting mouths. Both then wanted to give him their names and contact information.

I laughed quietly to myself and continued walking in the opposite direction. Must admit I had never seen a man raped in the middle of the street but in a manner which based upon his weakness in the knees after the attack must have been satisfying physically.

There was very amusing incident which occurred as I was walking down 8th Avenue. Remember this was the 1970's before they cleaned up the area. That section was referred to as the Minnesota strip because so many of the girls that had become whores worked that section of the avenue. I was looking for a particular vegetable market when suddenly I felt someone pulling the left sleeve of jacket. I turned, there was a short, over weight and not particularly attractive lady of the evening. As I looked at her she said:

"Hi honey, do you want a date?

Looking at he my response was immediate: "Sorry honey, you couldn't afford me!"

She tried to take a swing at me, but her arms were so short, I just leaned back slightly as her fist missed me.

Chapter 22

Carol's exciting sexual experience and Big Mistake

YOU MUST REMEMBER THAT at the time in the South Bronx I was hard up for cash. Still if there was a sale of any kind of meat I would take advantage of it. As mentioned turkey tails where a prime source of meat back then. One evening the local market must have a sale on either rostbratwurst or a bregenwurst, don't remember which one, all that is remembered was they were nor the long thin wursts but the very short but thick variety. The whole package had been cooked for dinner along with sauerkraut. There were two left over when Carol and I retreated to the bedroom for our usual evening activities void of any TV thus the focus was on mutual satisfaction. I had been making love to her for some time with special attention to her large breasts. Finally she wanted more than just her breasts to receive attention. By this time I was more than ready to comply. After proceeding to penetrate her, she was in a very randy state and was quickly matching my downward thrust with her own upward thrusts. Soon all control was lost and I came must faster than I would have liked.

Carol was laying there but wanted more. Since there were no dildos in the apartment, I thought of the leftover wurst. Rising it off I asked if she the idea, as I showed it to her. She nodded and spread her legs. I proceeded to go down on her and after a few minutes inserted the wurst into her. She between the wurst and my tough on her clit, she was going crazy. Her screams of passion was only exceed by the coupes vaginal juices that were streaming from pussy. Soon I could tell a major climax was approaching. Applying more attention to working the wurst and sucking on the protruding clit, she had a massive climax.

I withdrew the wurst. A full third of it was missing. The tenting effect of her climax had literally cut a third of it off and it was still inside her. I proceed to replace my fingers to where the wurst had just been pulled in an effort to withdraw the remaining section. My first two fingers were fully inside and not wanting her to realize what I was doing moved them in such a way to encourage additional organisms. She was thrashing and screaming with delight as I worked the fingers back and forth. But could not reach the missing part of the wurst. Soon all four fingers of my hand were inside her. I could now feel the missing part but still unable to grab it. I pushed further. Soon all but the thumb as inside her, At last maneuvering the fingers I was able to grab the missing piece, just as she has the most major climax yet.

I pull out the piece. She raised her head and was beginning to focus on me. Not wanting her to know what has just happened I popped the retrieved wurst into my mouth, showing her the remaining piece saying:

"That was the besting tasting wurst I have ever had!"

She give a gentile laugh and a huge kiss saying it was the most intense and wonderful sexual experience she had ever had. We both fell asleep that night fully satisfied.

Back to Boston and the one nighter. After meeting up with the woman from Southend Settlement for dinner. we went back to her apartment. She helped herself to a drink. By that time she realized I didn't drink anything alcoholic so she offered me a soda. We talked for a short time. There were a lot of issues she wanted off her chest. I complained about BU and the lack of support I was getting from the administration on my upcoming internship. But that opened up a flood gate of other thoughts which were buried in me, from the work in Ft. Apache to problems with my Mom, etc. After a while talking she simple said she was horny and wanted me to fuck her. She assured me she was on the pill.

We went into her bedroom. I stripped off her clothes as she did the same to me. Actually it was a very erotic start. But when I took her panties off and slipped them over her feet, I was totally turned off by the dirty ankles! There was what looked like caked on grime. The rest of her body appeared to be clean, there were no repulsive smells, but the ankles were terrible. Her body was very reminisced of Ruben's second wife. Standing around 5'6", shorter than Jane. She wore glasses. Again like Jane. The difference was she easily forty pounds heavier. Once exposed her breasts were huge. Easily 38" or more. What was interesting was they didn't droop very much for their size. That made up for some of the dirt. Her hips were also large but her thighs were not excessive. If she had been cleaner, physically, I would likely have been attracted to her. It had been a long time since I had screwed woman of her size. Carol was the last but not as well proportioned, as her breasts drooped terribly.

She took off my clothes and as she removed my pants started to suck my cock. She was actually doing a very good job at it. Outside of the physical pleasure, there was nothing attracting her to me. I just wanted to fuck the hell out of her and didn't care about her needs or response.

I did go down on her for a short time. When she was wet. I plunged my erection into her. I was fully buried in her pussy and started the usual piston like action. What was nice was being able to suck her large breast while fucking her. I didn't hold back and came within a few minutes. This was totally different than with the women I care for where I may take twenty minutes or more. She had not climaxed. I rolled off of her.

Expressions of disappointment was seen in both her eyes and body movement. I assured her I would have another erection soon. I actually started playing with myself to obtain a full erection again. She took my hand away and told me not to rush it. Her desires were not met. After talking for a few minutes, she started playing with me. First with her hand, then by taking my cock into her mouth. This turned me on, as it always does when a woman will suck me after I come.

We moved into a 69 position. I was on top licking her over flowing cunt, lapping up all the mutual juices dribbling down out of her. This actually turned me on. I became fully erect again. Switching around, this time fucking her from the back side, I again, proceeded with all the vigor and force of a man simply wanting to get his rocks off as quickly as possible. I did. Despite this being the second coming, it only took a few minutes more than the first. I laid on top of her back and played with the soaked pussy with my fingers.

Still she had failed to achieve a major climax, only mini organisms and again expressed her dissatisfaction. So I played and sucked her breasts, fingered her clit, then put my wet fingers in her mouth for her to suck the juices off. Again, something that usually turns me on. It did take some time to achieve a third erection. But eventually it became fully erect. Plunging back into her, missionary position, the passion was considerably lessened, not to say there was ever much to begin with. What was most enjoyable was at no time did she leave the bed. I have always been turned on by seeing sperm coming out of a vagina. Although the urge to lick it decreases shortly after, there is a time immediately after organism when I have this urge to go down on my partner. Not this time. Thus I came for a third time. Again not thinking of her pleasure.

Again she felt dissatisfied. At this point I didn't care. I realized this was not a good relationship. We dozed off for a short time. I woke up with her hand on my cock. I got an erection again. Again I was in her in a second. Almost with a desire to disappoint her I came again in her as quickly as possible, rolled over and returned to sleep.

This was the only time in my life where the pleasure of my partner didn't matter. It was if I deliberately performed badly just to ensure there was no continued desire on her part to ever see me again. It worked. After a brief breakfast and her complaint that we didn't address her issues, I left. There wasn't even a kiss good-bye.

Chapter 23

BU and Love Lost in 2ⁿᵈ Year

AFTER THE BOSTON SYMPHONY concert with Ann we returned to the dorm. My roommate was out of town so I had not fear of being interrupted. We started to make out. The kissing became very passionate. But Ann warned me she was saving her virginity for marriage. Still she kind of took pity on me for being deprived of sex after the break up. So we partly disrobed. I kissed and played with her wonderful breasts. Then she took my erection in her hand and started to fondle it. Eventually, respecting her wishes I simply got on top of her and dry humped her until I came all over her stomach. This was the first organism I had in since the split with Jane. I was fully satisfied.

Later I asked her if she had any real pleasure form it. She said not really and the guilt of having gone so far for the first time in her life kept her awake all night with a mixture of feelings. Should I have done that? Did I go too far? Did not go far enough? What does an organism feel like? Should I have allowed him to give me one.' All this at once was racing through her head all night.

I continued to be very interested in Ann. I wanted her to have a gift which would like us. I found two rutilated crystal in the form of pendants. Meditating on both together I visualized them being linked. One was given to Ann with the idea that they would forever link us. But the week after Christmas break Ann was worried about the depression one of the law students was going through. She went out with him several times that week. The impression it made was she was becoming more interested in him than me.

Since there was only a strong *friendly* attraction between us and not a love connection, I decided to move on. It was only after I started dating your mother did she ask why I was no longer interested in her. It was then she explained she was only interested in the law student's mental health and not romantically. But since I was dating someone else, I gave her a hug and kiss. That was the end of the relationship.

Only after graduation and leaving Boston while in a meditation the realization came to me that Ann was the woman I was meant to marry and be with. Here was a woman who would be remarkably successful in business. An accomplished artist. And from a religion which was close to a mystical form of Christianity. Not only that there was a psychic connection which could have been established between us. Later I heard she was dating a recently divorce man. Knowing her high moral character this surprised me. I never heard anything about her after that. What was interesting was the crystal which was meant to connect us was forever lost in one of my moves. This was perhaps one of the greatest errors in my life. But if that relationship had become a marriage, it is possible my daughter may not have come into existence. Thus the letters would have never been written. So just maybe it did work out, just in an alternative reality from what was meant to happen.

Being a new semester my former Texas roommate has moved out. My new roommate was an exchange student from Iran. Mohammad had not been accepted into the graduate program because he was not sufficiently fluent in English. BU had given him a semester to pass the English proficiency exam. He requested rooming with someone. He expected me to teach him English. But I made it clear that my graduate work came first. I did not have the time to work with him on his English. We would talk, but I began to avoid being in the room on days when I had a lot of work.

To solve this problem he purchased a huge (for then) color TV and placed it on his side of the room. This was a great distraction for my attempting to concentrate on my studies. As a result I was out of the room as much as possible. He may have been better than the Texan the previous semester, but was very distracting. I remember he told me how his family were reporters. But the Shah of Iran was terrible. If the they wrote about possible storms in the weather, the Shah's investigators would accuse them of making anti-government editorials disguised as weather forecast. "Anything would be better than the Shah!" was a comment he would often say. It was evident his family were leftists, if not socialists. But this was years before the Iranian Revolution, where the Ayatollah Khomeini took over and likely executed Mohammad's family if they remained in Iran.

Chapter 24

Your Grandmother enlists

MUST GO BACK TO a little more information about my mother. She continued working for Alice Bailey part time but there was not enough income coming from the Arcane School to support herself. Earlier the job with the fashion house was mentioned along with her being fired by Merrill Lynch after asking for a raise. There was simply no challenging jobs available for her. I told you how she signed up for the WACs (Woman's Army Corp). After all she was no longer married to Bernard, had no children and might actually be able to help in the war effort. So in late in 1944 she signed up.

In flight school she got her license no one doubted anything she said, nor her abilities as a pilot. The latter skill would come in handy later.

When finishing basic training someone took notice of her scores. Not just on the IQ test but the whole batter of tests she had taken. She was invited to go to Officer's Candidate School. But this was now the Spring of 1945. She had a tough choice. Go to OCS or ship off to Europe before the war was over. She decided on the latter. She did get her second strip on her uniform for the excellence she demonstrated during basic training.

On leave to NYC, she attended the AUM Masonic lodge and received her Fellow Craft Degree. She promised to return to receive the Master Mason's Degree the as soon as she returned from Europe. In the photograph of the inner circle of the Arcane School, she is the only one pictured in uniform.

Back to Florida she was assigned to the next transport headed to Europe. There was one problem, it was the last week in April. In or around May first, she boarded a ship headed to France. While in route there was an announcement over the ships public address system. It was May 10th. Germany had surrendered. The war in Europe was over. Everyone on the ship was elated, except your grandmother. She had really hoped to be in France before the end of the war. Still she was about to have many post war adventures which will have to wait.

Chapter 25

Back to Boston and graduate school

ONE AFTERNOON, TOWARDS THE end of the first semester, while working in the library, I noticed a slender nice looking young woman who I had seen walking to and from the other graduate dorm. Since I had thought Ann was no longer interested in me, I was on the lookout for other possible relationships. I came over and introduced myself noting that I had seen her coming from the graduate dorm next to mine. She said her name was Marisol. But outside of the artist I had never encountered a Marisol before and thought she had said Mary-Sal. We talked briefly. I learned she was a communications major. Hearing the accent, I asked her where was she from. When she said: "Puerto Rico." The image of a Catholic virgin immediately popped into my mind. This immediately dismissed her in terms of a relationship. Just didn't want a virgin, nor a Catholic!

However, from that time on, whenever we passed in the street I would say:

"Hello There" an expression I picked up from the comedy dual Marty and Rossy.

She would politely nod, but there was never any further exchange. Later I found out she didn't understand what I was saying thinking it was "Hello Dear!" At first she felt it was a little too familiar but after a few times just accepted it as my way of greeting her.

After a week of the second semester Mohammad, my new roommate, invited me to an Iranian student New Year's Party not far the dorm. We walked over to check out the party. There was some light food and a variety of non-alcoholic drinks, since most of the students were Islamic. We were both dressed rather casually, jeans and regular shirts. When looking around the room there must have been thirty of more men and only a half a dozen women. I turned to Mohammad and said:

"We don't have a chance here. Let's at least go back to the dorm and get dressed in the best clothes we have."

He agreed and we started back toward the dorm. Just then I spotted Marisol walking a short way ahead of us. I turned to Mohammad:

"I know her. She is in the dorm next door."

Mohammad literally pushed me towards her saying: "Inviter her to the party!"

Not sure of her name, yet, I started jogging toward her. Catching up with her I told her there was a party my roommate and I were going to, would she like to join us. She wasn't sure about having time to change into something more formal than the casual jeans and blouse she had on. I assured her that what she was wearing was fine. She agreed to come.

When we reached the dorms, Mohammad and I went in to change. Marisol went next door to drop off the books she was carrying. We agreed to meet in from of my dorm in ten minutes. In the mean time Mohammad and I dressed in the best pants and shirts we had. Neither felt a suit was appropriate, just nice casual look with decent duds. We put on our coats and waited only a minuter or two before Marisol joined us. As we walked back to the party.

The music was mostly Iranian. The men danced mostly by themselves in traditional steps. The few women were mostly looking on, rarely interacting with any of the men. There were few chairs to sit on. Since the music was not for couples dancing, I spotted one chair and invited Marisol to sit on my lap which she accepted. Over the next hour we chit chatted.

She found out I was in the School of Social Work while she was working on a Masters in Public Communication. Slowly my resistance to the possibility of dating a virgin Puerto Rican was breaking down. The next day I asked her out for a date. She accepted. This was the beginning of February.

Chapter 26

The blizzards of 1978

THE NEXT WEEK THE first of two snow storms hit. I was working at my internship at the Federal Administration on Aging downtown when the storm began to roar through Boston. Feeling the MTA would still be running and being less than a block from the station near Faneuil Hall it would be easy to get back to the graduate dorm. This was Friday afternoon. As the snow was getting worse, the advice coming over the radio and news stations was it was a snow emergency. Everyone needed to get off the street to let the snow plows complete cleaning the roads. I was told to get home. On the way I passed a sporting goods store. Just as a hunch I decided to purchase a pair of cross-country skies and boots, to enable me to get through the heavy accumulation on the streets.

I had little problems getting back to the dorm. The snow kept coming. By morning there was over twenty inches on the ground. Boston was at a stand still. I was able to get some groceries from the local market. Just wasn't sure if BU's cafeterias would be open. I seriously doubted the graduate cafeteria would be as it was the smallest and not as well known. Still we managed through the snow. Now I was helping my new girl friend get use her first experience with snow and helping her through the drifts.

The classes on Monday were delayed for the commuting students as there was still a lot of snow piled up in the side streets. I continued attending the usual classes. Then Wednesday came. It was the last three days of the week I would go to my internship. That week I was concentrating of the continued development of an elder law guide incorporating the legal regulations and guidelines from both the state and federal statues.

On Friday I continued to work at the Administration on Aging. My mentor suggested I go to the hearing in the capitol, only a few blocks away. There was to be hearing on proposed revisions of the Massachusetts elder care statues. As I proceeded to the Capitol the next blizzard was beginning to hit, and hit hard. The snow from the week before had just been cleared but huge piles of it were on many street corners.

I got to the hearing room. The Commonwealth's House of Representatives hearing was still questioning the state's official in charge of snow removal. State congressman Barney Frank was charing the hearing. While the public works official was answering the question, everyone in the hearing room could hear the storm getting worse by the minute. Representative Frank asked if there was sufficient funds in the budget to cover any additional snow storms for the remainder of the winter.

"As long as we have the normal three to seven inch snow fall there is sufficient funds to cover it. But if there is anything like last week we may be in trouble."

Suddenly a huge gust of wind and the sound of a blast of snow hitting the windows of the hearing room. The official almost at a whisper said: "We're in trouble, we're in trouble."

The hearing never got to the senior care issues. It soon adjourned because of the storm. As I walked back to the government building, it was evident the blizzard was getting much worse than the week before. The wind was gusting at lease sixty miles per hour or more. The snow was so heavy one could only see a few feet ahead. I was noticing the traffic on the street attempting to drive through the increasing snow. I spotted one woman walking on the sidewalk. A gust of wind suddenly lifted her off her feet and threw her into the street in front of a car. It was a miracle the driver was able to stop before running over her. Still she was on her side slightly under the bumper of the car. I helped he up and told her to take cover as the wind was too strong for her to walk in.

I managed to get back to the office. I told them the hearing was cancelled due to the storm. My boss told me to get home as everyone was released. Making back to the graduate dorm I purchased a few groceries before settling in. Most rice, canned beans, pasta and some canned sauces. Fortunately there was a stove next to the laundry machines in the basement of the dorm. I had brought a double boiler from home, just in case. That evening Marisol came over and along with Mohammad, my roommate we snuggled over to the main dorm and the large cafeteria. It would the last meal we had there for some time. Trudging though the ever thicking snow we made it back to the dorm, Mohammad and I to ours, and M to her's next door.

The storm increased in intensity that evening. About 10:30 the lights went out. Since most graduate students like to be prepared for a romantic evening, there were candles in almost every room. I told Mohammad to just put on an extra blanket and go to sleep, there being nothing we could do.

Saturday morning came. The storm had lessened but the wind was still very strong. I just pulled covers over my bed and tried to go back to sleep. After some thirty minutes the two graduate law students, Richard who I had already made an ass of and his friend were complaining that they couldn't get out of the dorm, the door was frozen shut. They were running up and down the halls and stairs trying to get everyone to call the maintenance to dig the dorm out. By this time the streets were totally impassable. The maintenance would just laugh at these two whining bitches and hung up on them. They called back threading a law suit. Same results—a laugh and a click on the other end.

After about an hour of hearing their complains which were approaching hysterical. They said without power they would freeze. Without access to the cafeteria they would starve. Without access to the library their grades would be threatened. These tirades were being shouted up and down the halls and on all the floors. They were trying to get everyone to complain to the maintenance and get them to take action.

I finally had enough. I got up and dressed appropriately for the storm. Having tried to open my room's windows it was apparent they were frozen shut. The temperature just before the worse of the storm hit was above freezing. The early snow was melting and getting into every crack and crevice of the doors and windows. Then the sudden drop of temperature froze everything tight. I went to the front door–shut tight. No way to budge it. Same for the emergency back door. All the windows and the first two floors where frozen. I went to the back staircase. There was chance that it being close to the other grad dorm next door, there was a potability it my be opened.

Sure enough, I was able to get it open. Now I had a way out. Problem was the wind was blowing the snow so hard one couldn't see anything. I had to have my ski mask. I asked Mohammad to get my mask, the shovel from the basement, and a chair. I could climb up to the window and crawl out. Figuring that although the window was about fifteen feet off the ground, and thinking there was likely at least a foot of snow to land on. I dropped. As I as falling I looked down. I was going to land on bare pavement. No snow! Knowing how to land I just dropped and rolled.

Even with the ski mask it was very hard to see in the alley. I walked to the front sidewalk. Almost no snow on it! You must be aware the shape of the buildings. The buildings had a U shape. They all had recessed entrances with about twenty feet between each walkway to the front doors. As I walked to where the entrance should have been, there was a wall of snow over six feet high. It was as if some stone mason had made a smooth barrier of snow. What had happened was the wind during the night crated a vortex between the building's entrances making the drifting snow into perfectly smooth walls even with the exterior of the building. Still this just didn't look right. I had a shovel but observing the wind was continuing to do, an idea crept into my head. I kicked to bottom of the snow wall. It came crashing down.

Now all I had to do was to shovel the walk and steps to the front door. The wind had done most of the job for me when it create the wall, after only a few minutes I was at the door. Sure enough the outer door was covered with ice. Chipping away at the larger pieces soon got it to open. The inner door more effort but by now the more civilized non hysterical graduate students were all able to apply some warmth to the cracks. Together with my chipping away the little ice that had gotten between the doors, the dorm was now available for anyone who wanted to egress from the comfort of a still relatively warm dorm to a frigate drift and blowing storm. I was the only one who was out. I cleared the entrance to the other grad dorm so they could get out. Thankfully it was a much easier task as their door was on the opposite the entrance of the next building where the snow was pilled up as it had been in my dorm.

Deciding to see if it was possible to get to Commonwealth Avenue and the rest of the dorms, cafeterias, and classes. I had Mohammed get my cross country skies. Looking at the corner half way down the block, one could see how deep the snow was. In some placed it must have been over five feet, mostly due to the drifting. I turned the corner heading toward the bridge that crosses the interstate. There on the next block over, I notices something unusual. It was another residential street, usually filled with parked cars on both sides. None were to be seen. Wiping the snow from the goggles, and taking a closer look I could see three or four inches of a car antenna about every ten feet. No cars were visible. Just antenna. Later when the snow plows started clearing the back streets, many a car was badly damaged by the plows, simply because most were so completely covered with snow the plows just couldn't tell where the cars were parked and where the center of the street was.

Over the next week Boston was plowed out. Things eventually began to take on a normal pace.

Chapter 27

Angelic Rescue (flashback)

VISITING MARIE DERAISMES AS often as possible the members were always glad to see me. Demetria who had been the Worshipful Master who gave me the Fellowcraft Degree related one of the more interesting cases of Masonic miracle. Her partner had a husband, Joel, who was mentally unbalanced. Not wanting to put him in an institution Annette, his wife cared for him at home. This home was just a few blocks from Demetria's residence. It was a typical townhouse on the upper East Side of Manhattan. Most houses had an outer and inner doors, which a small vestibule for coats and umbrellas to be placed during inclement weather.

One afternoon Annette called Demetria in a panic. Joel was having a violent episode. She needed help to clam him down and get his medicines. Not sure how Demetria could help, still she went over. Upon seeing her in the house, Joel grabbed a knife from the kitchen and started towards Demetria. Annette screams were added to those coming out of Demetria. A small crowd started to assemble outside on the sidewalk, all wondering what was happening.

Despite her excessive weight she was able to climb stairs to the second floor with Joel close behind. Out of pure desperation she gave the Grand Hailing Sign of a Master Mason as given in the Co-Masonic order. Suddenly a tall blond man appeared to come through the inner door. Seeing the situation and that Joel was getting closer to Demetria with the knife ready to be plunged, the blond leapt up and placed his hand on Joel. Joel immediately clammed as if asleep right there on the stairs. The young man helped Demetria up asking if she was alright. Demetria, though out of breath said she was unhurt. Upon hearing this and hearing some sirens coming from outside, turned and exited through the inner door.

Demetria beginning to recover mentally, got up and raced through both doors. She wanted to get the name of the man who saved her and Annette from the violent outburst. Looking in all directions up and down the street she didn't see him. When she asked those around the front steps:

"Did you see a talk blond man just leave here? I want to thank him for his assistance."

None in the crowd had seen anyone leaving the house. According to those outside, no one had emerged from the home, certainly not anyone fitting the descriptions Demetria was giving. It wasn't until some time later that Demetria related to giving the Grand Hailing Sign to the man's appearance. Her conclusion was that he must have been an angelic manifestation in response to a Mason's urgent need.

Chapter 28

A Fun class, Herb's book, flashback

THE CLASS ON SEXUALITY was a lot of fun. As Debby said in the beginning it was her favorite subject of the whole year. What was interesting was her descriptions of male erections. Recognizing the generations and that exceptions could be found she gave the following descriptions. Asian men were generally small. Blacks were pretty much what you see is what you will get. If not excited it's hanging down. When erect, it is about the same size, just stiffer and pointing at you. She noted her preference was caucasians. The reason was they were like a Jack-in-the-Box, you never could tell what would pop out! They could be tiny when relaxed but grow to more than a satisfying size when aroused.

At the time I was contemplating the possibility of becoming a sex councilor. But that would take a slew of additional courses. Most of which were not offered by B.U. School of Social Work. But my openness to discuss sex, inspired by these classes would land me in trouble years later when confronted by a very sexually repressed family that I happened to marry into. They just couldn't take any discussion related to sex or sexual relations. It was something I found very hard to handle, despite understanding the root cause for their problems.

I partly resolved this by signing up to be a sexual advisor in the Unitarian Universalist Church of Annapolis many years later. When editing this book I had signed up for on line courses and had already read one of the suggested readings for the qualification as a mentor to teens and young adults. But that will have to wait for some future book.

It was about this time that Herb Terrace came out with the Nim book. When I could I purchased the book and was really disappointed. Herb's argument was that since Nim was not putting his signing into a proper context, and simply responding to the requests of his teachers, his conclusion was chimpanzees were incapable to language.

My counter to Herb was multi fold. First, what human child at the age of four is fully capable of using proper syntax? Here was a chimp that was not using proper syntax, but yet he had many signs in his vocabulary. I also felt Herb's ego got in the way of unbiased analysis. There was a touch of 'if I can't do it, I'll be sure no one else will try.' The fact his focus was spending nights with Laura, came out in the documentary in 2011. Laura was very attractive and Herb wanted to take advantage of her working for the project by making her audition often in a horizontal position. This was evident as from my room above the kitchen I could see Herb slip out the front door early on some mornings after a night with Laura.

My second argument was many of the volunteers in the project would suddenly leave without explanation, at least too Nim. This would send him into a somewhat depressive state of mind. The clearest evidence of that is when I left the project to go to BU. His learning rate dropped dramatically. Yet for the few weeks I returned during the holidays, the rate of acquiring new signed picked up again. When I left to return to BU in January, I talked to him in normal vocal speech that I had to go again. I hoped he would behave and do well. This time when I left there was not the significant drop in learning new signs as had been the case a few months before.

A third point was Herb used the filming of Nim as part of the justification for the book's conclusions. Yet the filming didn't started after 3 closest house mates moved out, Amy, then Laura, and finally me. By this time all those who Nim was close too had disappeared leaving a very depressed chimp. The declining rates of learning indicate Nim just didn't care any more. The book also attacked Penny and Koko the sign language gorilla!

It was about half way through the second year when my favorite professor Debbie, father died. The problem was she was a pure Freudian and complete atheist. Yet three days after the death of her father she saw him in the hall of her home. She felt this was an illusion. She was suffering some much from his death, she was hallucinating. I tried to tell her it may have been real. That these is an astral form which can reappear to those close to those remain in the physical plane. What she was seeing was the astral form of her father, likely trying to say goodbye. She couldn't accept it. All her training and education created a pure atheists. I felt a little sorry for her but also for her father who was trying to communicate with her.

Another flashback T's Grandmother returns to the states

After returning to the states, it was easy for her to find a job with the secretarial experience in the WACs Being single again she was looking for a possible husband who she would be happy with. Most of the soldiers she had dated in Europe had returned to their home around the country. None to New York, where grandmother was. There was one man, a Milton Benesch who asked her out. He claimed to be working for an investment house. This was something your grandmother was involved with prior to the war, she started dating him. It was gradually becoming a serious relationship. Then he introduced her to his brother Walter.

You have to realize that Milton as a child contracted polio. His older brother was forced to drop out of school, having only completed the eighth grade to get a job and help pay for his younger brother's medical bills. This created a hidden hatred for Milton. When he was introduced to your grandmother, he figured out a way to get even. Steal her away from Milton.

Walter A had considerable charm when he wanted to apply it. Also unlike Milton, Walter was taller, much stronger, having been a life guard at Jones Beach and a semi-pro wrestler in his younger days. Like your grandmother he had been previously married. His wife died years before. Never found our how. Being free and wanting to get even with Milton he applied all his charms towards my mother. It succeeded. Sometime by 1947 they were married.

I suspect it was because he had gotten her pregnant as there was a child born later in the year. But it was months premature and died after two struggling days. Both wanting children they tried again. This time Mom sought out the medical doctor in New York.

You have to remember her first husband had forced her to have back alley abortions multiple times. This was the key reason why the first 'baby Benesch' didn't survive. Upon becoming pregnant again she told the doctor her history. Special care was provided, especially rest. It succeeded as related in the earlier book, but not without doubts. Remember I was only given a 50/50 chance of survival being premature myself. Ultimately karma favored me.

Back to her search for a job after the war. She contacted Alice Bailey who hired her as one of her personal secretaries. Even before the war, your grandmother was part of an inner circle of Alice's students of advanced meditators. These included several noted individuals, most of whom are now no longer remembered. One of the most outstanding members of the group was Marcia Moore, the daughter of Robert L. Moore the co-founder of Sheraton Hotels and sister to Robbin Moore, author of Green Berets and The French Connection. I once was dangling a vodka on the rocks under a limbo bar to Robbin to get under it during a family get together on Cuttyhunk Island. The island is off the New Bedford chain in Massachusetts. Robert Moore was very encouraging of Marcia's participation and became an important mentor for my Mom. Unfortunately his efforts fell through.

Still if was a close knit group. While Mom was secretary to Alice it was during a time when the last books were being dictated. Alice was receiving telepathic instruction for the books from the Master referred to as D.K. There have been any accounts of the dictations. Most inaccurate. This is what I was told.

Alice would be in her office. The door would be open. Mom could watch her from the adjourning room. She would see Alice at her typewriter typing what was being dictated by D.K. as if he was there in the room. Occasionally she would hear Alice say something like:

"This contradicts what was in the previous book. Well I know this is to be more advanced. Well alright, it is your book! I put down what you tell me."

Sometimes during these conversation Alice would actually get up from her desk and walk around it speaking directly to D.K. who was present in an astral form that only Alice could see.

Once Mom became pregnant first with the boy that did not survive and then with me, she curtailed her work with Alice. After I was born, she took me to Alice who gave me her blessing. It was a short time later that Alice died. What happen to the mediation group and the Arcane School, after her death is not subject here but interesting in itself as there was quite a conflict which ensured.

Chapter 29

Second semester second year and Leaving Co-M

IT WAS DURING THE second semester the head of Co-Masonry in America, Helen was pushing me to take on more responsibility upon graduation from BU. But she was promoting an individual who she felt would help the Philadelphia Lodge come back to life. Having had several discussions with this woman, a self proclaims minister, I realized this was not a good idea. I wrote to Helen telling her of this woman's narcissistic and exaggerated ego. That she just wanted to be the Master of the Lodge so the members would idealize her. There were members of Marie Deraismes who felt the same way I did. One satirically referring to her as 'That Holy Woman.'

Helen was furious about my position. She accused me of being myopic. After all she was far older and wiser than I. The last letter I received from her while in Boston was even more demeaning. I decided to show it to a theological graduate student who lived up stairs from my room in the dorm. He was also a Mason but a member of the more recognized order which dominates Masonry in the USA. He read it. His response was why should I put up with such un-Masonic accusations in the letter. Why not renounce my membership in Co-M and join regular Masonry.

I read the letter several times more. Boston University had a lodge associated with the university. After a few queries I found out they met in the Grand Lodge building on Tremont Street in downtown Boston. After contacting the worshipful master and describing my decision to join 'regular' Masonry, he was delighted. I was given the form for renouncing my 'irregular' Masonic affiliation. But noted according to the wording, I would not associate with them as long as I remained in the jurisdiction of the Massachusetts Grand Lodge.

It was easy to get a second signature on my petition. Several of the more intellectual members new of my history. The Worshipful Master told me not to spread it around to the other members as they might object to my becoming a member. After the required interview/investigation the petition was read, accepted and voted upon in the Lodge.

In late December of 1977 I was initiated into Boston University Lodge. Coming from a Co-M background I assumed that it would be at least 3 months before my taking the usual exam to become a Fellow Craft. Yet less than a month later at the January meeting I was asked if I was ready for the next degree. I had only attended one of the preparation classes since my initiation and was very unsure of the catechism of this slightly different ritual from the one I had become so familiar with. Here it is important to realize most lodges in the United States use a York Rite ritual. In Co-M they used a variation of the Scottish Rite ritual for the Blue Lodge. Similar but not identical.

When asked if I was ready, I told the lodge my answers may not be exactly what was expected but would give it a good try. Remember I had been examined on all the degrees first through the thirtieth in Co-M preparatory to receiving my 32°. The questions were close to what I was familiar with. But my answers far more elaborate and detailed they what was usually recited.

After the examination the lodge voted for me to receive the Fellow Craft

Degree that evening. During the post meeting dinner one of the older members who did not know of my background remarked to the Master where did this young man come from, he seems to know more about Masonry than most of the members. The Master just smiled. I was unable to make the February meeting but a similar routine took place in March with a similar examination and then be advanced to the Master Mason's Degree.

Chapter 30

The voice of a 1,000 characters

It was during my last semester at BU that Mel Blanc was a guest lecturer. This was after his serious accident. Still he gave a wonderful presentation showing many of the cartoons where he was the voice. Most didn't realize he was the original voice of Woody Woodpecker, also the vault and Maxwell car on the Jack Benny radio programs. His presentation was an overview of his career and the great characters he portrayed. Bugs Bunny being the most recognized. Bugs was the most characteristic of Mel himself as Bugs voice and mannerism were pure Brooklyn!

After the presentation I approached Mel. Not wanting to take up much of his time as I suspected he was tired, I just said how much I enjoyed the talk and all the years I had been aware of his great talent. Mel noticed the Masonic pin on my lapel. He immediately greeted me as a brother and sat down there in the front row of the auditorium to spend a little more time with a fellow Mason. It was exceptionally kind and greatly appreciated knowing I was in the presence of a truly thoughtful and giving individual.

Chapter 31

There final stage for the MSSS-Thesis

THE LAST REQUIREMENT OF the MSSS was a thesis. But this being a school social work, they required group thesis for all the graduate students. The team I was assigned to had four other students. At this stage I don't remember what the theme of the overall thesis was, all I remember was each of us was required to provide one chapter. The last weeks of class period was an intense focus on my completing my chapter. As a group we were required to help any of the other participants. There was one member of the team from South Africa. Her English was just bearable passable. But her ability to complete her chapter was way beyond her capacity.

Since I was the first to complete my chapter the rest of the team asked me to help with the outstanding chapter assigned to our African member. When I got with her she had no comprehension of how to write her chapter. After several hours we managed to get a basic outline. I would check with her on her progress the next day.

When I saw her the next day, she had made next to no progress. Taking the outline I sat at her typewriter and started writing her chapter. At this time all extra time was devoted to the thesis, both my and my team mates. Marisol was constantly asking when we would have time to be together again. I told her not until the thesis chapters were completed.

For the next two weeks all efforts were devoted to completing the two chapters and then work out an harmonizing effort with the remainder of the team. The thesis was likely the last of the whole graduating class to be submitted, but it passed and we were all passed to receive our respective degrees. MSSS for myself while the rest of the team received the traditional Masters of Social Work.

Graduate school work was completed!

Chapter 32

Graduation

MY MOM CAME TO the graduation ceremony and met Marisol for the first time. By my age she had already had married twice and was putting pressure on me to get married now that I was about to turn thirty. Marisol seemed like a nice choice should I want to get married to someone. I didn't take this exchange seriously, yet. But it was in the back of my mind as I went through the graduation ceremony.

Marisol was wearing her favorite hat, which was red and black in a semi Scottish pattern. I wanted my photo taken with the hat on as it was a perfect compliment to the BU master's collar of the same red. Marisol felt it was not proper to take such a photo and refused to lend me the hat. That should have been taken as warning but was set aside.

The academic year had come to an end. I had completed an elder law legal reference handbook as part of my internship and completed a paralegal course on Federal laws related to the elderly. It was shortly before graduation the Massachusetts Dept. Of Elder Affairs had just appointed a new director. My supervisor at AoA told me he needed help. After contacting the newly appointed as director of the Mass. Dept. Of Elder Affairs, George, I offered my services after graduation.

It is important to understand George obtained his job because he was very personable and outgoing. He was well known in the corridors of Beacon Hill including the Massachusetts House and Senate. Being black in a predominately white administration his appointment was to show the public they were not racists and that blacks could obtain status in the state government. In other words he was the trophy black for the state!

Upon the recommendation from my advisor, George was more than willing to meet me to see if I could help him. It was shortly after the our discussions began I realized he was a fish out of water. He have NO concept of Elder Law and had no idea how he should proceed as the director of a state wide program dealing with the seniors. I proposed two possible deliverables:

1) Legal reference handbook

2) An outline for training program

There was no budget for my work, so this was a pure pro-bono effort on my part. Still in the back of my mind it might look good on a resume and help be gain a position elsewhere. Since I had no other job prospects I told him if he could put me up somewhere, I would pull together the two deliverables in two weeks. He accepted and invited me to his house outside of Boston for the weekend to discuss more of what he needed and what I was willing to deliver.

In the meantime Marisol had been continuing in her program as the School for Communication was still in session. As a means of showing his thanks for what I had delivered to him, George invited Marisol and I to spend a weekend at his home. I asked Marisol if she was interested. Receiving a positive response from her, I accepted.

George picked us up and drove to his rather upscale home. It even had its own tennis court. Of course George prided himself as a decent player having taken lessons for several years. I was purely self taught but had always practices serving to the corners of the opponent's court. I did practice serves by placing a can on the corners on the opposing side of the net and try to hit them with my server. Rarely did I actually hit them, but I would come close!

We hit a few balls back and forth. He then challenged me to a match. I was able to return his serves with ease beating him in the first game. It was the power of my return shots shocked him. When it was my turn to serve, I usually aimed to the corners of service box and usually with both the accuracy and speed which George couldn't handle. After a score of 40 Love in my favor, he suggest we quit as it was getting hot. Thus ended the tennis match.

The three of us had a delightful dinner. Marisol and I were shown the guest room. It only had a single queen size bed. I noted that Marisol and I were not in a sexual relationship. We were expecting separate beds. None were available as this was the only guest room. I looked at Marisol and asked if this would be OK with her. She responded positively. We bid George goodnight and retired to our room with a separate bath.

After showering and getting prepared, I realized I never slept in pajamas, always in the nude. Marisol had brought a pair of pjs which she had on. When I returned from the bathroom I told her I never slept with clothing on. I was never sure of her feelings at that time, but she beckoned me to join her in bed. Off came my clothes and into the bed! Of course I was kissing her and getting an erection. She must have felt it as I was pressing her to me. Rather than resisting I felt she was getting excited. I remove her pjs, exposing her naked body to me for the first time. A slender and perfectly shaped petite female was laying next to me. Soon I rolled on top of her and started dry humping her to both our pleasure. No penetration but plenty of juices flowed from her as my climax coated her belly. This was a new and exciting experience for her, and a rather pleasurable one for me.

As for the assignment first was an adaptation of the legal reference handbook. It covered the laws and regulations from the Federal Government's AoA together with the additional rules and statues of Massachusetts laws related to the elder. Only a few additional paragraphs were needed from what I had created in AoA. Within 10 days I had a fairly complete reference book for him. It was both comprehensive, without being legalize. Writing in plain language and broken down into the various components I was quite proud of the resulting handbook with a slant toward the rules and regulations existing in the state of Massachusetts. I had created a specialized close to hundred page legal reference handbook for George within ten days.

The second item he required was a training program for him to develop the program he had been assigned to conduct. After talking with George I realized he had little or no understanding of what was needed in a train program. What was the needed was to draw up a training program for Dept. Of Elder Affairs. It was to have a dual focus. Part was to train the staff within George's department. The second part was external training for agencies and services to the elderly outside of the state government. By following the standard journalistic 5 Ws an outline of a training program was completed in the second week. It gave the 'who, what, when, where, why and how' of a state wide elderly program. I complemented it with what I had done in NYC with the intergenerational program. I pulled together about a twenty page outline which was actually quite detailed.

George almost ignored the legal reference handbook as he had little real interest in rules and regulations. He loved the training program guidance which I thought was the lesser of the two deliverables.

George was given both documents. Though the legal reference handbook was far more valuable for his job, he paid little attention to it. It was apparent he didn't understand its importance. What really caught his interest was the training program outline. This is what he felt he needed most. By that time I realized he had little to no managerial background this would be a critical piece of his program.

His eyes lit up. He immediately want to hire me. I pointed out the reference noting Dept. Of Elder Affairs had a quota system where a certain number of minorities had to be hired. Agency has quota system! I told him:

"You can't hire me–I'm white."

Thus ended all chances for a job in Boston.

Chapter 33

My Internship in Washington, D.C. and engagement

DURING THE SUMMER AFTER my graduations Marisol got an internship in DC. This was an excellent opportunity for her. She got an apartment in Falls Church with another woman who also had an internship in a different Federal agency. I decided to visit her for a few days to see where the relationship was capable of going. She was very happy to see me. I had the impression that she really wanted wed me as an excuse not to return to Puerto Rico.

The first night together I was fully aware of her desire to remain a virgin until marriage. But we were lying in bed together naked. Naturally heavy petting and erotic caressing advanced to me going down on her. This was a new and exciting experience for her, one which she had no objections to. Then she wanted to return the favor and started performing remarkably good oral techniques. Soon the feeling of a climax was being felt. I raised up her head and warned her if she kept it up I would be shooting a load into her mouth. She just smiled and went back to work. Sure enough, after only a minute or two I shot a huge load into this virgin mouth. She didn't hesitate but swallowed the whole load.

I immediately thought if she is so good orally as a virgin, she will likely be knockout once married. It was after this passionate session I considered proposing. She was very attractive with an exceptionally cute ass. Educated and open to new experiences, I felt that she would be an excellent spouse. Besides my mother was pressuring me to get married. I proposed and suggested we get married after her graduation in December. Unfortunately as far as sex is concerned she never swallowed again!

Where Next?

In the meantime Marisol had returned to Puerto Rico and informed her parents of our engagement. Having completed the volunteer work for George and the Massachusetts Department of Elder Affairs there was a new focus. Needing a real job! All possibilities of returning to NYC were out. They were still going through a fiscal crisis and laying off employees.

I returned to The Hill in Connecticut to plan my next move. Still considering the possibility of being hired by AoA at the Federal level, I asked my former mentor and co-workers in the Boston office if there was any possible openings. None! So the next was to examine what were the other possible ways to obtain employment in the Federal Government.

Looking at the Office of Personnel Management taking into consideration my education and experience I was qualified for be hired at the GS9 level. I completed the Federal Pace level application. It was submitted, leaving open any possible job opportunity which I would be qualified for.

The Department of Human Services (DHS) in the District of Columbia Government was in need of individual with my qualifications ASAP. The one saving factor was the D.C. Government was still under Federal service and control. I would be considered a Federal employee with the retirement and medical benefits of the Federal employees in the Federal government programs.

I found out the Government Accounting Office had done a review of the welfare program and determined their program was critically understaffed. The were ordered to hire over one hundred new employees to fill the vacancies which the program needed particularly in the welfare units.

The response was surprisingly fast. I was hired as a GS9 by welfare office - Dept of Human Services of the District of Columbia welfare agency. Off to Washington DC and new adventures and an upcoming marriage. What came was the next phase of my life. It was to be a surprise even to me.